ARISTOTLE
ON
TEACHING

Mary Michael Spangler, O.P.

University Press of America,® Inc.
Lanham • New York • Oxford

Copyright © 1998
Mary Michael Spangler

University Press of America,® Inc.
4720 Boston Way
Lanham, Maryland 20706

12 Hid's Copse Rd.
Cummor Hill, Oxford OX2 9JJ

Library of Congress Cataloging-in-Publication Data

Spangler, Mary Michael.
Aristotle on teaching / Mary Michael Spangler.
p.   cm.
Includes bibliographical references and index.
1. Aristotle—Contributions in education. 2. Aristotle—
Contributions in teaching. I. Title.
LB85.A7S73 1998 371.102—dc21 98-26328 CIP

ISBN 0-7618-1210-5 (cloth: alk. ppr.)
ISBN 0-7618-1211-3 (pbk: alk. ppr.)

⊖™The paper used in this publication meets the minimum
requirements of American National Standard for Information
Sciences—Permanence of Paper for Printed Library Materials,
ANSI Z39.48—1984

In gratitude to my teachers par excellence:

Sr. Mary Roman, OSF, all middle and upper elementary subjects,
Miss Eva Mae Moffatt, high school Latin and English,
Dr. Vincent E. Smith, graduate courses in Aristotelian Thomism,
Fr. Pierre Conway, OP, continual mentor in Aristotelian Thomism.

Contents

Preface

In this book we shall examine the doctrine of Aristotle to discover its relevance for the art of teaching. In this examination we shall restrict the meaning of teaching to the activity of explaining a given subject matter. Our meaning will not include those activities—such as disciplining, motivating, and testing—which, though useful for the instructor's explanation, are not the clarification itself. Rather the term *teaching* will denote the act of explaining the truth to those being taught. It is that act of the teacher leading the student from what he knows to that which is unknown to him. As we shall see, it proceeds either inductively or deductively and aims ideally at a knowledge of the causes of things.

To understand the activity of teaching, we shall employ the doctrine of Aristotle. Although he wrote no specific treatise on this art, Aristotle frequently uses the activity of teaching to clarify a particular problem. Thus, in showing that metaphysics is properly called wisdom, he points out that those who can teach are considered wise, and then he defines teachers as "those who tell the causes of each thing."[1] Again, in the discussion of intellectual virtue, Aristotle notes that "all teaching starts from what is already known,...for it proceeds sometimes through induction and sometimes by syllogism."[2] Statements on teaching, such as these just quoted, will give us clear indications of Aristotle's position concerning this activity.

Since Aristotle's references to teaching do not form a complete exposition of this art, however, we shall also use Aristotelian principles applicable to instruction but not directly related to this activity by the Philosopher. In fact, the majority of the principles used in this book to understand teaching were not directly applied to this art by Aristotle. These principles, nevertheless, do have a relevance for teaching and therefore are helpful in understanding the teacher's work.

Thus Aristotle's principle *art imitates nature* has a direct bearing on this activity;[3] for, by means of it, we can conclude that teaching, as an art, must always proceed in accord with the natural way that the student would acquire knowledge. Aristotle's doctrine on induction is also applicable to the art of teaching;[4] for the inductive procedure is the basic part of everyone's natural effort to acquire knowledge, and nature stands as an exemplar for every art. Therefore, since many of Aristotle's principles are quite relevant for an exposition on teaching, we shall utilize in this book not only his specific statements about this art but also in an even greater measure such parts of this doctrine as are applicable to the work of instruction.

Since we are utilizing various Aristotelian principles applicable to teaching, we shall use all of the major extant writings of the Philosopher. Some of these works, however, will contain more material for our purpose than others. From Aristotle's logical treatises we shall obtain many principles on induction and deduction, the two procedures of teaching; while the philosopher's work on psychology, *De Anima*, will provide insights on the natural way knowing occurs, a procedure teaching must imitate. Finally, Aristotle's *Ethica Nicomachea* and *Metaphysica*, as well as the opening methodological sections of his various works, contain many principles pertinent to teaching. Since Aristotle's basic principles recur many times, we shall need all of his major writings, although our chief sources will be the materials that we have mentioned.

In order to understand more clearly the above principles, we shall use the commentaries that Thomas Aquinas wrote on the works of Aristotle. Because of the brevity of the Philosopher's style, it is often difficult to grasp the full significance of the doctrine that he is expounding. For this reason, we shall utilize extensively Aquinas's commentaries, as well as his other texts treating the same principles. In working with both of these authors, we shall use exact quotations as much as possible so that the thinking of these philosophers will be more apparent.

By means of the foregoing texts, we shall attempt to understand the activity of teaching. Our purpose in this book is to learn about the nature of teaching by means of the doctrine of Aristotle. Our aim is not to explicate a position on teaching that the Philosopher formally expressed, but rather it is to understand teaching by means of Aristotelian principles.

To achieve this purpose, we shall follow a threefold plan: (1) We shall first give a general explanation of the art of teaching. (2) Since every art must imitate nature, we shall then discuss the natural acquisition of knowledge, treating first the objects of knowing, then its procedures, and finally the order in knowing. (3) Lastly, we shall examine the inductive and deductive procedures of teaching. Throughout these three stages of our plan, the emphasis will be placed on procedure, either that of the nature of knowing or that of the art of teaching.

Many individuals have helped to make this book a reality, whether by their instruction, assistance, or encouragement. Of this group, my first expression of gratitude belongs to Pierre Conway, OP, Dominican House of Studies, Washington, DC, for being a commentator par excellence of Aristotelian Thomism. Secondly, I am deeply grateful to Marie Granger, OP, my academic colleague for many years, whose application of Aristotle's theory for the preparation of student teachers was a constant proof of the soundness of his doctrine. Also, I must thank my community for the peace and quiet enabling me to complete the book. Above all, I have treasured the support of Sr. Stella, my sister, and my friends. Finally, I owe a special word of gratitude to Benedict Joseph, OP, for his never-failing encouragement and for his meticulous critique of the book.

In addition, grateful acknowledgment is made to the publishers for permission to use quotations from the following:

Aquinas, Thomas. *Commentary on Aristotle's De Anima*. Translated by Kenelm Foster and Silvester Humphries. New Haven: Yale University Press, 1951. Reprint by Dumb Ox Books, South Bend, IN, 1995.

_____. *Commentary on the Metaphysics of Aristotle*. Translated by John P. Rowan. 2 vols. Chicago: Henry Regnery Company, 1961. Revised unabridged edition by Dumb Ox Books, South Bend, IN, 1995.

_____. *Summa Theologica*. Translated by Fathers of the English Dominican Province. 3 vols. New York: Benziger Brothers, Inc., 1947-48. Reprint by Christian Classics, Inc., Allen, TX, 1981. Nonexclusive world rights in all languages granted by Burns & Oates, Ltd., Kent, England.

Aristotle. *The Works of Aristotle*. Edited by W.D. Ross. 1st ed. Vol. 1, *Analytica Posteriora*, 1928; vol. 3, *De Anima*, 1931; vol. 8, *Metaphysica*, 1928; vol. 9, *Ethica Nicomachea*, 1925. London: Oxford University Press, 1910-31. By permission of Oxford University Press.

Chapter 1

Teaching in General

A. Teaching's definition
    1. It moves from known to unknown
    2. It uses induction and deduction
    3. It strives for causal knowledge
B. Teaching's purpose
    1. The purpose: intellectual virtue
    2. Its value
        a. As education's goal
        b. As life's goal
C. Teaching's materials
    1. The student's potential
        a. This potential
        b. Need of this potential
    2. The teacher's knowledge
        a. Need of this knowledge
        b. Nature of this knowledge
    3. Teacher/student relationship
        a. Teacher's importance
        b. Student's attitude
D. Teaching's productive principle
    1. Teaching as practical
    2. Teaching as an art
    3. Teaching's productive principle

Teaching in General

Throughout this book our purpose is to discover what contribution Aristotle's doctrine can make in understanding the procedure that occurs when one person teaches another. By this procedure we do not mean the technique utilized to motivate the student so that he is willing to be taught, but the procedure proper to the act of teaching itself. Those who have been taught or who have assumed the role of the teacher know that an instructor finds himself involved in two kinds of activities: he must discipline and motivate, and he must also teach a given subject matter such as geometry. Neither of these functions can be omitted in the practical, concrete order, if the teacher wishes to accomplish his purpose.

It is with the function of teaching itself, however, that we are concerned. What is the general procedure that takes place whenever a teacher explains his subject matter to his students? This is our question, our problem, in this book. Therefore, whenever we use the term *teaching* throughout this study, we are restricting it to the actual activity which occurs when a given subject matter is being explained.

In order to accomplish our purpose, we shall first examine the Aristotelian principles related to teaching in general. To do so is in harmony with the way the human mind works, for "what is to us plain and obvious at first is rather confused masses, the elements and principles of which become known to us later by analysis. Thus we must advance from generalities to particulars."[1]

When we examine the general outline of teaching, we shall first state what this activity is like; i.e., we shall give a definition of it. Then we shall move into the procedure that occurs to bring such an activity about. In other words, we shall move from what to how. In doing so, we shall be following the order that Aristotle observed exists in the production of both natural and artificial things. Thus he says that the causes concerned in the generation of the works of nature are, as we see, more than one. There is the final cause and there is the motor cause. Now we must decide which of these two causes comes first, which second. Plainly, however, that cause is the first which we call the final one. For this is the Reason, and the Reason forms the starting-point, alike in the works of art and in works of nature. For consider how the physician or how the builder sets about his work. He starts by forming for himself a definite picture, in the one case perceptible to mind, in the other to sense, of his end—the physician of health, the builder of a house—and this he holds forward as the reason and explanation of each subsequent step that he takes, and of his acting in this or that way as the case may be.[2]

A. Teaching's Definition

What picture of teaching, then, does Aristotle hold forward as the explanation of each step taken later to make this activity a reality? Although he wrote no separate treatise on teaching, Aristotle has several statements which indicate the way in which he would define this activity. We shall first list them and then comment upon them:

1. All instruction given or received by way of argument proceeds from pre-existent knowledge.[3]
2. All teaching starts from what is already known, as we maintain in the *Analytics* also; for it proceeds sometimes through induction and sometimes by syllogism.[4]
3. The people who instruct us are those who tell the causes of each thing.[5]

1. It Moves from Known to Unknown

In the first quotation Aristotle maintains that teaching is a process which must be built on the knowledge possessed by the student. Obversely, he holds that the teacher cannot instruct his pupils if he proceeds from ideas unfamiliar to them. If the instructor wishes to clarify, for example, the principle *fungi are plants which obtain their food from an external source*, he must do so by utilizing particular kinds of fungi which are familiar to the students, such as mushrooms, puffballs, and molds. Only in this way can the teacher lead his students to new knowledge. In the words of Aristotle's commentator, Aquinas: "Anyone who teaches, leads the disciple from things known by the latter, to the knowledge of things previously unknown to him; according to what the Philosopher [Aristotle] says (*Poster*, i.1.): *All teaching and all learning proceed from previous knowledge.*"[6]

Aristotle is insistent that the teacher must proceed from ideas understood by the student because the latter only potentially knows that which he is trying to learn. In other words, the student is in a state of potency to the ideas presented in a given lesson. But what exists potentially must always be brought to actuality by an agent, which is an actual being. Hence what is potentially a man becomes actually a man as a result of the man who generates him, who is an actual being; and similarly one who is potentially musical becomes actually musical by learning from a teacher who is actually musical. And thus in the case of anything potential there is always some first thing which moves it, and this mover is actual.[7]

Since the potential is brought to actuality only by something actual, and the student only potentially knows that which he is studying, he can be helped only by something he actually knows. More briefly, the pupil, in potency to that which he is learning, must move into this unknown by means of what he knows. Only in this way can the student learn or be taught. For this reason Aquinas describes teaching as a process in which the instructor helps another "towards knowledge [by] leading him step by step from principles he already knows to conclusions hitherto unknown to him."[8] To be effective, the process of teaching must move from the known to the unknown.

2. It Uses Induction and Deduction

In the second quotation we have cited, Aristotle insists again that all teaching must start from that which is understood by the student. In addition to this principle, however, he points out that teaching utilizes both the inductive and syllogistic techniques. This means that teaching's movement from the known to the unknown can be either inductive or deductive. To explain what Aristotle means by this, let us make use of several illustrations.

If a teacher wishes to help a student learn some universal concept or principle by proceeding inductively, he will simply present the student with familiar examples falling under the knowledge to be taught. Thus, if a science teacher wishes to teach inductively the principle *friction produces heat*, he will give familiar examples of this truth. Thus he may show that particular cases of friction—such as rubbing the hands together, using roller skates, rubbing sticks together for a fire—produce heat. In this manner the student can be led to make the induction that the universal principle *friction produces heat* is true.

Aristotle himself shows the nature of this inductive process in the following example, in which he is clarifying the principle *everyone honors the wise*. He says that

everyone honours the wise. Thus the Parians have honoured Archilochus, in spite of his bitter tongue; the Chians Homer, though he was not their countryman; the Mytilenaeans Sappho, though she was a woman; the Lacedaemonians actually made Chilon a member of their senate, though they are the least literary of men; the Italian Greeks honoured Pythagoras; the inhabitants of Lampsacus gave public burial to Anaxagoras, though he was an alien, and honour him even to this day.[9]

From the above illustrations we can see that the inductive process in teaching is one in which we clarify a universal truth by means of examples, which are ultimately on the singular level. It is "a passage from individuals to universals, e.g. the argument that supposing the skilled pilot is the most effective, and likewise the skilled charioteer, then in general the skilled man is the best at his particular task."[10]

Deduction, on the other hand, is a movement, not from individuals to universals, but from general universal knowledge to more specific applications contained therein. Thus, let us suppose that the student is confronted with the following problem, or unknown: Is the earth round? When the teacher proceeds deductively to help the pupil solve this problem, he must utilize two things: (1) the student's knowledge of the specific case involved, namely, the earth; (2) the student's fund of general principles, one at least of which must be applicable to this case. Only by using these two knowns (which the student must first of all have), can the teacher help the pupil move from his general principles to specific applications. Thus, in our example, the teacher will proceed as follows:

1. He will aid the student to recall that on the surface of the earth a short distance causes a change in the horizon. If one would travel from New York to Florida, for example, one would see the stars in different positions.
2. Then the teacher will help the student to refer to the following general principle: Whenever a short distance causes a change in the horizon, a spherical surface must be involved. (This could be clarified by using small-scale examples.)
3. Immediately, then, the student should see that therefore the earth must be round. In other words, he now has a particular application of his general principle.[11]

From the above illustration we can see that the deductive process in teaching is one in which we solve a particular problem by our knowledge of the case involved and of the general principle applicable to it. In other words, it is a movement from known truths (the principle and the nature of the case) to an unknown application. More briefly, it is a movement from the known to the unknown, or from the general to the particular.[12] In the words of Aristotle: "Reasoning is an argument in which, certain things being laid down, something other than these necessarily comes about through them."[13]

Although we have stated that deduction is a process by which we move from the known to the unknown, we must still point out that the unknowns at which we arrive can have varying degrees of certitude. Thus, by the deductive process, we may conclude both of the following: (1) Material things are corruptible. (2) The Democratic Party is progressive. Without hesitation we can see that the former statement is more certain than the latter. Nevertheless, both statements can be obtained by the deductive process.

Therefore we can see that this process does not, by means of the nature or form of its procedure, lead always to conclusions of absolute certitude. In other words, the process of deduction, formally considered, does not necessarily lead to certain conclusions. This certitude also demands the use of known material, or principles, of at least equal certainty. Thus only certain principles, as well as the correct deductive process, can lead to the conclusion *all material things are corruptible.* We do not, by means of the deductive process alone, always arrive at certain or causal knowledge.

Rather the process of deduction includes all types of conclusions, no matter whether they are rhetorical, dialectical, or demonstrative. For this reason Aristotle says that "not only dialectical and demonstrative syllogisms are formed by means of the aforesaid figures [of the syllogism], but also rhetorical syllogisms and in general any form of persuasion, however it may be presented."[14]

Having described briefly the inductive and deductive processes proper to teaching, we must point out that induction is the more basic of the two, simply because all of our knowledge starts from the senses. The starting point, therefore, in the teaching process is the inductive procedure. Any real progress is ultimately dependent upon it. Thus Aristotle says that "induction is the starting-point which knowledge even of the universal presupposes, while syllogism proceeds *from* universals. There are therefore starting-points from which syllogism proceeds, which are not reached by syllogism; it is therefore by induction that they are acquired."[15] Induction, as being the movement from sense to the universal, is our contact with reality, is our way of staying in touch with the world around us.

3. It Strives for Causal Knowledge

In addition to pointing out that teaching employs both induction and deduction, Aristotle says that "the people who instruct us are those who tell the causes of each thing."[16] Why does he speak in this manner? In saying that the teachers impart the knowledge of the causes of a thing, he is still indicating that they help the student acquire knowledge; but he does so by stressing the best kind, namely, the knowledge of causes. In other words, for Aristotle, the teacher is one who helps the student attain the best kind of knowledge, that of the causes proper to a thing.

Thus, if the teacher would explain to the student that the sum of the angles of a triangle is equal to two right angles, he must show him the reason or cause for such a truth. This he can accomplish by constructing an angle falling outside the triangle and formed by one of its sides, for such a construction makes it evident that the very nature of a triangle would lead to such a conclusion about the sum of the angles. By a construction the teacher can help the student see the truth of the theorem, a truth which rests on the very nature or definition of the triangle.

Why does Aristotle hold that the best kind of knowledge is that of the proper causes of a thing? The answer rests in the fact that genuine knowledge is found in the truth about any given object. But the truth about such a thing lies in its causes, "for the principles of the existence of a thing and of its truth are the same."[17] Since these principles of a thing's existence are precisely its causes, then the truth, wherein lies genuine knowledge, is found in the causes of a given object. Because, then, the truth lies in a thing's causes, Aristotle holds that the knowledge most desirable is that concerning the causes of a thing.

Thus, concerning the fact that the sum of the angles of a triangle is equal to two right angles, the knowledge most desired is that of the proper reason or cause of this fact. To illustrate that causal knowledge is best, Aristotle points out that "we suppose artists to be wiser than men of experience (which implies that wisdom depends in all cases rather on knowledge); and this because the former know the cause, but the latter do not."[18]

Again, Aristotle shows that causal knowledge is real wisdom by explaining that the one knowing causes can teach, and that teaching is a sign of the wise person or of one who really knows. It is he who knows the answers who can teach and be called wise. Aquinas's commentary on this insight of Aristotle is as follows:

> A sign of knowledge is the ability to teach, and this is so because each thing is perfect in its activity when it can produce another thing similar to itself, as is said in Book IV of *Meteors*. Therefore, just as the possession of heat is indicated by the fact that a thing can heat something else, in a similar way the possession of knowledge is indicated by the fact that one can teach, that is, cause knowledge in another. But men who have an art can teach, for since they know causes they can demonstrate from these; and demonstration is a syllogism which produces knowledge, as is said in Book I of the *Posterior Analytics*. But men who have experience [only] cannot teach; for since they do not know the causes, they cannot cause knowledge in someone else.... Hence, it is clear that men who have an art are wiser and more knowing than those who have experience.[19]

To have an understanding of the causes of a thing is to possess scientific knowledge, according to Aristotle. Thus he says that "we suppose ourselves to possess unqualified scientific knowledge of a thing, as opposed to knowing it in the accidental way in which the sophist knows, when we think that we know the cause on which the fact depends, as the cause of that fact and of no other, and, further, that the fact could not be other than it is."[20] One knows, therefore, a given fact scientifically if one knows it in the following way: (1) The cause of the fact is known. (2) This cause is known as the cause of the fact. (3) One knows that, given the cause, the resulting fact cannot be otherwise (i.e., one does not have the case where the cause is posited but the effect need not necessarily follow).

To illustrate the nature of scientific knowledge, let us take the kind of knowledge that we can possess about the eclipse of the moon. At first we see that the moon is eclipsed, and we wonder about the cause of this phenomenon. We do possess a knowledge of the cause when we are able to say that the eclipse occurred because of "the interposition of the earth, or the turning of the moon, or the extinction of its light."[21] We do not possess, however, a knowledge of the cause of the fact until we know which of the reasons we have is the proper cause. When we know, however, that the cause of the eclipse of the moon is the interposition of the earth between it and the sun, then we know not only the cause but that this is the cause of the fact. When we know also that, given this cause, the effect (an eclipse) will follow, then we have the three conditions necessary for scientific knowledge. Then we possess science about the fact of the eclipse of the moon.

It is scientific knowledge that Aristotle says the teacher must strive to give to the student. Naturally, it is not always possible to arrive at such a perfect understanding of a given thing, but this is the ideal toward which the teacher must aim. In the Philosopher's short statement that "the people who instruct us are those who tell the causes of each thing,"[22] we have a description of the activity of teaching at its best. To tell the student what are the causes of a thing is the real work of a teacher, though many times one can do no more than approach such a goal.

We can now summarize the knowledge that we have from Aristotle about the meaning of teaching. We know that it is a movement from the known to the unknown, that it proceeds both inductively and deductively, and that, at its best, it gives a knowledge of causes. It is this understanding of teaching that we will employ throughout this book. We shall speak of teaching in general as a movement from the known to the unknown, but we shall keep an awareness of its twofold procedure and of the goal toward which it should strive.

B. Teaching's Purpose
1. The Purpose: Intellectual Virtue

Having set down Aristotle's definition of teaching, let us now elaborate upon its purpose. From the material that we have already treated, we know that the purpose of teaching is to give the student science or knowledge of causes. Most simply expressed, it is to help the student to know. If possible, the student should acquire a scientific knowledge of a given subject or at least an educational acquaintance with it, for, as Aristotle says,

> every systematic science, the humblest and the noblest alike, seems to admit of two distinct kinds of proficiency; one of which may be properly called scientific knowledge of the subject, while the other is a kind of educational acquaintance with it. For an educated man should be able to form a fair off-hand judgement as to the goodness or badness of the method used by a professor in his exposition. To be educated is in fact to be able to do this; and even the man of universal education we deem to be such in virtue of his having this ability. It will, however, of course, be understood that we only ascribe universal education to one who in his own individual person is thus critical in all or nearly all branches of knowledge, and not to one who has a like ability merely in some special subject. For it is possible for a man to have this competence in some one branch of knowledge without having it in all.[23]

As we can see from the above quotation, the student's knowledge admits of different degrees or levels. The ideal, of course, would be that the teacher would help him to be scientifically equipped in relation to all of knowledge. At this point he would be considered wise, for "in general we all consider those especially to be wise who know all things, as the case demands, without having a knowledge of every singular thing. For this is impossible, since singular things are infinite in number, and an infinite number of things cannot be comprehended by the intellect."[24]

To possess wisdom, the student must understand the science which considers first principles and causes, namely, the science of metaphysics. He must possess a causal knowledge of things culminating in a knowledge of the First Cause of things because

> the more a man attains to a knowledge of the cause, the wiser he is.... [Thus] the man of experience is wiser than one who has sensation alone without experience; and the artist is wiser than any man of experience; and among artists the architect is wiser than the manual laborer. And similarly among the arts and sciences the speculative are more scientific than the practical.[25]

Such wisdom is not easy to obtain, for it presupposes the knowledge of all the subjects subordinate to metaphysics, chiefly logic, mathematics, natural science, and moral science. It is, however, the goal toward which all teaching and learning should strive. Expressed in Aquinas's words, the knowledge of the First Cause "constitutes the goal to which the things studied both in this science [metaphysics] and in the other sciences are directed."[26]

Although the student may not attain to wisdom, it is hoped that he will at least possess a scientific knowledge of one of the subjects subordinate to metaphysics. Insofar as he does, he will be able to think easily about such a subject; his intellect will be well disposed to handle the knowledge under consideration. In other words, he will be one whose "intellect has the power to bring itself into action at will."[27] We can say, therefore, that such a person possesses intellectual virtue, since in general "every virtue or excellence both brings into good condition the thing of which it is the excellence and makes the work of that thing be done well; e.g. the excellence of the eye makes both the eye and its work good; for it is by the excellence of the eye that we see well."[28] If, then, one's intellect is well disposed to perform its work well, to act according to its nature, such a one possesses intellectual virtue.

Therefore we can say that the purpose of teaching is to help the student acquire intellectual virtue. As should be clear from what has preceded, Aristotle has already implied this when he said that those "who instruct us are those who tell the causes of each thing."[29] He makes a more explicit connection, however, between teaching and intellectual virtue when he says that "intellectual virtue in the main owes both its birth and its growth to teaching."[30]

The purpose of teaching, therefore, can be expressed in various ways: to help the student to know, to help him arrive at the causes of things, to help him acquire intellectual virtue. The ideal, of course, running throughout all of these expressions is that the student arrive at the highest knowledge of all, that of the First Cause. Only with such knowledge will he be satisfied, for even

> the scanty conceptions to which we can attain of celestial things give us, from their excellence, more pleasure than all our knowledge of the world in which we live; just as a half glimpse of persons that we love is more delightful than a leisurely view of other things, whatever their number and dimensions.[31]

2. Its Value

Having seen that intellectual virtue is the purpose of teaching, let us relate such a purpose to the goals of education and of life itself. To the extent we see that the goals of all three are the same, we shall understand more fully the value of the activity of teaching, for the end of life "must be the good and the chief good."[32] If the purpose of teaching coincides with the human being's reason for living, then the work of the instructor has a true importance.

a. As Education's Goal

In order, then, to see how closely the purpose of teaching is related first to the end of education, let us begin by defining the latter. Aristotle holds that education is the development of the human being, over and beyond that provided by nature. This development is basically twofold, for, although human powers are irrational (or vegetative), appetitive, and rational,[33] it is chiefly the latter two which are open to education. Therefore education can be described as a process for developing the human appetitive and rational powers. In the words of Aristotle: "All else [beyond that provided by nature] is the work of education; we learn some things by habit and some by instruction."[34] In this quotation *habit* refers to the appetitive powers, while *instruction* indicates the rational faculties.

More accurately, however, Aristotle's position on education is that it is the acquisition of moral and intellectual virtue. This is so, for education should promote a sound development of the appetitive and rational powers.[35] Since virtue is that which "both brings into good condition the thing of which it is the excellence and makes the work of that thing be done well,"[36] then education, striving for a sound development of human powers, is the acquisition of moral and intellectual virtue.

The process of education must include both moral and intellectual virtue; neither can be excluded if this process is to be effective. Moral virtue is needed in the student's education, for it is an indispensable prerequisite for the acquisition of intellectual virtue. Without the virtues of attention and docility, for example, the student's advance in the intellectual life would be most difficult. This basic position of the moral virtues in the educative process is emphasized in the following quotation:

Now, in men rational principle and mind are the end toward which nature strives, so that the birth and moral discipline of the citizens ought to be ordered with a view to them.... Wherefore, the care of the body ought to precede that of the soul, and the training of the appetitive part should follow: none the less our care of it must be for the sake of the reason, and our care of the body for the sake of the soul.[37]

Neither moral nor intellectual virtue can be excluded from the process of education, for the latter is its end or purpose. Aristotle makes this clear in the above quotation, when he says that "in men rational principle and mind are the end towards which nature strives."[38] He holds that intellectual virtue is the primary goal of education, for such virtue perfects the intellect, the highest human faculty. This faculty is best, for it makes human nature to be what it is. "For even if it be small in bulk, much more does it in power and worth surpass everything. This would seem, too, to be each man himself, since it is the authoritative and better part of him."[39] That intellect is of his very essence can also be seen by the fact that the human being is defined as a rational animal.

Since intellectual virtue perfects the highest human faculty and the perfection of this power is the aim of education, then we can conclude that intellectual virtue is the purpose of this process. The development of the human being's best faculty is the aim of education because "that which is the best in each thing is the end and that for the sake of which something is done."[40] If the best is always the end, the development of each person's highest faculty is the purpose of education. Since intellectual virtue perfects this faculty, then the acquisition of this virtue is the goal at which education aims.

We have pointed out the purpose of education in order that we might see the value of teaching. Insofar as the purpose of teaching is the same as that of education, we can see the significance of the instructor's work, for education is vital to one who lives by reason rather than by instinct.[41] Since the goal of both teaching and education is intellectual virtue, then the work of the teacher is a most important one.

b. As Life's Goal

The importance of teaching can also be noted from the fact that its end is the same as the end of life, namely, intellectual activity in accordance with virtue. Aristotle is led to the conclusion that such activity must be the end of life by a very deliberate process of reasoning. He sees that to find this end he must discover the proper human function, "for just as for a flute-player, a sculptor, or any artist, and, in general, for all things that have a function or activity, the good and the 'well' is thought to reside in the function, so would it seem to be for man, if he has a function."[42]

Aristotle then reasons that the proper human function will not be one which he shares with other living things, such as the activity of growth or sensation, but one peculiar to him alone, namely, the activity of reason. Such activity, however, must be that which is performed in a virtuous way. Aristotle sees the necessity of this further specification, for human actions admit of mediocre or excellent performance, and the latter is of more worth. If, then, virtuous activity is better, "human good turns out to be activity of soul in accordance with virtue, and if there are more than one virtue, in accordance with the best and most complete."[43]

The highest type of virtuous activity will be that of speculation or contemplation, for such activity is both in accord with each person's nature and reaches out to the highest object, namely, the First Cause of all things. Aristotle sees many reasons why such activity should be the proper human function and thus the end of life. Among these we find him saying that

> this [contemplative] activity is the best (since not only is reason the best thing in us, but the objects of reason are the best of knowable objects).... And we think happiness has pleasure mingled with it, but the activity of philosophic wisdom is admittedly the pleasantest of virtuous activities; at all events the pursuit of it is thought to offer pleasures marvellous for their purity and their enduringness, and it is to be expected that those who know will pass their time more pleasantly than those who inquire.... And this activity alone would seem to be loved for its own sake; for nothing arises from it apart from the contemplating, while from practical activities we gain more or less apart from the action [such as money and power].[44]

Since that activity which is for its own sake, is most pleasant, and is best, will be the end of all human desires, then Aristotle reasons that contemplative activity in accordance with virtue must be the end of life.

If virtuous contemplative activity is the end of the human being, then again we can see the dignity of teaching. Since the purpose of the instructor is to lead his students to intellectual virtue (ideally to the virtue of wisdom), teaching is a most important human activity. It is true that the teacher may help his students acquire both the practical arts, such as engineering, and the speculative sciences, such as theoretical physics; but his work is geared ultimately to help his students gain, insofar as they are able, the speculative knowledge of the First Cause. In this respect, teaching can be considered an activity of great dignity, for it aims at the same purpose as that of life, which "must be the good and the chief good."[45]

C. Teaching's Materials

Having discussed the purpose and value of teaching, we shall now point out the materials with which it works. This accomplished, we shall then be prepared to treat the procedure utilized to bring about its purpose. In following this order, we are adhering to the thinking of Aristotle, who says that

> if a house or other such final object [such as intellectual virtue in the student] is to be realized, it is necessary that such and such material shall exist; and it is necessary that first this and then that shall be produced, and first this and then that set in

motion, and so on in continuous succession, until the end and final result is reached, for sake of which each prior thing is produced and exists.[46]

What, then, are the materials with which teaching works? In order to arrive at his goal, the teacher must work with both the student and his own fund of knowledge. If he is to teach, the instructor needs, besides his own knowledge to guide him, the student who is to be formed in intellectual virtue. In other words,

in the act of teaching we find a twofold subject matter, and as an indication of this, two accusatives are used as objects of the verb which expresses the act of teaching. This is so because the subject which one teaches is one kind of subject matter of teaching, and the one to whom the knowledge is communicated is another type of subject of teaching.[47]

Thus we might say that we teach geometry to the student.

1. The Student's Potential
a. This Potential

Let us begin, then, by describing the possibilities that the student, as one of the needed materials in teaching, furnishes in order that this art may accomplish its purpose. According to Aristotle, the pupil is not simply passive in this process, as a piece of clay might be; for, if he were, no growth in knowledge would occur. This observation—that the student is more than passive in the process of acquiring knowledge from a teacher—is further substantiated by the fact that he is able to acquire knowledge by himself. For this reason we can say that the student furnishes active potential for the process of teaching. Thus we find Aristotle saying that "the soul is so constituted as to be capable of this process [that of arriving at the first principles of all knowledge from sense perception]."[48] Again he says that "he who is learning must, it would seem, possess some part of the science."[49]

Before we say anything further about the active potential of the student, we must distinguish between the meanings of active and passive potential. Aristotle points out that the term *potential* or *potency* has both an active and a passive denotation. Thus, in the active sense *potency* or *power* can be used to mean a principle of motion or change. We can speak, for example, of the power of a diesel engine to pull a freight train. Aristotle defines this type of potency precisely as

a source of movement or change, which is in another thing than the thing moved or in the same thing *qua* other; e.g. the art of building is a potency which is not in the thing built, while the art of healing, which is a potency, may be in the man healed, but not in him *qua* healed.[50]

We can also use *potency* in the passive sense meaning that potency is a principle whereby a thing can be moved or changed. Thus we may speak of a forest, especially in a dry season, as having the possibility, or potency, for catching on fire. Such a potency, very properly called passive potency, is defined by Aristotle as "the source of a thing's being moved by another thing or by itself *qua* other. For in virtue of that principle, in virtue of which a patient suffers anything, we call it 'capable' of suffering."[51] Thus, repeating the above example, we see that the forest is capable of suffering, is capable of being burnt up.

From this we can realize that there are at least two kinds of potency: active and passive. Active potency is the "source of movement or change, which is in another thing than the thing moved or in the same thing *qua* other.... [Passive potency is] the source of a thing's being moved by another thing or by itself *qua* other."[52]

As we examine these two definitions of potency, we see that Aristotle is very careful to note that both potencies have a reference to another thing, either something entirely external to the potency or, if in the same thing as the potency, something different from the given potency. Thus in active potency, for example, he says that the art of building is distinct from the thing built and that the art of healing, as being in the intellect of the doctor who heals himself, is distinct from that which he heals, namely, the sick organ. In other words, these two types of potency are distinct from the things to which they have reference, either because that to which they refer is external to the potency or because the thing to which they refer, if in the same thing as the potency, is a different part of the thing from the potency.

Why does Aristotle hold that the potency, whether active or passive, must be distinct from that to which it has reference? Why does he, for example, maintain that, if the active potency of healing is in the man who is healed, it must be a different part from that which is healed? Why, in the same thing, must the potency be a different part from the part to which it has reference?

Aristotle lays down this specification, for he sees that "everything which is moved [passive potency] is moved by another,"[53] and conversely that everything which moves (active potency) moves something other than itself. The truth of such a principle is most evident, Aristotle says, "in things that are in motion unnaturally, because in such cases it is clear that the motion is derived from something other than the thing itself."[54] Thus we can observe, for example, that the ball thrown into the air is moved by something other than itself. Since the mover and the moved are always distinct, we can see why Aristotle must define active and passive potency as he does.

Having clarified the two definitions of potency, we can state that the active potential of the student is that which is a source of movement or change, specifically, the source of the movement toward knowledge.[55] Is it, however, in another thing than the thing moved or in the same thing *qua* other? In other words, is the principle of change in some other thing, such as the teacher, or is it in the student himself, but in a different part of him from that being moved toward

knowledge? Aristotle asserts that the source of movement is in the student himself when he says that "the soul is so constituted as to be capable of this process
[that of arriving at the first principles of all knowledge from sense percep-
tion]."[56] Within the person learning there is a principle by which he is able to
advance in knowledge by his own efforts.

Not only does the student have an active principle of knowing but also (because of the nature of active potency) this principle is distinct from that which
receives its action. In other words, there must be both an active and a passive
principle within the student who advances in knowledge. In the words of Aquinas, there is "(1) a factor akin to the matter which, in any given class of things, is
potentially all the particulars included in the class; and (2) another factor which
operates as an active and productive cause, like art with respect to its material."[57]

Although we shall treat these two factors in more detail in chapter 3, we must
now at least indicate what they are. The passive principle within us, called the
possible intellect, is that whose "nature is simply to be open to all things."[58]
According to Aristotle, it is that principle in the intellect which is lacking all
things in the material world. Such a principle must be proper to the human intellect, for at birth it only potentially understands all that it is destined to know.
Since whatever is in a state of potency to a given object is automatically lacking
that object, then the intellect must have a principle which is

> lacking in every bodily nature; just as the sense of sight, being able to know col-
> our, lacks all colour. If sight itself had any particular colour, this colour would
> prevent it from seeing other colours, just as the tongue of a feverish man, being
> coated with a bitter moisture, cannot taste anything sweet.[59]

While the passive principle in the human intellect is that which is open to all
things, the active principle, called the agent intellect, is that power in the human
intellect which abstracts the natures of sensible things from their individuating
principles. It "actualises the intelligible notions themselves, abstracting them
from matter, i.e., bringing them from potential to actual intelligibility."[60] Thus it
is the agent intellect that abstracts the nature *rational animal* from the individual
persons encountered. Its chief work being abstraction, it can be compared to a
light which penetrates to the nature of the individuals concerned. Because of
this, we may speak of it as the light of reason, a light which is only a "participation in the intellectual light of separated substances."[61]

By means of this abstractive power of the agent intellect, one is able to understand the nature of sensible things, to arrive at that common notion which
pervades every singular of a given type. This power is exercised first of all on
those concepts and principles which underlie all other knowledge.[62] These
function as the

> seeds of knowledge..., which by the light of the agent intellect are immediately
> known through the species abstracted from sensible things. These are either com-

plex, as axioms, or simple, as the notions of being, of the one, and so on, which the understanding grasps immediately. In these general principles, however, all the consequences are included as in certain seminal principles.[63]

These general principles, as well as the universal knowledge subsequent to them, can be abstracted from the sensible singulars only by the power of the agent intellect.

b. Need of This Potential

Having seen that the student possesses within himself both an active and a passive principle for advancing in knowledge, we must point out that one could not teach another if the student were not so equipped. We say this because the teacher instructs another or communicates his knowledge to him by means of sensible signs, chiefly the spoken word. For this reason Aristotle says that "rational discourse is a cause of instruction in virtue of its being audible."[64]

Sensible signs, however, are discernible by the sense powers. As such, they are not the proper object of the intellect, which reaches beyond the sense order into the inner nature of things. Thus a particular patch of color or a given instance of sound is the proper object of a sense power, but not of the intellectual power. Therefore it seems that the teacher, utilizing sensible signs, would be unable to reach the student's intellectual power. If so, it appears that the teacher could not accomplish his purpose, namely, to help the student acquire intellectual virtue. If the teacher instructs by sensible signs, how can he help his student obtain universal knowledge?

In spite of his inadequacy, the teacher can instruct the student, for the latter has the power to abstract the nature or essence from whatever his senses present to him. By means of his active principle, the agent intellect, the student is able to penetrate into the sensible signs presented to him and to arrive at the nature of the thing involved. Because the student has this power, the teacher can instruct him; without this active principle, the teacher could not achieve his purpose. Thanks to the agent intellect, however, the teacher is able to set "before the pupil signs of intelligible things, and from these the agent intellect [of the pupil] derives the intelligible likenesses and causes them to exist in the possible intellect."[65]

From this we can see that the teacher, in order to achieve his purpose, must depend upon the light of reason within the student. In this respect he stands as a helper in the student's acquisition of science. In this he resembles the doctor, who only assists the sick person in his efforts to regain health. The reason is that

just as there is in the sick person the natural principle of health, to which the doctor lends aid for the perfecting of health, so in the student there is the natural principle of science, namely, the *agent intellect*, and the *self-evident first principles,* while the teacher furnishes certain helps, by deducing conclusions from the self-evident principles....

And just as health in the sick person is not produced according to the power of the doctor, but according to the faculty of nature, so also science is caused in the student not according to the power of the master, but according to the faculty of the one learning.[66]

Since the acquisition of science in the student depends basically upon the faculty of the one learning, the teacher must exercise his art with a constant awareness of the active principle within the material with which he is working. He must also remember that there are individual differences in the group of students before him. One pupil, for example, has a greater native capacity, a better ability to abstract and reason, than another. The teacher, in his activity, must never forget this, for "actions and productions are all concerned with the individual; for the physician does not cure *man*, except in a incidental way, but Callias or Socrates or some other called by some such individual name, who happens to be a man."[67] In terms of the activity under discussion, the teacher does not instruct student in general, but John and Mary, who happen to be students.

2. The Teacher's Knowledge
a. Need of This Knowledge

Having examined the type of material that the student presents for the activity of teaching, let us now see what Aristotle says about the second type of material, namely, the knowledge of the teacher. As the following listing shows, he emphasizes that the instructor must know his subject matter:

1. Teaching necessarily implies possessing knowledge, and learning not possessing it.[68]
2. [A person] starting with the power to know learns or acquires knowledge through the agency of one who actually knows and has the power of teaching.[69]
3. In general it is a sign of the man who knows and of the man who does not know, that the former can teach....

   ...[Also] the people who instruct us are those who tell the causes of each thing.[70]

Aristotle holds that the teacher must know because his work is to help the student advance in knowledge. In other words, he must help the student move from potential to actual knowledge. To do this he must possess the knowledge himself,

for what exists potentially must always be brought to actuality by an agent, which is an actual being. Hence what is potentially a man becomes actually a man as a result of the man who generates him, who is an actual being; and similarly one who is potentially musical becomes actually musical by learning from a teacher who is actually musical. And thus in the case of anything potential there is always some first thing which moves it, and this mover is actual.[71]

For this reason Aristotle says that the teacher, as a cause of the student's moving from potency to act, must possess actual knowledge of the subject matter.

Not only does Aristotle hold that the teacher must know his subject matter, but, conversely, he maintains that the sign of one who knows is the ability to teach. His reason for this position is that

> each thing is perfect in its activity when it can produce another thing similar to itself.... Therefore, just as the possession of heat is indicated by the fact that a thing can heat something else, in a similar way the possession of knowledge is indicated by the fact that one can teach, that is, cause knowledge in another.[72]

Realizing that the teacher must know his subject matter and that the activity of teaching is a sign of his knowledge, we can conclude that the student does not teach himself. It is true that he is able to discover things by his own efforts, but this cannot be called teaching. The reason is that "this is a contradiction, because a teacher has a science but a learner does not."[73] For this reason a person studying by himself can be called a discoverer, but he cannot be called a teacher in relation to himself.

b. Nature of This Knowledge

Having seen that the teacher is one who knows, let us now point out what kind of knowledge he must possess. Since the goal of teaching is to lead the pupil to science and wisdom, the teacher should have not only a scientific knowledge of his subject matter but also the ability "to form a fair off-hand judgement as to the goodness or badness of the method used [in all subjects]."[74] In other words, he should both know his own subject scientifically and also be able to make sound evaluations about the procedures of the other subjects. Ideally, he should be a wise person, knowing first causes and principles; "for the more a man attains to a knowledge of the cause, the wiser he is."[75]

What do we mean when we say that the teacher must know his subject in a scientific way? This implies that the instructor, concerning the necessary and universal truths of his subject, will know them in this way. To do so, he must know the proper causes of these truths; for to know scientifically is to "know the cause on which the fact depends, as the cause of that fact and of no other, and, further, that the fact could not be other than it is."[76] Thus the mathematician, in order to know scientifically that the exterior angle of a triangle is always equal to the two opposite interior angles, must understand the reason for this theorem. Helped by a geometrical construction, he must see that the very nature and definition of the triangle lead to such a conclusion.

It is also necessary for the person of science to know the basic principles of his subject matter; for it is only when "the starting-points are known to him that he has scientific knowledge, since if they are not better known to him than the conclusion, he will have his knowledge only incidentally."[77] Thus it is necessary for the arithmetician to know the definition of the unit, the starting point of his science. Then, having a knowledge of this basic principle, he can proceed to demonstrate the conclusions proper to his subject.

The teacher who knows his subject scientifically must also be aware of the method which is appropriate for his science. He should not demand the same precision or the same amount of information in all subject matters. The person who studies the science of politics, for example, should not demand the same certitude that is found in mathematics. The reason is that

> fine and just actions, which political science investigates, admit of much variety and fluctuation of opinion, so that they may be thought to exist only by convention, and not by nature. And goods also give rise to a similar fluctuation because they bring harm to many people; for before now men have been undone by reason of their wealth, and others by reason of their courage. We must be content, then, in speaking of such subjects and with such premises to indicate the truth roughly and in outline, and in speaking about things which are only for the most part true and with premises of the same kind to reach conclusions that are no better. In the same spirit, therefore, should each type of statement be *received*; for it is the mark of an educated man to look for precision in each class of things just so far as the nature of the subject admits; it is evidently equally foolish to accept probable reasoning from a mathematician and to demand from a rhetorician scientific proofs.[78]

If possible, the teacher should know not only the method proper to his subject but also that which is appropriate for the various subject matters. He should know, for example, that the method of mathematics is more certain than that of natural science. If he can do this, he can be considered, according to Aristotle, a person of universal education. At this point he is capable of making critical evaluations not only of the conclusions of his own subject, but also of those of all or nearly all branches of knowledge. We could say that he is learned, that he is one who knows. If he perfects his knowledge in the study of first causes and principles, found in the science of metaphysics, he is a person of wisdom.

Thus far we have seen that the teacher, in order to be one who knows and who can produce knowledge in another, must possess the following:

1. Ideally, he should know his subject in a scientific way. This means that he must know the proper causes of his subject, since these causes (the definitions of the subject) are the means whereby one arrives at the conclusions of the science.
2. He should know the appropriate method for his science.
3. He should also know the methods proper to the various subjects.
4. If possible, he should have an understanding of the science of metaphysics.

If the teacher understands his subject in the above way, we can say, with Aristotle, that he is one "who actually knows and has the power of teaching."[79] Is such a knowledge of the subject matter sufficient for the person who wishes to teach, or must he also have an understanding of the art of teaching, i.e., of the methodology of instructing another? As the above quotation implies, Aristotle holds that the teacher, truly knowing his subject matter, has also the theory (but not the practice) of the art of teaching. Why does he speak in this way? Why does he maintain that the person knowing the general and special methods of the various subjects has the theoretical principles of the art of teaching?

In order to understand that the person possessing the knowledge of the general and special methods of the various subjects has at least the theoretical principles of the art of teaching (as explaining, not motivating), let us first point out that the general method for all the sciences is logic. Thus we find Aquinas, when commenting on Aristotle's doctrine, saying that "logic considers the general method of procedure in all the other sciences."[80] The art of logic has this function because it gives the general rules for thinking, the process indispensable in all the sciences. Therefore we can see immediately that the teacher truly understanding the general method of the sciences would know the art of logic.

In addition to this general method found in logic, the sciences also have their own individual procedures, which vary from subject to subject. Thus the following quotation shows the distinction in procedure between physics and dialectical reasoning:

> A physicist would define an affection of soul differently from a dialectician; the latter would define e.g. anger as the appetite for returning pain for pain, or something like that, while the former would define it as a boiling of the blood or warm substance surrounding the heart. The latter assigns the material conditions, the former the form or formulable essence; for what he states is the formulable essence of the fact, though for its actual existence there must be embodiment of it in a material such as is described by the other.[81]

Such procedures as these are simply refinements of the art of logic. They, as well as the general rules of the art, should be learned before the teacher attempts to acquire a scientific understanding of his subject, for

> it is absurd for a man to try to acquire a science and at the same time to acquire the method proper to that science. This is why a man should learn logic before any of the other sciences, because logic considers the general method of procedure in all the other sciences. Moreover, the method appropriate to the particular sciences should be considered at the beginning of these sciences.[82]

When we have seen that the teacher well equipped in the general and special methods of the various subjects knows the art of logic, then we can understand that such a teacher has at least the theoretical principles of the art of teaching. The reason that such a teacher is so prepared is that the two basic procedures in the art of logic, whether it concludes demonstratively, dialectically, or rhetorically, are induction and deduction. Thus Aristotle remarks that "not only dialectical and demonstrative syllogisms are formed by means of the aforesaid figures [of the syllogism], but also rhetorical syllogisms and in general any form of persuasion, however it may be presented. For every belief comes either through syllogism or from induction."[83]

Aristotle speaks in such a fashion because logic, as the art of thinking, is modeled after the way the human mind operates. What is this mode of operation? In order to advance in knowledge, the learner must rely on what is given him by his senses and on the way of inquiry proper to his reason. In the former case, he is proceeding inductively, and in the latter, deductively. The reliance of the learner upon these two processes is seen in the following quotations:

> Since according to common agreement there is nothing outside and separate in existence from sensible spatial magnitudes, the objects of thought are in the sensible forms, viz. both the abstract objects and all the states and affections of sensible things. Hence...no one can learn or understand anything in the absence of sense.[84]
>
> ...It is proper to man to come to an understanding of intelligible truth by the way of rational enquiry; whereas the immaterial substances, which are in a higher degree intellectual, apprehend truth immediately without having to reason about it.[85]

When we have realized that the basic procedures of logic are inductive or deductive, then we can understand its value for the teacher, since such procedures are those used by the instructor. Thus, if we recall, Aristotle points out that "all teaching starts from what is already known, as we maintain in the *Analytics* also; for it proceeds sometimes through induction and sometimes by syllogism."[86] That these procedures of induction and deduction should be the basic methods of the teacher (as explaining, not motivating or disciplining) is understandable when we remember that the teacher must work in accordance with the nature of the material that he has at hand, namely, the mind of the student. Since the student, as we have just mentioned, proceeds inductively or deductively, then we can understand why these procedures are the basic methods of the teacher.

In addition to this, since the art of logic works with the same procedures, then we can see that this art contributes much to the methodology of the teacher. If to propose to the student "some sensible examples, either by way of likeness or of opposition, or something of the sort, from which the intellect of the learner is led to the knowledge of truth previously unknown,...[or to show] the disciple the order of the principles to conclusions,"[87] is the work of the teacher, then we can understand why the art of logic should be most helpful to him.

With the knowledge that the art of logic does much for the teacher in an understanding of his art, we are now prepared to see why the teacher equipped in the general and special methods of his subject has the theoretical knowledge of how to teach it. We say this, for the general method of all the sciences is nothing other than the art of logic, since it gives the general thought procedures common to all the sciences. Therefore we can say that a teacher really understanding his subject, by knowing its principles, the proper causes of its conclusions, and its method, will have the theoretical principles for the art of teaching it. In the words of Aristotle: "In general it is a sign of the man who knows and of the man who does not know, that the former can teach."[88] He speaks in this way, for the man who knows, knowing also the method of his subject, knows theoretically how to teach it.

We say *knows theoretically* because another important factor for the teacher besides scientific knowledge of his subject is the possession of experience. In fact, says Aristotle, "with a view of action [in which teaching culminates] experience seems in no respect inferior to art, and men of experience succeed even better than those who have theory without experience."[89] Aristotle places such value on experience in relation to any kind of practical activity, including that of teaching, because action takes place in the concrete, in terms of singular cases. Thus, as we mentioned before, the teacher instructs John and Mary, not student in general.

In addition to this, we must remember that the association of several memories of singular cases constitutes experience. Thus, we can say that we have experience in a certain activity, such as playing tennis, after we have practiced the game in many single instances. To profit from these instances and to be considered experienced, however, we must do more than go through the routine of attempting to play the game. We must remember what we did well or poorly and gradually associate these memories of individual trials into a unified technique or procedure which qualifies us as experienced at the game. We must associate our memories of the game into a unified view.

This view, however, remains on the singular level, for it sees only these memories as a unit and does not yet have a knowledge of the game of tennis in general, does not have a universal view of tennis. When such an insight occurs, we no longer have just experience in the game but now it has become for us a real art. We have left the singular level and have moved to the universal level of art and science.

That the association of several singulars is proper to experience is pointed out in a classic example of Aristotle, which is explicated by Aquinas as follows:

> For when a man has learned that this medicine has been beneficial to Socrates and Plato, and to many other individuals who were suffering from some particular disease, whatever it may be, this is a matter of experience; but when a man learns that this particular treatment is beneficial to all men who have some particular kind of disease and some particular kind of physical constitution, as it has benefited the feverish, both the phlegmatic and the bilious, this is now a matter of art.[90]

If, then, the association of singular cases constitutes experience and the teacher's action is always in terms of individual students, it should be clear why it is most valuable for him to have experience, as well as theory, in the art of teaching. It is through experience that the teacher will be able to sense the problems and questions of individual students and to lead them, by means of his own knowledge, to a satisfactory solution.

To say that the teacher needs experience in no way discredits the fact that he should also have a scientific knowledge of his subject matter. The ideal, naturally, would be that the teacher both know his subject and have experience in teaching it. If he has only the theory, however, he is less effective in actual teaching (because of its practical nature) than the person of experience. "For men of experience act more effectively than those who have the universal knowledge of an art but lack experience."[91] In turn, the person with experience only is less effective than the teacher possessing both the knowledge of his subject and experience.

3. Teacher/Student Relationship
a. Teacher's Importance

Having indicated the qualifications required in order that the teacher be able to explain the subject matter, let us now point out that the teacher is a most important instrument in the student's acquisition of intellectual virtue. Though it is true enough that the student is able to acquire knowledge by his own efforts, such a process is both laborious and time consuming. The reason for the difficulty of this process is that the mind of the student at first only potentially knows that which it sets out to acquire. "It is like a sheet of paper on which no word is yet written, but many can be written."[92] For this reason (as well as the intellect's initial weakness) Aquinas, commenting on Aristotle, says that "error seems to be even more natural to animals, as they actually are, than knowledge. For experience proves that people easily deceive and delude themselves, whilst to come to true knowledge they need to be taught by others."[93]

The teacher is most necessary in helping the student acquire knowledge, for he knows the subject matter and can show his pupil the steps to take in mastering it. Thus the teacher knows both the starting points of the science and its chief conclusions. With such knowledge he is prepared to

> help him [the student] towards knowledge, leading him step by step from principles he already knows to conclusions hitherto unknown to him. Nor would this external aid be necessary if the human mind were always strong enough to deduce conclusions from the principles it possesses by nature.[94]

This, however, is not always the case; therefore "intellectual virtue in the main owes both its birth and its growth to teaching."[95]

b. Student's Attitude

If the teacher is so important to the student, with what attitude of mind should the student receive the doctrine of the teacher, especially in the beginning of his intellectual education? As we ask this question, we stress the beginning of the process deliberately, "for the beginning is thought to be more than half of the whole."[96] The reason is that all that comes after is virtually contained in the beginning. Thus the conclusions of a science are virtually contained in its basic principles. Therefore, all that follows will be colored by the beginning, just as the direction that a traveler is taking is indicated by his first steps down the road. With good reason, then, we ask what is the student's intellectual attitude toward his teacher in the beginning.

At the outset of his education the only possible intellectual attitude of the student toward the doctrine of the teacher is one of belief. As Aristotle expresses it, "the learner should take things on trust."[97] If a person takes driving lessons, for example, at first he can only believe the directions of the instructor. Later he will understand whether or not his instructions are sound, but in the beginning he can only trust the directives given. In this example we have an indication of the fact that the student begins his intellectual education with an attitude of belief toward the teacher.

The student assumes such an attitude toward his teacher because human faith or belief is synonymous with opinion. Thus we might say synonymously: "I believe that it will rain," or "It is my opinion that it will rain." As such, belief has the same meaning as opinion, which is defined as an act of the intellect in which "reason inclines wholly to one side of a contradiction, with fear of the other."[98] In other words, opinion is defined as that kind of knowing in which we have probability, rather than the certitude of science, and an assent mixed with fear, rather than the firm assent of divine faith. Thus, when we state an opinion on something such as the weather, we see the probability of what we are holding, such as the possibility of rain, and yet we retain a fear that such an event might not occur.

Since natural belief or opinion has not the certitude of science nor the firm assent of divine faith, it is at best an imperfect kind of knowledge. As such, it is the type that the student has in the beginning of the process of learning from a teacher. The student must first believe, before he can attain to true scientific knowledge.

The reason that the student begins by believing is that learning is a gradual process, is a quality which is slowly generated in the student.[99] As such, learning is a process in which the student is imperfect in the beginning and slowly matures to perfect knowledge, and then only by the guidance of the perfect, i.e., by the guidance of the teacher. That this is the case can be seen from the fact that in all things which acquire perfection gradually, a given

thing is brought from imperfection to perfection only through the activity of something perfect. Nor does the imperfect thing at once in the very beginning fully receive the action of that which is perfect; at first it receives it imperfectly and, later, more perfectly. And it continues in this way until it reaches perfection. This is evident in all physical things, which acquire a perfection gradually.[100]

Since things gradually acquiring perfection move from the imperfect to the perfect, and learning is such a gradual process, we can understand that the student must begin with an imperfect kind of knowledge, must begin with an attitude of belief. At the outset of his attempts to learn from the teacher, the student, being imperfect in knowledge, can only place his belief in the truths proposed to him, a belief which has the possibility of maturing later into full scientific knowledge. Thus, at the beginning of his study of the science of mathematics, the student accepts the fact of continuous and discrete quantity both from his own experience and from the authority of his teacher. Only later, as he becomes mature enough for the study of metaphysics, will he understand these two kinds of quantity scientifically.

When we say that the student must begin by believing the teacher, we do not mean that he places a blind assent in the doctrine of his instructor with no hope of future clarification. Rather the student's first act of belief is one which should mature into a real understanding. In the beginning the student believes in the teacher's ability to lead him easily and surely to the truth that he is seeking. He trusts that the teacher knows the subject and that he knows the road over which to lead the student. As the teacher explains the various steps for the student to take, however, the student should gradually see and understand what is being proposed to him. It is true that the student must first believe in the procedures of the teacher and in his knowledge of the subject matter, but in the end the student should understand the proposed subject matter by himself.

Therefore, although the act of belief is indispensable at the outset of the student's seeking for knowledge, we can say that it need not be more than a transitory state; for the student, as he sees the correspondence between the given facts (as substantiated by their examples or reasons) and the reality of things, can move from conditional belief to knowing. The student himself can begin to understand the nature of the teacher's doctrine and see whether or not it conforms to the way things are. He can begin to see whether or not the teacher's doctrine on the human soul, for example, actually conforms to the nature of such a soul.

This ability to judge of a doctrine, however, demands some experience with it. For this reason Aristotle says that "each man judges well the things he knows, and of these he is a good judge."[101] Such needed experience for the student is obtained much more easily from a teacher, who knows the nature of the subject matter, than from the learner's own efforts. Since the student relies so heavily on the teacher, we can understand why, if the student hopes eventually to be able to make sound judgments about a doctrine, he must begin by making an act of faith in the ability of the teacher to help him.

At this point we have completed our explanation of the nature of the materials utilized in the activity of teaching, namely, the potential of the student for learning and the knowledge of the teacher. We have seen that the student has an active and a passive principle for the acquisition of knowledge and that the teacher needs both knowledge of his subject matter and experience in the art of teaching it. Prior to our treatment of these materials, we pointed out the definition of teaching and explained more fully the purpose given in the definition. One factor of the process of teaching now remains to be treated, namely, teaching's principle of production.

D. Teaching's Productive Principle
1. Teaching as Practical

To speak about the principle behind the product at which teaching aims is most important, for teaching is a practical kind of activity. Before we show, however, why teaching is this kind of operation, let us explain briefly Aristotle's distinction between speculative and practical activity. The Philosopher bases this distinction upon the two fundamental purposes for which the human being uses his rational faculty, namely, to know the truth about reality or, with an awareness of such truth, to produce changes in those things which are contingent or open to change, such as natural resources or even the human will.

Thus the human being, gifted with the power of reason, is able not only to know the order of the natural world but also to produce changes in this given order. The members of a chemical laboratory, for example, are able both to know the molecular structure of a given element and also, by means of this knowledge, to so change or combine this element with other chemicals that a new drug can be produced. In the former case these persons are speculative in their activity, while, in the latter, they are practical. That both kinds of activities are open to human beings stems from the fact that the rational faculty is able not only to know the order present in nature but also, by considering this order, to bring about a new order, such as that found in artificial things. In the words of Aristotle: "There are two parts which grasp a rational principle—one by which we contemplate the kind of things whose originative causes are invariable, and one by which we contemplate variable things."[102]

As we have just mentioned, when the human being studies the things of reality just to find out the truth about them, his activity is speculative. We might say that he is simply speculating about the nature of things. When, however, his primary purpose, even if some study is involved, is to produce something, he is practical. In other words, whether he is building bridges, painting pictures, or producing peace among nations, he is a person involved in practical activity, a person of the active life.

Therefore we can say that speculative activity is simply a consideration of the truth, which is pursued in order to learn about reality and ultimately the First Cause of all reality. On the other hand, practical activity is that which, although it does involve study, is aimed at production, a production which may occur within the minds and wills of human beings or in things external to them, such as the natural resources of the land.

In the same way as we define speculative and practical activity, so do we describe the knowledge about such activities. Thus Aquinas says that

> theoretical, i.e., speculative, knowledge differs from practical knowledge by its end; for the end of speculative knowledge is truth, because it has knowledge of the truth as its objective. But the end of practical knowledge is action, because, even though "practical men," i.e., men of action, attempt to understand the truth as it belongs to certain things, they do not seek this as an ultimate end; for they do not consider the cause of truth in and for itself as an end but in relation to action, either by applying it to some definite individual, or to some definite time.[103]

Since the end of speculation is the truth about things and that of practical operation is production, one working in these two orders must never forget their proper purposes. This means that the research worker must diligently pursue the truth, while the person of action, whether he is a factory worker or a teacher, must aim for actual production. One whose task in society is the bringing about of some needed product cannot afford to rest in theory, just as the one dedicated to the pursuit of truth should not dissipate his energies in the practical order. Both the individuals of action and of contemplation have indispensable roles which must be fulfilled. The importance of this principle is illustrated in the following quotation about the true outcome of moral science:

> The end of the science concerned with practicable matters is not to know and investigate individual things, as in the speculative sciences, but rather to do them. And since we become virtuous and doers of good works in accordance with virtue, it is not sufficient for the science whose object is man's good that someone have a knowledge of virtue. But he must try to possess it as a habit and practice it.[104]

Having pointed out the distinction between speculative and practical activity and the importance of the fulfillment of the proper role of each, let us now return to the statement that teaching is a practical activity. There might be some question as to whether teaching is speculative or practical, for, as we pointed out in a previous section of this chapter, it has a twofold subject matter, namely, the particular subject being explained and the student to whom it is taught. If one thought of teaching solely in terms of the truth which the instructor must consider, then one might classify teaching as a speculative activity.[105] Is the consideration of such truth, however, the proper purpose of the teacher, or does he consider such truth in order that he may impart it to others? According to the thinking of Aristotle, the teacher prepares his subject matter so that he may guide others to the same truth.[106]

Teaching is primarily a practical activity, for it is a work of helping another to find the truth, a work of action for another. Since such external actions or operations are practical in nature, then with good reason teaching belongs to the practical order. It is true that the teacher in considering his subject matter is performing a speculative action, but the activity of teaching finds its fruition in helping another, which is an active work, a part of the practical order.

Since the end or "that for the sake of which other things are tends to be the best and the end of the other things,"[107] then the activity of teaching, terminating in an active work, is primarily a practical activity. We do not classify teaching by the speculation which it uses but by that in which it rests, namely, the leading of a student to truth. Teaching is practical simply because "teachers think they have achieved their end when they have exhibited the pupil at work."[108]

If teaching is practical, then, to be true to the nature of such activity, it must lead to actual production. In other words, the teacher must aim, not simply to know the truth, but to help others to acquire intellectual virtue. Since actual production is the goal in the work of teaching, the principles guiding such a process must be understood and followed. Put in another way, the teacher must know the basic principles of production, must know the principles relative to the method of teaching. The reason, of course, is that "the end of the science [such as the art of teaching] concerned with practicable matters is not to know and investigate individual things, as in the speculative sciences, but rather to do them."[109] What, then, is teaching's basic principle of production?

2. Teaching as an Art

In order to answer this question, let us begin by pointing out that teaching is an art. If any person intends to engage in this activity, he must exercise a real skill. This need may be recognized only because of its absence, but, nevertheless, it remains that teaching happens, not by chance, but by art. An activity that fulfills its purpose not just because of sheer luck nor again just because nature is at work (as, for example, in the growth of a plant), teaching can produce results only when it works at the level of art.[110] We can easily note the artistic quality required of teaching in the following quotation:

> In general it is a sign of the man who knows and of the man who does not know, that the former can teach, and therefore we think art more truly knowledge than experience is; for artists can teach, and men of mere experience cannot.[111]

When we say that teaching is an art, we must remember that Aristotle holds that "*art* is identical with a state of capacity to make, involving a true course of reasoning."[112] Art is a good habit of the mind whereby the intellect has the firm disposition to be able to direct the making of things in a reasonable fashion. Thus one, working easily with the reasonable rules for building with wood, possesses the art of carpentry. Again one who possesses the art of perspective can represent three-dimensional reality on two-dimensional canvas.

When we inquire further into the nature of art, we see that it deals with those things which are contingent, with those things which can either be produced or not be produced. Thus the carpenter's product might be a chair, which could have been made or not made according to the desire of the carpenter. For this reason Aristotle says that "all art is concerned with coming into being, i.e. with contriving and considering how something may come into being which is capable of either being or not being, and whose origin is in the maker and not in the thing made."[113] In this quotation Aristotle points out not only that art deals with the contingent but also that the source of such things is not in them, but in the artist. Thus a particular piece of art, such as a chair, is not only something that can either exist or not exist but also a thing that has come about because of something external to it, namely, the artist.

Because art is concerned with those contingent things brought into being by something external to them, it deals "neither with things that are, or come into being, by necessity, nor with things that do so in accordance with nature (since these have their origin in themselves)."[114] In other words, because art is concerned with those contingent things produced by an external source, it does not deal with eternal things, nor with things that will necessarily begin to exist, nor finally with those things which have a natural origin. Thus the object of the artist is not God or the separated substances, nor such things as an eclipse of the moon (which necessarily follows when the earth is interposed between the sun and the moon), nor anything stemming from a natural origin, such as the generation of a child from its parents. The things of art are those which can either be produced or not produced and which have their source in an artist, but not in themselves.

Art, then, "is nothing else but the *right reason about certain works to be made*,"[115] works which can either be produced or not produced by the artist. More briefly expressed, art is a reasonable making or producing. Insofar as it deals with making it does not concern itself with acting. This distinction can be made, for Aristotle maintains that making and acting have a basic difference. Acting, or activity, is simply the use of the powers capable of action, such as the activity of the power of sight is seeing, while that of the intellect is thinking. Making, on the other hand, is the use of a power in order that some product may be brought about. Thus the use of one's intellect in order that a house may be built is called a making, not an acting. Aquinas alludes to this distinction when he says that

> the ultimate goal or end of some active potencies consists in the mere use of those potencies, and not in something produced by their activity; for example, the ultimate goal of the power of sight is the act of seeing, and there is no product resulting from the power of sight in addition to this activity. But in the case of some active potencies something else is produced in addition to the activity; for example, the art of building also produces a house in addition to the activity of building.[116]

Because of this distinction between making and acting, we can see that acting remains within the person actualizing his power, while making passes over into the thing made, the former being an immanent operation and the latter, a transient one. In other words, "action is an operation that remains in the agent itself, as choosing, understanding and the like…, whereas production is an operation that passes over into some matter in order to change it, as cutting, burning and the like."[117] Seeing, for example, is a perfection in the power of sight, while building passes from the powers at work to bring to perfection some external thing, namely, a house.

With an understanding of the distinction between making and acting, we are better prepared to comprehend Aristotle's doctrine that art is a good habit that deals with the reasonable making of things, whether one is building a chair or producing an educated student. Art, whether that of carpentry or of teaching, deals with the contingent, specifically the contingent brought about by an external agent. In this area it is concerned with the contingent as it is made, not as it is related to action. In addition, it is a making stemming from reason, rather than from a lack of reason. In the words of Aristotle: "Art…is a state concerned with making, involving a true course of reasoning, and lack of art on the contrary is a state concerned with making, involving a false course of reasoning; both are concerned with the variable."[118]

All of the above characteristics we can detect in the art of teaching; otherwise it would not be worthy of the name *art*. Thus we see that teaching is concerned with the contingent, for the student is one who can be educated or not educated.[119] In addition to this, the education of the student (by the process of learning, not of discovery) is brought about by an external agent. This is most evident in the fact that such a process (namely, that of teaching and learning) demands both an instructor who knows and a student who only potentially understands. Aristotle brings out the fact that these two are needed when he says that "[one] starting with the power to know learns or acquires knowledge through the agency of one who actually knows and has the power of teaching."[120]

Finally, teaching is a making according to reason. This can be seen if we consider that the purpose of teaching is to "tell [another] the causes of each thing."[121] It is a process whereby, through the help of the teacher, the reasoning power of the student reaches that knowledge which it did not possess before.[122] In other words, teaching is a process whereby the instructor is instrumental in producing intellectual virtue in the mind of the student. As a process culminating, not just in the act of thinking on the part of the teacher, but in the production of intellectual virtue in the student, the activity of teaching consists in a making, a making which must work according to reason if good results are desired.

Before we indicate the basic principle whereby teaching produces intellectual virtue in the student, let us point out that it is proper for the human being to live at the level of art, rather than at that of mere instinct or experience. More specifically, the person who hopes to be a qualified member of the teaching profession must be an artist, and not just a person of experience. This is so, for the human being, possessing reason, has the possibility of arriving at art, rather than of remaining at the experiential level. Unlike the lower animals, who are guided by instinct, the human person lives by reason.

With this power the human being can arrive at the best way to perform the different tasks needed in life. Thus, by means of his reason, he can discover the best way to build his houses, to cook his food, and to construct his roads. These are none other than examples of the various arts, arts which are possible because of reason. Gifted with such a power, each person should live at the level of art, rather than at that of experience. That this is the thinking of Aristotle can be seen from the following quotation:

> As Aristotle says in the beginning of the *Metaphysics*, the human race lives by art and reasoning, in which the Philosopher is seen to touch upon a certain property of man wherein he differs from the rest of the animals. For the other animals are led to their acts by a certain natural instinct; but man is directed in his acts by the judgment of reason. Whence it is that for the purpose of easily and in an orderly way accomplishing human acts there are different arts. For an art seems to be nothing else than a sure ordination of reason whereby, through determinate means, human acts attain to a due end. [123]

If the human being must be an artist, rather than one who operates at the level of singular experiences, how does he arrive at such knowledge? In other words, how do the arts come about, or, more specifically, how does one arrive at the art of teaching? According to Aristotle, the various arts, whether of cooking, carpentry, or teaching, grew originally from a process of trial and error, from a process of repeated experiences. Thus one might experiment with various ways to build a chair until he finally arrived at some definite rules on the matter. These rules, or universal principles, are nothing other than the principles of the art of chair making. The one possessing them, now qualified to be called an artist, arrived at such principles by means of many singular experiences. In a word, Aristotle holds that the principles of art come from experience. He says that

> art arises when from many notions gained by experience one universal judgement about a class of objects is produced. For to have a judgement that when Callias was ill of this disease this did him good, and similarly in the case of Socrates and in many individual cases, is a matter of experience; but to judge that it has done good to all persons of a certain constitution, marked off in one class, when they were ill of this disease, e.g. to phlegmatic or bilious people when burning with fever—this is a matter of art. [124]

3. Teaching's Productive Principle

Thus far we have seen three things about art, namely, its definition, its distinctive human quality, and its origin from experience. Let us now return to the question initiating our discussion about art, the question concerning the nature of teaching's basic principle of production. What is this principle that guides the art of teaching, a practical activity, in its efforts to arrive at actual production? Most simply expressed, it is the doctrine of Aristotle that all art, whether that of carpentry or of teaching, must imitate nature.[125] This principle *art imitates nature* furnishes the basic rule for production in all art, whether it is one that produces chairs or educated students. Unless this doctrine is observed, no art can hope to achieve its purpose in any kind of reasonable way. More specifically, unless the teacher imitates the natural way the mind of the student operates, he cannot hope to help him arrive at intellectual virtue.

If the fact that all art must imitate nature is the basic methodological principle for the teacher, let us examine it more carefully. First of all, what do we mean by this principle? When we say that all art must imitate nature, we do not mean that art copies nature, or that it is a mere facsimile of the natural order of things. If this were so, the things of art would not be necessary, since they, being mere copies of nature, would have no reason for being produced.

Rather the meaning of the principle *art imitates nature* is that art looks to nature for its materials and for the basic rules of procedure with these materials. In other words, art finds in nature both its materials and the sound ideas on how to use them. Nature, as it were, stands to art as an exemplar and as the source of its materials. As Aquinas expresses it:

> Nature, indeed, does not perfect those things which are of art, but only prepares certain principles and furnishes an exemplar for the work in a certain way to the artisans. Art, for its part, is able to look at the things which are of nature, and use them to bring about its own work; but it cannot bring about the things of nature.[126]

That the relationship existing between art and nature is of this type can be seen in the work of any true artist. The doctor, for example, studies carefully how nature works in the healing of the human body and, utilizing the healing materials offered by nature, performs his art with a constant awareness of the natural principles he has learned. In like manner, the painter, having studied nature's laws about perspective, color, and so forth, employs ingredients furnished by nature to bring about his artistic representations. Even the simple processes of broiling and boiling, as Aristotle points out, work in accordance with the laws of nature and with her materials. He says that

> broiling and boiling are artificial processes, but the same general kind of thing, as we said, is found in nature too. The affections produced are similar though they lack a name; for art imitates nature. For instance, the concoction of food in the body is like boiling, for it takes place in a hot and moist medium and the agent is the heat of the body.[127]

From the observation of various kinds of art we can see that all art imitates nature in order to produce fruitful results, but why is this so? Why is it that the artist, if he hopes to be successful, must first observe nature and then proceed with his work? The answer is not hard to find. It rests on the fact that all art comes from human reason, which ultimately is dependent on the world of sense. Let us listen to Aquinas's words on the matter:

> The reason for saying that art imitates nature is as follows. Knowledge is the principle of operation in art. But all of our knowledge is through the senses and taken from sensible, natural things. Hence in artificial things we work to a likeness of natural things. And so imitable natural things are [i.e., are produced] through art, because all nature is ordered to its end by some intellective principle, so that the work of nature thus seems to be the work of intelligence as it proceeds to certain ends through determinate means. And this order is imitated by art in its operation.[128]

In the preceding quotation we note not only the reason why art imitates nature but also the cause of nature's being imitable. There is an order in nature, stemming from the Divine Intelligence, which permits imitation. Expressed negatively, if nature possessed no definite order and were composed of only accidental relationships, it would present no natural laws or principles to the artist, but only a random picture. Such chaos, because of its very instability, would be impossible to imitate. This condition, however, does not exist in nature. On the contrary, it "is nothing but a certain kind of art, i.e., the divine art, impressed upon things, by which these things are moved to a determinate end. It is as if the shipbuilder were able to give to timbers that by which they would move themselves to take the form of a ship."[129]

Nature then, as the divine art, furnishes the artist with his materials and acts as an exemplar for his work. For this reason we say that teaching, as the art of leading students from the known to the unknown, must work in accordance with the natural way that the student acquires knowledge. Teaching's basic principle of method or production is that the instructor must imitate nature.[130] If, for example, the teacher neglects the fact that the student is naturally dependent on his senses for knowledge and omits the use of examples, he cannot expect to lead those he instructs to knowledge. The teacher, to really possess the art or method of leading others from the known to the unknown, must observe first how every person naturally moves from what he knows to what he does not know.

If, then, in order to master the art of teaching, it is imperative that the teacher observe nature, we shall assume this task in our succeeding chapters. Only after we have studied the nature of knowing carefully, will we be able to formulate any rules about the art of teaching. Let us see, then, what Aristotle can tell us about the way that the human being naturally arrives at knowledge.

Chapter 2

Natural Objects in Knowing

A. Sense objects in general
    1. Their classification
    2. Their relation to truth
    3. Their principle for knowing
    4. Their individuality
    5. Their importance for teaching
B. Specific external sense objects
    1. Sight for distinction
    2. Hearing for learning
    3. Touch for certitude
C. Internal sense objects
    1. Those for common sense
    2. Those for imagination
    3. Those for cogitative power
    4. That of memory
D. Object of the intellect

Natural Objects in Knowing

A. Sense objects in general
B. Specific external sense objects
C. Internal sense objects
D. Object of the intellect

Having established that the art of teaching must imitate the student's natural procedure in moving from the known to the unknown, let us now observe what this natural procedure is. Since this art is built upon the human being's natural way of knowing, we must examine the knowing process carefully. What is the nature of this activity? What takes place when one knows something?

To begin our analysis of the Aristotelian doctrine on the process of knowing, let us treat first that which is obvious to the knower, namely, the objects which are sensed and understood. These objects—such as the colors, sounds, images, memories, and essences of things—are more evident to the one knowing them than the nature of the activity by which they are known. Thus the knower can ascertain that he sees color, but how he does this is still another question. Therefore, in attempting to understand the knowing process, let us move from the objects of knowing to the nature of the activity. Expressed in terms of an example, we shall move from a discussion of color to the way that seeing color takes place.

In addition to the obvious character of these objects, there is a more penetrating reason behind the decision to move from object to activity in learning about the acquisition of knowledge. Aquinas, commenting on Aristotle, notes that all activities are determined or specified by their objects. Thus color makes seeing a certain kind of activity, while flavor determines tasting as the type of operation that it is. This observation is important for us, since whatever determines the nature of a given thing will help in the understanding of it. If we have found the determining factors of a given species of flower, for example, we have discovered those causes giving us real knowledge of this species. Therefore, the objects of an activity such as knowledge, being its determining factors, will help in the understanding of that activity.[1]

That objects do determine the activities connected with them may be seen from the fact that every activity stems from either an active or passive power of the soul. Thus the activity of growing stems from an active power within the living thing enabling it to reach a certain size. The activity of seeing, on the other hand, is proper to the power of sight, which is passive in that it "is potential with respect to its object; for it receives sensible impressions."[2]

Now the object of a passive power, such as that of sight, is related to such a power as the moving cause or agent, as that which initiates this power into its proper activity. Thus color moves the power of sight to take up its activity of seeing. On the contrary, the object of an active power, such as that of growth, is related to such a power as a term or an end, for in this case the object is that which is finally realized by the particular power. Thus the power of growth arrives at its object, the measure of quantity proper to a given species allowing for individual differences,[3] as the termination or end of its given activity.

Therefore the objects of the soul's activities are either moving causes or final terms. Expressed more specifically, the object of the activity of seeing is its causal agent, while the object of the operation of growing is its final term. "In both respects they [these objects] specify those activities. For, obviously, specifically diverse causal agents do specifically diverse things—as heat heats and cold chills. And so also with the final term of activity: becoming well or becoming ill differ as 'doings', because health differs from illness."[4] Consequently, since whatever specifies a thing will help in its understanding, the objects of any activity will help one to know more about it.[5]

For this reason we shall approach the problem of how the human being naturally acquires knowledge by examining the objects of knowing first. Here we shall move from the more to the less obvious, from the objects of external sensation through those of the internal senses, and finally to the object of intellection. Then we will be prepared for an understanding of how the activity of knowing takes place on both the sense and intellectual levels.

A. Sense Objects in General

Knowing is found in its lowest degree in the activity of sensation, which is proper to both irrational and rational animals. In fact, it is precisely this kind of knowing that constitutes these living things as animals,

> for we call those things *animals* (not just living beings) which have sensation, even if they are fixed to one place. For there are many such animals whose nature restricts them to one place, but which have the power of sense, e.g. shell fish, which cannot move from place to place.[6]

Within sensation there are both external and internal powers, a division based on the location of the sense organ involved. Thus sight is classed as an external power, while memory falls under the internal senses. We shall treat the objects of these powers in general first, for such objects are the most basic in human knowing. Especially in the sense of touch we can note the fundamental quality of these sense objects,

[for] it is in feeling resistance to touch that we are first and most vividly aware of what is 'outside the mind.'... It is in the feel of being buffeted by reality in resistance to our touch that we have the most vivid experience of existence. It is the sense, the touchstone, upon which the most elaborate theories of mathematical physics must continue to rely. Without it we could not reach even existence in the sense of truth that is essential to every science.[7]

The external senses are adequately and completely divided into the powers of seeing, hearing, smelling, tasting, and touching, as Aristotle proves before entering into a discussion of the internal senses. The normal human being is familiar with these powers and their objects from his daily experiences with the external world. Thus he sees the color of an apple, together with its shape, size, and oneness. In holding it in his hand, he touches its texture, while his senses of smell and taste can appreciate its aroma and flavor. He can also hear the sound that it makes when it falls from a tree, as well as see the motion of falling.

With these sense objects, as exemplified above, we will now concern ourselves, limiting our discussion to some general observations, since a detailed treatment is not within the scope of this book.

1. Their Classification

In examining the sense objects, Aristotle first notes what the term *object of sense* designates. He says that it is used in three ways: one referring to objects only incidentally sensed, and the other two referring to either proper or common essential sense objects. In other words, there are three types of sense objects: proper, common, and incidental.[8] Examples of these, such as color, size, and the individual, are familiar to us, but perhaps we have never reflected on the way in which Aristotle has classified them. Let us, then, give a brief explanation of his threefold division.

A proper sense object is one that

is perceived by one sense and by no other, and in respect of which the perceiving sense cannot err; thus it is proper to sight to know colour, to hearing to know sound, to taste to know flavour or savour. Touch, however, has several objects proper to itself; heat and moisture, cold and dryness, the heavy and the light, etc. Each sense judges the objects proper to itself and is not mistaken about these, e.g. sight with regard to such and such a colour or hearing with regard to sound.[9]

These are the objects most of us associate with the senses, but they are not the only ones perceptible by these powers. In addition, the common sense objects are essentially perceived by the external senses. They are five in number: "movement, rest, number, shape, and size. These are not proper to any one sense but are common to all; which we must not take to mean that all these are common to all the senses, but that some of them i.e. number, movement and rest, are common to all. But touch and sight perceive all five."[10]

At this point the question might arise concerning whether the external senses actually do perceive the common sense objects. The fact that these powers sense their proper objects is easily acceptable, but there might be some doubt about the direct perception of the common sense objects. Aquinas answers this problem very clearly and, at the same time, gives the reason for the distinction between essential and incidental sense objects. He says that whatever "enters sensation precisely by disturbing the sense-organ is directly, not indirectly, sensed; for to sense directly, is simply to receive an impression from a sensible object."[11] "But whatever makes no difference to the immediate modification of the faculty we call an incidental sense-object. Hence the Philosopher [Aristotle] says explicitly that the senses are not affected at all by the incidental object as such."[12]

The common sense objects, however, do disturb the sense organs. "Size, for example, is obviously sensed in this way: it is the subject of such sensible qualities as colour or savour, and no quality is able to act in separation from its subject."[13] In other words, size disturbs the sense organs, for it is the subject of sense objects which do affect the organ. Thus a size of six inches may be the subject of a given patch of red. Now the subject of these sense qualities automatically accompanies them in their activity, as the size of six inches, for example, is part of the action of red upon the organ. Since this is so, and the sense qualities do disturb the sense organ, then, size, as their subject, also affects it.

Not only size but also all the other common sensibles, however, disturb the organs of sense. This can be seen if we remember that all the common sensibles "are either quantity (like number and magnitude), modalities of quantity (figure, movement, rest), or reducible to quantity or to a modality of it (as time is to movement, and *situs*, i.e. position or order of parts in place, to external figure)."[14] Since quantity is the immediate subject of the sensible qualities[15] and the subject accompanies these qualities in their activity, then all the common sensibles are part of the action of the sense qualities. Since the action of these proper sensibles disturbs or affects the sense organs, then the common sensibles also have such an effect. As red, for example, disturbs the eye, so the subject of this color has the same effect.

Having seen that the common sensibles do disturb the sense organs, we can now answer the question concerning whether these sensibles are directly perceived by the external senses. Since we know that whatever disturbs the sense organs is directly sensed and that the common sensibles do have such an effect, then we can conclude that all of the common sensibles are directly perceived by the external senses. These powers react directly not only to the proper sensibles but also to the common sense objects. Thus the sense of sight perceives directly not only color but also such common sensibles as size and shape.

In addition to the proper and common sensibles, Aristotle has a third type of sense object called incidental. This particular type must fulfill the following qualifications:

It must first be connected accidentally [to be incidental] with an essential sense-object; as a man, for instance, may happen to be white, or a white thing happen to be sweet. Secondly, it must be perceived by the one who is sensing; if it were connected with the sense-object without itself being perceived, it could not be said to be sensed incidentally.[16]

This perception, however, is not on the part of the external senses, or these objects would be essential sense objects. To be an incidental sense object, then, the thing must be only accidentally connected with an essential sense object and must be perceived by a faculty other than the external senses.

What then is an incidental sense object? We know that we do perceive something over and beyond the colors and sounds reflected or emanating from surfaces, for we would never admit that color or sound is all that we know when we have such an experience. Thus this white is sensed as in this surface and as in this man. Our sense experience does not occur in isolation from any individual subject. Then what distinguishes an incidental sense object?

As Aquinas clarifies, this object is not apprehended by an external sense. Rather it is found only in "what is at once intellectually apprehended *as soon as a sense-experience occurs*. Thus, as soon as I see anyone talking or moving himself my intellect tells me that he is alive; and I can say that I see him live. But if this apprehension is of something *individual*, as when, seeing this particular coloured thing, I perceive this particular man or beast, then the cogitative faculty...is at work."[17] Thus, repeating the above example, we sense not only this white but also, through our cogitative power, this man.

Apprehending such an object, our cogitative power is higher than natural instinct, for it "apprehends the individual thing as existing in a common nature, and this because it is united to intellect in one and the same subject. Hence it is aware of a man as this *man* and this tree as this *tree*."[18] Briefly, then, a key incidental sense object is properly the individual thing as existing in a common nature.

Having described the incidental sense objects, let us now summarize Aristotle's classification of the sense objects. His division is threefold: proper, common, and incidental. By the proper sense objects he means those which are "perceived by one sense and by no other, and in respect of which the perceiving sense cannot err."[19] On the other hand, the common sensibles are those which are common to all the senses to the extent that some of them (number, movement, and rest) are common to all. Lastly, the incidental sense objects are those individual intentions found in immediate intellectual apprehension, but not perceived by the external senses.

2. Their Relation to Truth

Since the sense objects are the ultimate source of all our knowledge whether we learn by ourselves or are taught, we must note to what extent our sense impressions can be trusted. Aristotle answers this by saying that "each sense has

one kind of object which it discerns, and never errs in reporting that what is before it is colour or sound (though it may err as to what it is that is coloured or
where that is, or what it is that is sounding or where that is)."[20] The senses, in
other words, do not err about their proper objects, although they may judge
falsely about their common or incidental objects.

More specifically, we have much more assurance about the colors and
sounds sensed that we have about the sizes of things or about the kind of individual perceived. Thus the object across the road we may readily assert to be
green, but whether it is taller than we are or whether it is an oak tree is still another matter. Aquinas explains this assurance we have about the proper objects
of our senses as follows:

> Sense-perception is always truthful with respect to its proper objects, or at least it
> incurs, with respect to these, the minimum of falsehood; for natural powers do
> not, as a general rule, fail in the activities proper to them; and if they do fail, this
> is due to some derangement or other. Thus only in a minority of cases do the
> senses judge inaccurately of their proper objects, and then only through some or-
> ganic defect, e.g. when people sick with fever taste sweet things as bitter because
> their tongues are ill-disposed.[21]

Although our senses do not usually fail in respect to their proper objects precisely because these are the objects proper to them, they can be deceived about
the common and incidental sense objects, for these are perceived, not in a spon-
taneous fashion, but indirectly or "by means of a certain comparison."[22] Thus
one deciding the size of a tree at a certain distance has to compare it with what
one remembers about the actual size of trees at that particular distance. The size
of heavenly bodies is another very pertinent example of the way that we use
comparison in arriving at the common sensibles.

We also apprehend the incidental sense objects by a kind of a comparison.
Thus we use sensible qualities or figure to indicate what kind of an individual is
before us. In winter, for example, we may see a patch of white on the ground
and judge it to be snow, when in reality it may be a white sheet; or we may see a
tall figure in front of a store and judge it to be a doorman, when actually it is
only a mannequin. From these illustrations we can note that the incidental sense
objects, and also the common sensibles, are reached by an indirect method, by a
kind of comparison.

But where there is a comparison, wherever there is a combining or separating
of things, then one has the possibility of truth or falsity. Then error can enter
into the knowing process.[23] Thus, when one begins to judge that the human person is or is not a social being, then one can correspondingly say that such is or is
not true. Since, then, comparison opens the possibility of error and the common
and incidental sense objects are apprehended by a comparative method, they
therefore can be perceived erroneously. In other words, because of the manner
in which they are perceived, the common and incidental sense objects can be
apprehended incorrectly. This is not usually the case with the proper sense ob-

jects; for they, being the proper objects of the external senses, are arrived at spontaneously. For this reason Aristotle says that each sense "never errs in reporting that what is before it is colour or sound (though it may err as to what it is that is coloured or where that is)."[24]

3. Their Principle for Knowing

Having seen that the different kinds of sense objects have varying relations to truth, let us examine these objects to see what is their principle of knowing for the sense powers. In other words, by means of what principle in these objects do we know them?

To answer this, let us recall briefly that the objects of the material world are composed of matter and form. By matter, we mean a passive or potential principle; by form, a determining or specifying principle.

> Matter is that which is not as such a 'particular thing', but is in mere potency to become a 'particular thing'. Form is that by which a 'particular thing' actually exists. And the compound is 'the particular thing' itself; for that is said to be a 'particular thing' (i.e. something you can point to) which is complete in being and in kind; and among material things only the compound is such.[25]

Aristotle illustrates matter, form, and the composite in his discussion of these three as related to first or particular substance. Aquinas comments on this section as follows:

> To clarify this part of his division he draws an example from the field of artifacts, saying that bronze is as matter, the figure as "the specifying form," i.e., the principle which gives a thing its species, and the statue as the thing composed of these. This example must not be understood to express the situation as it really is but only according to a proportional likeness; for figure and other forms produced by art are not substances but accidents. But since figure is related to bronze in the realm of artifacts as substantial form is to matter in the realm of natural bodies, he uses this example insofar as it explains what is unknown by means of what is evident.[26]

Having noted that the particular things of the material world are composed of matter and form, let us return to the problem stated above: By means of what principle in sense objects do we know them? To answer this it will not be necessary to confine ourselves solely to sense objects, for what we say will pertain to anything knowable.

If we were asked to speculate what makes a thing knowable, we might venture the suggestion that at least a thing must exist, for how can we know what is not there in any respect at all?[27] In other words, a thing must have being or be actual in order to be known. Aquinas expresses this truth from both a positive and negative viewpoint:

Those things are more knowable by nature which by reason of their own nature are capable of being known. Now these are the things which are more actual and are beings to a greater degree. And these lie outside the scope of sensation....

...Those things which are...first in the process of knowing, are often only slightly knowable by nature. This happens because they have little or nothing of being; for a thing is knowable to the extent that it has being. For example, it is evident that accidents, motions and privations have little, or nothing of being, yet they are more knowable to us than the substance of things; for they are closer to the senses.[28]

Contrariwise, that which is not actual, but potential, is unknowable to the extent that it possesses this quality. Aristotle illustrates this by explaining that it is not enough for geometrical constructions to be potentially drawn in order to arrive at a conclusion; they must be actually constructed. He says that

it is by an activity also that geometrical constructions are discovered; for we find them by dividing. If the figures had been already divided, the constructions would have been obvious; but as it is they are present only potentially. Why are the angles of the triangle equal to two right angles? Because the angles about one point are equal to two right angles. If, then, the line parallel to the side had been already drawn upwards, the reason would have been evident to any one as soon as he saw the figure.... Obviously, therefore, the potentially existing constructions are discovered by being brought to actuality.[29]

We see, then, that the actuality of things is the principle which makes them knowable, but, as we have already stated, "form is that by which a 'particular thing' actually exists."[30] This is the very nature of form; to be the principle by which a thing has being, to be that which determines the thing to be what it is.[31] Therefore we can conclude that the form of the thing makes it knowable. Thus the form of red makes this proper object knowable to us; we do not sense it by means of its matter or by means of the composite, since "form or actuality is chiefly the principle of knowing."[32] We sense this red object, but we sense it by means of its form or specifying principle.

4. Their Individuality

Granted that it is by means of its form that the sense object is knowable to us, we must still answer whether the sense object is known as an individual thing or not. In other words, in sensing, do we know the sense object as a singular thing or do we know the whatness of this individual sense object? To illustrate, do we know this individual patch of red, or do we know the whatness of red?

It is necessary for us to ask this question, for the objects we know admit of such a distinction: they can be known as objects of sense or as having a nature. The reason is that our proper object of knowledge is the material thing.[33] Thus it is proper for us to know, not about the angelic natures, but about the essences of trees, elephants, and so forth.

Now, as we said before, any material thing is composed of matter and form. Another way of expressing this is that in the material thing the form exists in matter. As so existing, the form or species is restricted by its matter to one thing. Thus the essence, rational animal, is restricted by a certain amount of matter to one particular individual called Tom Jones. As Aquinas states it: "When received in matter, the form is determined to this one particular thing."[34] "In so far as a thing is *material*, it is restricted by its matter to being this particular thing and nothing else, e.g. a stone."[35]

In other words, matter is the principle which, together with a given form or species, constitutes an individual. It is because of the material element in human beings that there can be many members of the human race.

> The specific nature is individualised through matter.... But where the form does not exist in matter, where it exists simply in itself, there can be nothing except the essence; for then the form is the entire essence. And in such cases, of course, there cannot be a number of individuals sharing the same nature; nor can the individual and its nature be distinguished.[36] [On the other hand] insofar as matter has certain designated dimensions it is the principle by which a form is individuated. And for this reason a singular thing is numerically one and divided from other things as a result of matter.[37]

If it is clear that in the material thing the form is restricted to this particular individual by means of the matter, then it should be understandable that "any form, taken in itself, is naturally disposed to exist in many things."[38] Thus the form or specific nature of cows, as a form not existing in its own right, is naturally disposed to exist in matter or in many individual things. To express this another way, "form is made finite by matter, inasmuch as form, considered in itself, is common to many; but when received in matter, the form is determined to this one particular thing."[39]

Therefore Aristotle maintains that, in the material thing composed of matter and form, the form or nature of this thing, considered in itself, is common to many. However, this same form, as actually existing in matter, is restricted by this matter to actualizing this individual thing. It is from the tendency of form to be common to many and from the tendency of matter to restrict to one that we have in material things the possibility of any one of them being an individual and also having a specific nature shared by all the individuals. We can truly say, therefore, that a given patch of red is this individual patch and also has the specific nature of red.[40]

If any material thing is an individual and also has a specific nature, it is possible for us, whose proper object of knowledge is the essence of the material thing, to know both the individual and the specific nature. Therefore it is necessary to ask if we sense the proper, common, and incidental sense objects as individual things or as having a specific nature.

Aristotle points out that we sense these various sense objects as individual things. As he expresses it, "what actual sensation apprehends is individuals."[41]

Thus the red that we sense is not an abstract notion of red, but a concrete surface of red appearing somewhere in space with its own particular degree of vividness. The sensation we have of this patch of red applies only to it; that is, in sensation we know only this singular thing. We do not, by just our sensations, possess within us something that applies to many red objects, as an idea of red would. If we tried to apply it to many, we would lose its quality of being this red, of being this individual sense object.[42]

To the realization that we sense the various sense objects as individual things we may add, because of the material given in the previous section, that we know these by means of the form existing in each. Since form is the principle of knowing and we know these sense objects as individual things, it is proper for us to say that in sensation we know by means of form as subject to materiality and consequent individuality. Thus we know this red by means of its determining principle, a principle subject to conditions such as this space, this particular surface, and this degree of vividness.

Here we do not mean that the form we receive in sensation is a form as existing in matter, but that it is a form as subject to material conditions. To illustrate this: in the former case we have the particular patch of red itself; in the latter we have the principle of knowing, the form of this red, which conveys to us its particular degree of vividness, its position in space, and so forth. In Aquinas's words, we sense by means of "the form of the thing known, without matter indeed, but subject to material conditions."[43]

This way of knowing sensibles is in contrast to the way we know intellectually, for here we abstract "the species not only from matter, but also from the individuating conditions of matter."[44] When we sense, however, we do so by means of a form, without matter, but with its individuating material conditions. We must emphasize that this is a form without matter; otherwise, we would receive in sensation the actual thing itself. Thus we would receive the particular patch of red as it exists out there. Such a reception is in direct opposition to the doctrine of Aristotle.

In pointing out that the various sense objects are known by means of a form subject to material conditions, we are laying the foundation for the next chapter in which we will explain Aristotle's position on the way that knowing takes place. There we will see that "all knowing is produced by an assimilation of the knower to the thing known."[45] In order to understand how this is possible, we must realize that the object is known by its form, whether as individuated or as abstracted from such conditions.

5. Their Importance for Teaching

At this juncture let us also note the importance of what we are discussing for the art of teaching. Thus far we have covered the following Aristotelian principles about the objects of sensation:

1. The objects of sensation are those proper to a given sense, those held in common by these senses, and those accidentally connected with the proper and common objects, i.e., the incidental sense objects.
2. The external senses usually do not err about their proper objects (although error is common in relation to the common and incidental objects), since a power generally does not fail in the activity proper to it.
3. These objects are sensed by means of their form, for this principle causes the particular thing actually to exist.
4. It is possible for any material thing to be known as an individual or as having a nature, since it is composed of matter and form. Aristotle points out that these sense objects are known as individual things. They are known by means of their form as subject to individuating material conditions.

To understand something of the nature of these sense objects is helpful to the teacher because these objects are the ultimate basis of all knowing. Without them no further knowing is possible.

These sensible qualities are what we know first and...no matter how far investigation may lead us away from this familiar realm, it continues to be the indispensable starting-point of all our knowledge about nature, and one to which we must always return. Unless anchored in sense experience, the study of nature [and of any other subject] can never keep to the right track, nor lead towards the truth.[46]

If it is true, then, that these sense objects are basic to all knowing, then an understanding of them is most valuable to the teacher, who can construct his art only after an observation of the nature of knowledge. Let us see, then, why Aristotle holds that sense experience is the starting point in any investigation we might make. Afterwards we will note which specific powers of external sensation are most helpful for learning.

Aquinas points out that the highest kind of knowledge possible to us, intellectual knowledge, cannot be obtained without a reliance upon sense. He gives two indications of this: one, our inability to understand something because of the lesion of the organ of a cognitive power; the other, the need of forming images for ourselves or of receiving examples from a teacher when we are trying to understand. The text of his first argument is as follows:

In the present state of life in which the soul is united to a passible body, it is impossible for our intellect to understand anything actually, except by turning to the phantasms. And of this there are two indications. First of all because the intellect, being a power that does not make use of a corporeal organ, would in no way be hindered in its act through the lesion of a corporeal organ, if for its act there were not required the act of some power that does make use of a corporeal organ. Now sense, imagination and the other powers belonging to the sensitive part, make use of a corporeal organ. Wherefore it is clear that for the intellect to understand actually, not only when it acquires fresh knowledge, but also when it applies knowledge already acquired, there is need for the act of the imagination and of the other powers. For when the act of the imagination is hindered by a lesion of the corporeal organ, for instance, in case of frenzy; or when the act of the memory is hindered, as in the case of lethargy, we see that a man is hindered from actually understanding things of which he had a previous knowledge.[47]

The reason that the intellect is dependent upon the senses is that we, as beings composed of body and soul, know properly material things, which exist in matter. But these things, as individuated by matter, are knowable properly by the senses. Therefore we can never bypass sense knowledge. Aquinas's explanation of this is as follows:

> He [Aristotle] observes that, since all of the objects of our understanding are included within the range of sensible things existing in space, that is to say, that none seems to have that sort of distinct existence apart from things of sense which particular things of sense have apart from one another, it follows that all these intelligible objects have their beings *in* the objects of sense; this being true not only of the objects studied by natural science, the properties and modifications of things of sense, but even of mathematical abstractions. It follows then that without some use of the senses we can neither learn anything new, as it were for the first time; nor bring before our understanding any intellectual knowledge already possessed.[48]

This sense knowledge, especially that of the proper sense objects, is so immediate to us that we can explain it only by indicating an instance of it, which the inquirer must be able to share.

> When asked what is meant by 'warm,' we can only convey our meaning by inviting the questioner to share our experience of warmth. Actually we can do no more than interpret the word by designating an instance of a special object or proper sensible; in so doing, we refer to a particular kind of experience which the other must be able to share if he is to know what the word stands for. To a man born blind, it will never be possible to convey what is meant by the proper sensible 'colour.'[49]

Not only are the proper sense objects the beginning of all of our knowing, but also they are in a very real sense its termination. Aristotle indicates this when he says that the final issue, "which in the case of productive knowledge is the product, in the knowledge of nature is the unimpeachable evidence of the senses as to each fact."[50] By this he means that the evidence of our senses gives us a final judgment on the truth of what we know about nature. The reason is that our senses are the source of our knowledge, and all that follows is dependent upon those beginnings.

But whatever influences the whole of knowledge can stand in judgment on the conclusions obtained. Because of this, our sense knowledge is not only the beginning but also the termination of all that we discover or learn. No matter how advanced the matter, such as the theory of relativity or of transfinite numbers, it still owes its origin to sense knowledge and therefore must accord with this unimpeachable criterion. Aquinas stresses this when he says that

> since the senses are the first source of our knowledge, we must in some way reduce to sense everything about which we judge. Hence, the Philosopher says that the sensible visible thing is that at which the work of art and nature terminates, and from which we should judge of other things.[51]

As not only the beginning but also the termination of all knowing, the sense objects are fundamental in understanding reality. It has been very truly said that "just as we could not know what a sensation is without having a real one, so we could not know anything real without having a sensation."[52] Because of this, an analysis of these objects will interest the teacher, for the way the human being naturally learns about reality forms the basis of his art. The truth, for example, that the senses do not err generally in relation to the proper sensibles will point the way to the use of such things as colored figures in illustrating a lesson. The realization that sense is the beginning and termination of all learning will urge the teacher to have a ready supply of good examples.

B. Specific External Sense Objects

Throughout this section on the sense objects in general, we have examined them from the viewpoint of what they possess in common, making no detailed reference to the object of any specific power, such as sight or hearing. We have done this deliberately, for an elaborate treatment is beyond the scope of this book. Since, however, some of Aristotle's insights into the specific powers of external sensation have much to offer the teacher, we shall explain briefly the following truths:

1. [Sight], most of all the senses, makes us know and brings to light many differences between things.[53]
2. Indirectly, however, it is hearing that contributes most to the growth of intelligence.[54]
3. Touch takes place by direct contact with its objects, whence also its name.[55]

1. Sight for Distinction

Aristotle notes that sight, more than any other sense, makes us know and brings to light many differences in things. If we were asked which external sense we prize most highly, we would probably choose sight. There is good reason behind this, for sight is the sense of clarity and distinction. By sight and touch, but especially by sight, we have our most extensive knowledge of the sensible things around us, for these senses perceive not only their proper sensibles but also all the common sensibles. Thus these powers can detect the movement and rest of an orange, its oneness, its shape, and its size. The reason is that sight and touch sense qualities, such as color, warmth, and coldness, that remain in the physical thing and do not emanate from it, as sounds or smells do.

Because of this, the perception of these two powers reaches to the thing, and not just to qualities that might be a distance from the thing. Thus by our perception of color we are in contact, so to speak, with the colored thing; while sound, as emanating from a thing, does not do this for us. In thus reaching the physical thing, sight and touch perceive how it is disposed corporeally, noting, for example, whether it is near or far away, whether it is large or small. But these corporeal dispositions are the common sensibles. Therefore it should be evident that sight and touch, as perceiving qualities remaining in the physical thing, detect not only its proper but also its common sensibles.[56]

Sight, however, has a superiority over touch in this regard for

> quantity and those [accidents] which naturally follow from it, which are seen to be the common sensibles, are more closely related to the object of sight than to that of touch. This is clear from the fact that the object of sight belongs in some degree to every body having some quantity, whereas the object of touch does not.[57]

By this last statement Aquinas means that light, which illuminates the transparent medium so that color can be seen, is common to both the heavenly and earthly bodies, such as the sun and fire. On the contrary, the tangible objects, such as the dry and the wet, are properties of earthly things in a solid or liquid state, such as earth and water.[58]

Thus we see that light, the quality needed so that one can sense the object of sight, can be found to a degree in any type of body having quantity, while the object of touch is not. When we realize, in addition to this, that quantity (number and magnitude) or some mode of it (figure, movement, rest) constitutes the common sensibles, then we can see that sight has the superiority over touch in relation to the common sensibles. Thus only sight perceives some of the bodies that are always actually lucent, such as the heavenly bodies. Therefore sight gives the most extensive knowledge of the sensible things around us.

2. Hearing for Learning

In addition to being superior to touch in this regard, sight is also more excellent than hearing in knowing about the differences found in sensible things. Aristotle notes this when he says that

> the faculty of seeing, thanks to the fact that all bodies are coloured, brings tidings of multitudes of distinctive qualities of all sorts; whence it is through this sense especially that we perceive the common sensibles, viz. *figure, magnitude, motion, number*: while hearing announces only the distinctive qualities of sound, and, to some few animals, those of voice.[59]

Therefore sight is superior to hearing because of its more extensive knowledge, when one compares their objects directly, i.e., considers the visible in relation to the audible.

"Indirectly, however, [as we pointed out above] it is hearing that contributes most to the growth of intelligence."[60] This statement may seem surprising because of the limited scope of the audible, but it in no way denies that sight is superior to hearing when one compares their objects directly. The reason that Aristotle attributes growth in intelligence chiefly to the sense of hearing is that such growth takes place to a much greater degree from a teacher than from one's own efforts, since the instructor knows the subject matter and the way to master it best. Now the teacher uses as his instrument words, which signify the knowledge that he possesses. He may use motions, diagrams, pictures, or the actual things themselves; but words, as being signs of ideas and thus representing the intellectual order, are his chief instrument.[61] Therefore growth in intelligence, relying so heavily upon a teacher, correspondingly is helped by the instrumentality of words.

Immediately we can add that growth in intelligence is also aided chiefly by hearing, since the sounds of words are perceived by this sense. This growth comes only indirectly or per accidens from this sense, however. Thus Aristotle says that "indirectly, however, it is hearing that contributes most to the growth of intelligence."[62] Nevertheless, it is still through the avenue of this sense that the greatest intellectual growth is achieved.

The reason that this sense is only indirectly the way to intellectual growth is that the word as audible is the object of hearing. The fact that the word may carry meaning for the human being is incidental to the sense of hearing as such. In other words, the meaningfulness of the word is only indirectly the object of the sense of hearing. The audible quality of the word is the per se object of this sense, while the meaning that the word carries is a per accidens object of hearing.

It is, however, the meaning as standing for some object in reality that the intellect seeks. Since this has only a per accidens connection with the sense of hearing, we can understand why Aristotle says that intellectual growth is achieved by hearing only indirectly. Nevertheless, it is still through this sense that the human being makes the greatest progress intellectually. The reason, of course, lies in the fact that the human person, to make real progress in the intellectual order, must rely upon a teacher, who shares his knowledge with him by the instrumentality of words. When, however, one progresses only by his own efforts, then the sense of sight would be more useful; for here one is dealing directly with the objects of reality, rather than with words, as signs of this reality.[63]

3. Touch for Certitude

Although the senses of sight and hearing give us much in relation to our growth in knowledge, Aristotle holds that from one aspect the sense of touch has a superiority over these, for through it we arrive at our greatest certainty about the existence of external reality. In relation to this truth, it is noteworthy to recall that Dr. Johnson, by striking his foot against a stone, refuted Bishop Berkeley's position on the nonexistence of matter. Because of the assurance given by touch, it has been called the sense of certitude, while sight and hearing have been designated respectively the senses of distinction and of learning.

Touch gives us assurance, for it takes place by direct contact with its objects. "That is why it is so named: it is 'contact' *par excellence*, whereas the other senses perceive by a sort of contact, indeed, with their objects, but through a medium, not immediately. Only touch perceives of and by itself, and no mediuim."[64]

To substantiate this fact, Aristotle examines the other types of sensation. He notes that colors, sounds, and odors are detected through a medium, most commonly through the air. Flavors, however, cannot be included in this listing, for it is evident that the sense of taste contacts food directly. It seems, then, that touch is not the only sense that perceives by direct contact.

This difficulty is solved by the fact that "taste also is a sort of touch; it is relative to nutriment, which is just tangible body; whereas sound, colour, and odour are innutritious.... Hence it is that taste also must be a sort of touch, because it is the sense for what is tangible and nutritious."[65] Thus we see that taste, as perceiving the tangible, is a sort of touch.[66] It is in this respect that this sense perceives by direct contact. Therefore Aristotle says that touch, as including taste insofar as it is a kind of touch, alone perceives by direct contact.

But it is precisely this contact with the tangible that gives us assurance, that makes us certain that what we sense is really there. We know that there are times when seeing a thing does not satisfy us; in addition, we must hold it in our hands. Our sense of touch, as providing us this contact, gives us the assurance that we seek. We find in this sense a certainty that none of our other senses gives us.

> Sight, notwithstanding its accuracy of discernment and its certitude of distinction, yields less assurance than touch. The words "phantom" or "ghost" usually stand for things visual, yet unreal and intangible.... Even when not doubting the things we see but cannot touch, we somehow feel more at home when they are brought within our reach, as is proved by the large numbers of people in this century ready to face any risk in order to set foot on the moon.[67]

This completes our discussion of Aristotle's doctrine on the objects of external sensation, in which perhaps the most important points are that these objects are known by means of form as subject to individuating conditions, and that sensation is basic to all knowledge, whether it gives us certitude, the many differences in things, or the instrumentality of the teacher. It cannot be stressed enough that "without some use of the senses we can neither learn anything new, as it were for the first time; nor bring before our understanding any intellectual knowledge already possessed."[68] When we do not remember this, we become "too ready to dogmatize on the basis of a few observations,"[69] and then, holding such views, are too resolved, "to bring everything into line with them."[70]

C. Internal Sense Objects

In addition to our external sensory equipment, Aristotle holds that we have four internal senses: common sense, imagination, the cogitative power, and memory. We profit by the objects and activities proper to all of these powers, but perhaps our reflective awareness of some of them is greater than of others. Thus we may realize that we have images of absent things and that we remember past events, but we may not have associated the perception of things as beneficial or harmful with a distinct sense called the cogitative power. Yet we must admit that, in our individual sense experience, we can be aware not only of the sensible qualities in the thing but also of the value it has for us. Thus we sense the external appearance of our neighbor, and, at the same time, realize that he is friendly toward us.

1. Those for Common Sense

Even more basic than our ability to imagine, to evaluate, and to remember (and perhaps for this reason not too noticed by us) is our power to distinguish among the objects of our external senses. Thus we are able to discriminate between the white and the sweet, the loud and the cold. Without such ability, which Aristotle refers to the common sense, the many aspects of external reality knowable to us would appear to be exactly the same.[71] From this we can see the importance of this sense, so called because it is the "common root and term of all sensitivity."[72] From it "sensitivity flows to the organs of all the five senses [as] from one common root, to which in turn are transmitted, and in which are terminated, all the sensations occurring in each particular organ."[73]

To be able to so discriminate must be the ability of a sense power, "for to know sense-objects as such is a sensuous activity; the difference between white and sweet is for us not only a difference of ideas, which would pertain to the intellect, but precisely a difference between sense-impressions, which pertains only to some sense-faculty."[74]

Granted that we distinguish among our external sense objects by a sense faculty, why does Aristotle maintain that it must be a power different from our external senses? Why cannot they perform this function for the one acquiring knowledge? Why, for example, cannot taste and sight together tell us the difference between sweet and white? The answer lies in the principle that "what discerns between two things must know both."[75] Thus the man judging the capabilities of two men working for him must know both of them. But the external senses know primarily their own proper objects, such as white or sweet. "Wherefore the discerning judgment must be assigned to the common sense; to which, as to a common term, all apprehensions of the senses must be referred."[76]

We see the necessity, then, of the power called the common sense to terminate and thereby to distinguish all sensation of external things. Considered as the termination of all the particular senses, it knows all their objects; but regarded as the single power that it is, it discerns the differences in these objects. It is "a certain common medium between all the senses, like a centre upon which lines from a circumference all converge."[77] Here sensation finds its greatest unity, for the common sense lies at the very root of sensitivity.[78]

Not only does the common sense distinguish among the various external sense objects, but also it perceives that the actions of the various particular senses are occurring. By our speech we indicate that we have the power to do this, for we remark that we know when we are seeing, imagining, dreaming, or remembering. That our external senses cannot do this themselves stems from the fact that they are powers in a material organ. "Since an organ is composed of matter which has its parts extended outside of each other, there can be no perfect reflection upon itself by the power of such an organ. At most, one part can reflect upon another that is joined to it."[79] This the common sense does with respect to the activities of the external senses.[80]

This awareness of the actions of the various senses, a function performed by the common sense, is most necessary for the human being in both the practical and speculative orders. Without it one could not tell whether one were actually sensing or were just imagining that he was. One would then have great difficulty performing the practical activities necessary for survival, such as providing for one's food, clothing, and shelter. One would also be hard pressed to know whether the things sensed actually existed, an understanding upon which one's further acquisition of knowledge must rest. We can thus see the importance of our common sense from both a practical and speculative standpoint. Without it we would not be aware of our own life and consequently could not survive, or find out about things, or be taught.[81]

2. Those for Imagination

It is evident, then, that not only our external senses but also our common sense is necessary for the proper reception of the sensible forms of things. We do more, however, than receive these individuated forms into our sense powers; we also retain these forms as images when the external thing is absent. Thus without any difficulty we can imagine a room in our own home or the face of one of our friends. These images are always concrete, sensible representations of the external object. As such, they are related to a given quantity and to a particular time and place. An image, for example, might be of a large tree we saw yesterday standing in the front yard.

This function of retaining images is the work of our imagination, a power related to the sensible order, since the images formed are always concrete and particular. In fact this power is defined as a "certain movement caused by the senses in their act of sensing."[82] Aquinas says that Aristotle concludes this because he sees the affinity between the imagination and the senses, since both are related to the concrete, particular order. In addition he realizes that

> the act of sensation can give rise to a sort of movement, in accordance with the principle...that a thing moved may move another. Actual sensation is a being moved by a sensible object; and the movement of the actuated sense itself causes another movement which, as it proceeds from sensation must resemble sensation; for every agent as such is a cause of its own likeness. And that which, being moved, moves another, must cause a motion similar to its own.[83]

Since, then, sensation can give rise to a movement, which must be similar in nature to it, and imagination has this similarity, it must be nothing other than a "certain movement caused by the senses in their act of sensing. It cannot exist without sensation, nor in insentient being."[84]

Moved or impressed by the actuated external senses, the imagination acts as a storehouse for the forms thus received. Because it retains these forms, it can reproduce them or form for itself images of what is absent. "Its proper object is something absent, for it supposes the persistence of sense impressions after the stimulus which produced these impressions is removed."[85] This absent thing, of which we now form an image, may have been a sound, an odor, or any of the objects of the external senses. We most commonly associate the work of our imagination, however, with the formation of visual images. This should not indicate to us that this power is restricted to this type, but only that we may not be making the best use of our imagination.

Not only does Aristotle maintain that the imagination forms phantasms of reality as it was actually sensed, but also he holds that it can make new combinations out of the forms received from the external senses. Thus we can form for ourselves an image of a centaur from our past sense experiences of horses and men. Our imagination may do this

> either on account of some bodily transformation (as in the case of people who are asleep or out of their senses), or through the coordination of the phantasms, at the command of reason, for the purpose of understanding something. For just as the various arrangements of the letters of the alphabet convey various ideas to the understanding, so the various coordinations of the phantasms produce various intelligible species of the intellect.[86]

This creative function of our imagination is particularly valuable in the acquisition of knowledge. It is not enough for the artist and scientist carefully to observe nature and retain in their imaginations that which their senses have given them. They must also be able to imagine various combinations of what they have sensed, for nature does not yield her secrets easily. By means of such ability, research workers can more easily set up working hypotheses and artists sketch the beginnings of their paintings. Since a beginning well made is more than half the whole, we can easily see the advantage of a good imagination in both practical and speculative activity. Thus all great scientists—such as Archimedes, Copernicus, and Galileo, to name only a few—must have relied upon it constantly.

Although a good imagination is a most useful tool in finding out about things, it must be handled carefully, for it is more subject to error than the external senses. The reason is that

> the movement of imagination, being derived from the actuated senses, differs from...sensation as an effect from its cause. Thus, just because effects, as such, are weaker than their causes, and the power and impress of an agent is less and less evident the further away are its effects, therefore imagination is even more liable than are the senses to fall into the error which arises from a dissimilarity between the sense and its object.[87]

If the imagination is not kept under control, the scientist and artist will lose the contact with reality so indispensable to them. Then, not an advance in, but only a retrogression from, knowledge is possible.

3. Those for Cogitative Power

Thus far, in our discussion of the internal senses, we have seen that the common sense completes the work of receiving the individuated forms of the sense objects, while the imagination retains and even rearranges the forms received. This is not all that occurs in sensation, however, for the animal is capable of perceiving, in addition to the proper and common sense objects, the external thing as harmful or beneficial.

Thus we note that "the sheep runs away when it sees a wolf, not on account of its color or shape, but as a natural enemy: and again a bird gathers together straws, not because they are pleasant to the sense, but because they are useful for building its nest."[88] In our lives we also have countless examples of this, such as our perception of the friendliness of people, of the danger to be found in violent thunderstorms, of the advantages of certain foods that we eat, and so forth.

Since these harmful or beneficial impressions are part of a sense experience and yet they are not proper to the external senses,[89] they are the objects of some other power, but one still in the sensible order. In animals it is called instinct, while in the human being it is termed the cogitative power. In animals the power of instinct proceeds in a fixed pattern, directed by the Intelligence that governs nature. One sees, for example, that certain species of birds instinctively perceive their natural enemies and manifest certain ways of protecting themselves. There is here no process of development as a result of experience or training, although there may be an accidental perfecting through exercise. By means of their instinct, animals sense spontaneously the external thing as beneficial or harmful.

In the human being, however, the perception of things as advantageous or disadvantageous undergoes a gradual development. By means of his cogitative power, a person sees, for example, that this glass of milk is beneficial to his physical well-being. This initial awareness of the value of this food is then stored in his memory, which is stimulated to retain this awareness precisely because of the value it has.[90]

The first perception, however, is only a beginning, a stable unit, so to speak, around which are gathered enough later occurrences of the same type until one has a distinct realization of the fact that milk is beneficial for one's health. There is a gradual growth in the awareness of the value of things, for we do not operate instinctively, as the animals do. We have the power to grow in this direction, but we do it by the process of comparing circumstances of a similar nature until we see clearly that a thing is either harmful or beneficial.

Because we perceive the value of things by comparing one occurrence with another, the power which performs this function for us "is called *cogitative*, which by some sort of collation discovers these intentions. Wherefore it is called the *particular reason*,...for it compares individual intentions, just as the intellectual reason compares universal intentions."[91]

As a result of this comparison of many memories by the cogitative power, we arrive at experience. As Aquinas expresses it, "experience arises from the association of many singular [intentions] received in memory. And this kind of association is proper to man, and pertains to the cogitative power."[92] Experience thus comes about, for it

> is seen to be nothing other than to receive something from many things retained in the memory. But nevertheless experience requires some ratiocination about particulars, through which one is related to the other, which is proper to reason. For example, when someone remembers that a certain herb has many times saved many from fever, this is said to be experience that such a herb is curative of fever.[93]

Since Aristotle holds that experience comes about from the comparison of many memories, he does not maintain that animals are experienced, but rather instinctive; for they do not have the power to correlate individualized notions. The reason that our cogitative power is so superior to the lower animals' instinct is that it is the faculty of a rational being, and thus has some share in the life of the intellect. It is

> that which is highest in the sensitive part of man, and, thus, sense in some way comes in contact with the intellective part so that it participates in something of that which is lowest in the intellective part, namely, discursive reason. This is in accord with the rule of Dionysius that contact is established where the lower begins and the higher leaves off.[94]

From the above we can see that an important object of the cogitative power is the thing as it is beneficial or harmful to the human person. A full awareness of this object is not arrived at spontaneously or instinctively, but is the result of this power's comparison of what has been stored in the memory precisely because it had a value attribute. This refinement of the sense knowing of the cogitative power is properly called experience. Strictly speaking, experience is not proper to the lower animals, for the association of singulars performed by the cogitative power is peculiar to human beings. But, "since animals are accustomed to pursue or avoid certain things as a result of many sensations and memory, for this reason they seem to share something of experience, even though it be slight."[95]

Not only does our cogitative power provide us with experience but also its manner of perceiving the individual thing is the means "that from apprehension of sense there should be caused in us the knowledge of the universal."[96] The reason is that this power "apprehends the individual thing as existing in a common nature, and this because it is united to intellect in one and the same subject. Hence it is aware of a man as this *man*, and this tree as this *tree*."[97]

In this it differs from instinct which knows the individual thing only insofar as it is "the term or principle of some action or passion. Thus a sheep knows this particular lamb, not as this lamb, but simply as something to be suckled; and it knows this grass just in so far as this grass is its food."[98]

That we should be capable of sensing the individual thing as existing in a common nature, while the lower animals know it only as the term or principle of some action or passion, stems from the fact that we, as intellectual beings, have a higher end in life than the brute animals have, namely, the contemplation of the First Cause. "For perfect happiness the intellect needs to reach the very Essence of the First Cause."[99] Therefore, since the end determines all the other causes operating in a thing,[100] it is only fitting that our sensations, as the material cause of our intellectual knowledge,[101] should in some way contain that to which they lead, the knowledge of the universal terminating in the essence of the First Cause. This is not necessary for the brute animals, for "knowing belongs to these animals, not for the sake of knowing, but because of the need for action."[102]

From the ability, then, of the cogitative power to sense the individual as existing in a common nature, we, as intellectual beings, are able to arrive at the universal level in knowing, at the level of art and science. Aquinas expresses it thus:

> For it is plain that the singular is sensed *properly* and *per se*, but nevertheless sense is in a certain way even of the universal. For he knows Callias not only as he is Callias, but also as he is this man, and likewise Socrates as he is this man. And thence it is that when such a grasp of the sense preexists, the intellective soul can consider man in both. But if it were such that the sense only apprehended that which was of a particular nature, and in no way apprehended with this the universal nature in the particular, it would not be possible that from the apprehension of sense there should be caused in us the knowledge of the universal.[103]

From this we can see the importance of our cogitative power in our acquisition of knowledge. Without it we would have neither experience nor that apprehension of the universal nature in the particular thing leading to the universal level in knowing. With good reason Aquinas calls it our highest power in the sense order. It forms a very vital link in the chain extending from sense to intellectual knowing, for it is on the boundary of these two orders, where the lower touches the higher. No discovery or teaching could take place without it.

4. That of Memory

The last of our internal senses is memory, whose object is a sense experience insofar as it is past. Aristotle reasons that "there is no such thing as memory of the present while present, for the present is object only of perception, and the future, of expectation, but the object of memory is the past. All memory, therefore, implies a time elapsed."[104]

In his reasoning Aristotle observes that memory is a state relative to either perception or conception, conditioned by a lapse of time. Because of this time element, the ability to remember belongs to a sense, rather than to an intellectual, faculty. This is understandable if we remember that "past, as past, since it signifies being under a condition of a fixed time, is something individual."[105] But, as we observed in the beginning of this chapter, it is the individual that is known by our sense powers. With this in mind, we can see that memory is a sense, rather than an intellectual, faculty.[106]

This sense power remembers certain things from the past precisely because, at the time that these things were sensed, they were perceived as having some significance or value. The things that stand out in our memory are those that affected us favorably or unfavorably, as an examination of a time period, such as that in which our schooling occurred, will indicate. We can also note this characteristic of what we remember in the fact that, in order to train our memories, we are told to "be anxious and earnest about the things we wish to remember."[107]

When we realize that memory retains a given singular because it has somehow affected us, we can see a direct relationship between this sense and the cogitative power, which perceives the thing as harmful or beneficial. In fact these two work hand in hand, because

> for the apprehension of intentions which are not received through the senses, the *estimative* power is appointed: and for the preservation thereof, the *memorative* power, which is a storehouse of such-like intentions. A sign of which we have in the fact that the principle of memory in animals is found in some such intention, for instance, that something is harmful or otherwise. And the very formality of the past, which memory observes, is to be reckoned among these intentions.[108]

Having remarked previously that the imagination was the storehouse for the forms received by the external senses, we must make certain that the functions performed by memory and imagination are not confused. Perhaps an example will clarify the fact that the latter preserves the forms perceived by the external senses, while the former preserves those individuated forms not perceived by these senses, such as whether a thing is harmful or beneficial.

A satisfactory illustration to show this difference might be found in our attendance at a particular lecture. The general appearance of the lecturer, including his distinct mannerisms and the quality of his voice, is stored in our imagination. This is sufficient to make us wonder why the man seems familiar to us if we should meet him at a later date, even though we are forced to admit that we cannot remember why we now have this impression. This is the way with many things that bombard our senses daily and affect us personally only a little, or in no way at all.

Let us suppose, however, that the speaker mentioned above was an unusually fine one and had a distinct effect upon our thinking about a certain topic. Without any difficulty we can remember many things about this man, such as his manner of delivery and the value of what he had to tell us. Memory is functioning now, for the form received had an effect upon us. We can recall what we experienced, and, in doing so, we can revive the many particulars about it, such as its time, place, and value.

It must also be mentioned that, just as the cogitative power is superior to brute instinct, sense memory in human beings can operate in a higher way than it does in animals, simply because the lower human powers share in some way in the life of the intellect.[109] By this we mean that "man has not only memory, as other animals have in the sudden recollection of the past; but also *reminiscence* by syllogistically, as it were, seeking for a recollection of the past by the application of individual intentions."[110] We see this ability in ourselves, for we have experienced searching through certain memories of a situation in order to find a particular aspect of it that we need. According to Aristotle,

> recollection is, as it were, a mode of inference. For he who endeavours to recollect *infers* that he formerly saw, or heard, or had some such experience, and the process [by which he succeeds in recollecting] is, as it were, a sort of investigation.[111]

Animals, not sharing in the life of reason, are unable to do this, but are stimulated to remember by their physical surroundings, as, for example, their remembering pain because of the presence of the one who inflicted it.

Needless to say, the ability to remember is essential for the acquisition of knowledge. Without the storehouse provided by memory, all advance by discovery or learning is impossible, for the human being moves to new knowledge only by means of that which he knows. Thus knowing cannot possibly be present without the faculty of memory. It is a power which forms an integral part of the foundation laid for a life of learning. Although memory is essential throughout the whole process of growth in the intellectual virtues, it has an especially important place at the beginning of this process; for here the raw materials of these virtues, so to speak, are being gathered. The teacher who remembers this truth will do much to aid the intellectual advance of his students.

This section on memory completes the discussion of our external and internal senses in relation to their objects. Therefore, let us summarize briefly what is known by each power. In doing this, we must always keep in mind that the various objects are known as singular things, not as having a nature:

1. The external senses know the proper and common sensibles, such as color and shape.
2. The common sense distinguishes the different proper and common sensibles and perceives the actions of the various particular senses.
3. The imagination preserves the forms of the proper and common sensibles received by the external senses and constructs images of them. It can also rearrange the forms received.
4. The cognitive power perceives the individuated forms or intentions not sensed by the external senses, such as whether a thing is harmful or beneficial.
5. The memory preserves the forms apprehended by the cogitative power. Its object is that which is past, insofar as it had some value for us.

From this we can see that our senses perceive those accidental characteristics of the thing classed as its qualities or quantities, and also those incidental factors, such as its harmfulness or helpfulness. In every case these objects are sensed as individual things such as, for example, this red or this triangular shape.

D. Object of the Intellect

By means of his senses, the human being obtains knowledge of an object as a particular material thing. This sense knowledge, however, is not the only kind available to a person, for, according to Aristotle, he is also capable of knowing the nature or essence of a thing. What indications do we have of this? In his speech, a person reveals that he can know the thing not only under its individuating material conditions but also in terms of its nature. Thus he might ask, "What is this thing? What kind of thing is this?" These inquiries seek more than sense knowledge of the object; they search instead for the thing's whatness. Thus, if asked about a human being, these questions are not satisfied with a concrete image of a person; rather they seek to know what is common to all individual persons, to know what specific kind of thing the human being is.

This being-a-specific-kind has been variously named, according as one or another aspect of it has been stressed. The expression *what it is*, or *whatness*, is probably most familiar to persons who have not given much thought to the matter. This terminology emphasizes something in the thing by means of which it can be defined. Aristotle uses the word *quiddity* to designate this aspect of the thing. An indication of such word usage can be found in the following quotation: "He [Aristotle] says that the quiddity of each thing, which the definition signifies is also called its substance."[112]

Even more basic than *quiddity*, however, is the word *essence*, which emphasizes either something by which the thing can be distinguished from other types of things or, most especially, something by reason of which the thing is what it is. A third word is *form*, which stresses something which is the complete determination or whole perfection of the thing. Lastly, the word *nature* is used, which emphasizes either something by which the thing is intelligible or something by which the thing is ordered to its proper activity.[113]

From this short explanation we see that we have four ways of expressing that something in the thing which is not its individuality. We may say *essence*, *quiddity*, *nature*, or *form*, as one or the other aspects of this something are emphasized. This wealth of terminology reveals that the thing (which is also an individual) contains the following: that by which it is what it is; that by which it is distinguished from other types of things, that by which it is defined; that by which it is intelligible, that by which it is ordered to its proper activity; and that which is its whole determination.

When we know the essence or nature of a thing, we have a different type of knowledge from that which our senses give us. As Aristotle expresses it: "What actual sensation apprehends is individuals, while what knowledge apprehends is universals."[114] By means of our senses we arrive at a knowledge of the thing which is concrete and particular, while through our intellectual power we attain a knowledge which is abstract and universal. In the former case, we have an image or phantasm; in the latter we possess an idea or concept, which can be refined into a definition.[115]

To illustrate the difference between an image and an idea, let us take the example of a maple tree. Our image is of a particular maple tree with all the peculiarities proper to it. This will include such things as a certain height and breadth, a given amount of foliage, any striking peculiarities in limb structure, and the particular place that it is growing. Such an image is concrete and particular: it applies to only this material thing. Our idea of a maple tree, however, abstracts from all such individuating conditions. Perfected in a definition, it can be stated as follows: "Any of a large genus (*Acer*) of trees of the maple family, grown for wood, sap, or shade."[116] This definition has abstracted from the peculiarities proper to the maple tree as an individual and thus has a universality about it. It can be applied to any maple tree. Thus we may say that it is both abstract and universal.

In our section on the sense objects in general, we brought out why, in material reality, "the thing and its essence are not quite identical. Socrates is not his humanity."[117] Therefore we will not repeat that explanation now, but we must point out that the essences which we know are the essences of material things. Aristotle very carefully specifies this because he was faced with extreme positions on the problem, positions which helped him to understand the nature of the proper object of our intellect.

One position, that of the early philosophers, held that things are simply material, having no intelligible nature. Therefore one cannot have any certain knowledge of the nature of things. The other position, that of Plato, maintained that there is a separate genus of being called Ideas, and that we know these, rather than the nature of the material thing. Aquinas summarizes these positions as follows:

> The early philosophers, who inquired into the natures of things, thought there was nothing in the world save bodies. And because they observed that all bodies are mobile, and considered them to be ever in a state of flux, they were of opinion that we can have no certain knowledge of the true nature of things. For what is in a continual state of flux, cannot be grasped with any degree of certitude....
>
> After these came Plato, who, wishing to save the certitude of our knowledge of truth through the intellect, maintained that, besides these things corporeal, there is another genus of beings, separate from matter and movement, which beings he called *species* or *ideas*, by participation of which each one of these singular and sensible things is said to be either a man, or a horse, or the like. Wherefore he said that sciences and definitions, and whatever appertains to the act of the intellect, are not referred to these sensible bodies, but to those beings immaterial and separate: so that according to this the soul does not understand these corporeal things, but the separate species thereof.[118]

In contrast to these positions, Aristotle held that we know the essence of material things. He destroyed the opinion of the ancient philosophers by showing that there is a formal cause in things.[119] That this type of causality had not been clarified previously is indicated when he says that "the essence, i.e. the substantial reality, no one has expressed distinctly. It is hinted at chiefly by those who believe in the Forms [Platonists]."[120]

In addition, Aristotle shows the falsity of Plato's opinion that we know the essence by itself, in separation from things, when he explains

> that quiddities are only accidentally distinct from singular things. For example, a white man and his essence are distinct just in so far as the essence of man includes *only* what is specifically human, whereas the thing called one white man includes something else [the individual accidents] as well.[121]

If the essence is only accidentally distinct from the individual thing, then "the 'proper object' of our intellect is not, as the Platonists held, something existing outside sensible things; it is something intrinsic to sensible things."[122] In other words, what we know is the essence of material things. Granted that there is an essence in material things and that we can know it, it seems only misleading to say that our knowledge is of an essence separated from material reality.

> It seems ridiculous, when we seek for knowledge of things which are to us manifest, to introduce other beings, which cannot be the substance of those others, since they differ from them essentially: so that granted that we have a knowledge

of those separate substances, we cannot for that reason claim to form a judgment concerning these sensible things.[123]

The reason that Plato was led to this error is that he did not discern the ability of the mind to abstract the essence from its individuating conditions. Because of this he "thought that mathematical objects and the essences of things were as separate from matter in reality as they are in the mind."[124] Aristotle saw that the doctrine of separated substances did not conform to the nature of material reality, and thus he rejected it. From this he came to postulate an active force in the intellect capable of abstracting the essence from its individuating conditions. We shall discuss this power, called the agent intellect, in the following chapter after we have treated the doctrine that in both the sense and the intellectual orders there is a movement from potency to act.

At this juncture, however, we will point out that our ability to know the essence of things gives us an indication that we have a power within us that is more than sense. Here is an object that, being both abstract and universal, is completely distinct from the concrete and particular objects of sensation. If we remember that powers are determined by their objects, then we can see why it is possible for us, knowing that essences and the objects of sensation differ, to conclude that we have a power in ourselves that is more than sensation.

The above conclusion is a most important part of Aristotle's theory of knowledge. We shall therefore quote his reasoning on this position, reasoning which relies heavily on experience and places the emphasis on the activity of the power, rather than on the object:

> That perceiving and practical thinking are not identical is therefore obvious; for the former is universal in the animal world, the latter is found in only a small division of it. Further, speculative thinking is also distinct from perceiving—I mean that in which we find rightness and wrongness—rightness in prudence, knowledge, true opinion, wrongness in their opposites; for perception of the special objects of sense is always free from error, and is found in all animals, while it is possible to think falsely as well as truly, and thought is found only where there is discourse of reason as well as sensibility.[125]

Our ability to know the essence of material things, then, gives us an indication that we possess an intellectual power. As Aristotle puts it, by our ability to think practically and speculatively, we demonstrate that we have a power capable of such activity. If this is so, then a whole new level is opened for the one acquiring knowledge whether he does it by his own discovery or by being taught. Now the human being, capable of knowledge on the universal level, can arrive at the causes of things.

But to help the student arrive at a knowledge of causes is the raison d'être for the profession of teaching, as we pointed out in chapter 1. Therefore we can see the importance of this section for the teacher. Without an ability on the part of the student to know the essences of things, the instructor would be forced to redefine the nature of his work, for knowing would take place only in the sense order. At best, there would be, on the part of both instructor and student, the life ruled "by memory together with activity that has become habitual through training."[126]

At this point we have completed the first part of our treatment of Aristotle's doctrine concerning the way the human being naturally knows: the discussion of the objects which are sensed and understood. We stated, in opening this section, that our intention was to move from the more to the less obvious, from the objects of knowing to the way in which this activity occurs. Having completed the former matter, we shall now investigate how the human being knows. The forthcoming problem might be phrased in this way: How does the knower become assimilated with the object of his knowledge?

Chapter 3

Natural Way Knowing Occurs

A. Nominal definition of knowing
B. Way sense knowing occurs
   1. Platonic solution
   2. Early philosophers' solution
   3. Aristotle's solution
      a. Senses in potency
      b. Senses as acted upon
      c. Senses receive form without matter
      d. Why things know and are knowable
      e. Knower in act/known in act
      f. Knowing as oneness of knower and known
   4. Value of this insight for teacher
C. Way intellectual knowing occurs
   1. The possible intellect
   2. The agent intellect
   3. Value of this insight for teacher
   4. Way intellectual knowing occurs
      a. Origin in sense order
      b. Process of abstraction
      c. Abstracted nature as universal
      d. Actualized possible intellect as knowing
      e. Formation in possible intellect
      f. Intelligible species as vehicle
   5. Threefold activity of intellect
   6. Value of this insight for teacher

Natural Way Knowing Occurs

A. Nominal definition of knowing
B. Way sense knowing occurs
C. Way intellectual knowing occurs

To begin our understanding of the way in which Aristotle says knowing occurs, we will give a brief description of the end of this process. In other words, we will begin by describing what the end product, knowing, is. In this way we can gain some insight into the kind of activity needed to achieve such an end, for we shape our activity in relation to the end required, not conversely. Thus, if one plans to take an overseas trip, one's preparatory actions will be determined by the goal at hand.

A. Nominal Definition of Knowing

Our first task, then, is a description or definition of Aristotle's position on the nature of knowing. Although this activity is part of the experience of every normal human being, it is not an easy thing to define. "Knowing, like the most obvious things, resists definition."[1] If asked, one might say that knowledge is a grasp somehow of what a thing is, but this is a restriction of knowing to the intellectual order, a restriction that does not consider the fact that animals can know. Our manner of speaking about them indicates this, for we remark that a certain dog knows his master, that the mother animal knows her offspring. To define knowing, then, as grasping the idea of a thing is not adequate.

What definition of knowing, then, does Aristotle hold which includes both the sense and the intellectual orders? What meaning of knowing does he posit that is common to both sensing and understanding, although these two kinds of knowing do have distinct differences? For Aristotle, knowing is described in a general way as that activity in which the knower possesses something. As Aquinas expresses it: "The thing known is, in some fashion, in the possession of the knower."[2] Again, "all knowing is produced by an assimilation of the knower to the thing known, so that assimilation is said to be the cause of knowledge."[3]

In order to understand this description of knowing, we can use the example of what occurs when we know something intellectually. After a period of careful study of a given topic, we can assert to any inquirer that we know what we have studied. This assertion we might express in the following way: "Yes, at last I have it." In this expression there is an indication of Aristotle's position on the meaning of knowing, for he holds that it is that activity in which the knower possesses something.

If knowing is that operation in which the knower is assimilated to something, then it is evident that both the knower and the known are needed. These two must remain distinct so that there will be something to possess and something to be possessed, so that there will be someone to know and something to be known. At the same time there must be a possession, must be some sort of union. It is of this union that Aquinas speaks when he says that "any act of sense is identical in being with the act of the sensible object as such."[4] If there were no assimilation of the knower and the known, how could knowledge take place? When one is isolated from the objects of reality, there can be no knowing. The man who is blind and deaf is shut off from all color and sound, indicating that knowing cannot occur where there is isolation, pointing out that knowledge demands some kind of union.

Therefore Aristotle's understanding of knowing as the knower's possession of something emphasizes the necessity of three things: the knower, the known, and the union of the two. That these three are needed is quite clear, but how they can all be present in knowing is much more difficult to understand. How is it possible that the knower and the known can be assimilated and yet remain? Before giving Aristotle's answer to this problem, let us eliminate solutions that have proved unsatisfactory.

Before proceeding to those solutions, however, we must attempt to allay a question which may be in the mind of the reader: Of what value to the teacher is an understanding of the way in which the knower and the known are assimilated? This is a question which must be answered, but, since our understanding of knowing is yet only a nominal one, it is best if we postpone our response until the problem itself has been clarified. Therefore we shall show the teacher how he can benefit from understanding the way in which the knower and the known are assimilated after we have explained what we mean by the process itself.

B. Way Sense Knowing Occurs

Let us return now to the unsatisfactory solutions concerning this general process of knowing. One way to explain the assimilation found in knowledge is to posit, not that the knower and the known become assimilated, but that the knower has always possessed in some way the object of his knowledge. Then one would not have to worry about how assimilation occurs; one can dismiss it by saying that it has occurred, that the knower and the known have always been united in some fashion. Both the early natural philosophers and Plato subscribed to this viewpoint, the former believing in a material union and the latter holding to an innate possession of all forms. "The early natural philosophers

[held] that the soul knows all things because it is composed of all things, but...Plato's opinion [was] that the human soul is by nature in possession of a universal knowledge which only its union with the body has caused it to forget."[5]

1. Platonic Solution

Plato held to an innate possession of all forms because he believed that

the soul, then, as being immortal, and having been born again many times, and having seen all things that exist, whether in this world or in the world below, has knowledge of them all; and it is no wonder that she should be able to call to remembrance all that she ever knew about virtue and about everything, for as all nature is akin, and the soul has learned all things, there is no difficulty in her eliciting, or as men say "learning," out of a single recollection, all the rest, if a man is strenuous and does not faint; for all inquiry and all learning is but recollection.[6]

In order to demonstrate this point, Plato

introduces someone who is wholly unacquainted with the art of geometry, and who is interrogated in order concerning the principles from which a certain geometric conclusion is concluded, beginning with self-evident principles. To all of these he who is ignorant of geometry answers what is true, and thus by leading the questions down to conclusions, he answers what is true in each case. From this Plato wishes to hold that even those who appear unacquainted with certain arts have knowledge of them before they are instructed in them.[7]

On the surface it does appear that the interrogated person, to the extent that he can answer each new question, does know the material he is exploring, and that, therefore, he has always been in possession of a universal knowledge. Aristotle shows, however, that it is not accurate to conclude that one has always had actual knowledge because of his ability to respond to a given order of questions. Rather it seems much more plausible that the student has only virtual, potential, or general knowledge of the new material. "There is nothing to prevent a man in one sense knowing what he is learning, in another not knowing it."[8]

That the student in the beginning possesses only virtual knowledge can be seen from the fact that the new material follows as an effect from the student's previous knowledge. Effects, however, preexist only virtually or potentially in that which causes them. Thus the oak tree preexists only virtually in the acorn from which it comes. Therefore the new material is foreknown by the student in only a virtual or potential way, not in an actual mode, as Plato believed.[9] If the student has only potential knowledge of that which he is about to learn, then the problem of how the knower becomes assimilated to the known, of the way in which knowing occurs, remains.

2. Early Philosophers' Solution

Before Plato, the natural philosophers attempted to solve this problem about the process of knowing by saying, not that the soul actually possessed all forms, but that it was composed of the elements of all material things. Thus the constituents of the soul were actually such elemental substances as earth, air, fire, and water. Because of this, knowing could be described as a case of like being acted upon by like, as a case of the fire in the soul being acted upon by the external reality, fire.

These philosophers, one of whom was Empedocles, came to this conclusion, for they were aware of the truth that "knowledge is caused by the knower containing a likeness of the thing known; for the latter must be in the knower somehow."[10] Thus the person perceiving a tree contains it in some manner within himself. As we remarked before, the knower and the known are united, are assimilated to each other, in knowing. If there is no assimilation, there is no knowledge. How can this assimilation take place?

These philosophers were not aware of the fact that a thing is knowable by means of its form, and that, as so known, it exists differently in the knowing power from the way it does in physical reality. Not seeing this truth, they did not have it as a possibility for explaining the assimilation in knowledge that their experience told them occurred. Therefore they thought that knowledge of a thing could be had only if that thing were in the knower according to its material mode of existence. Now this could happen if the knowing powers were actually the basic elements or principles out of which all things were constituted, such as earth, air, fire, and water; for these, as belonging to the essence of all things, would give a true knowledge of them. Thus, "as Empedocles said, earth knows earth, fire knows fire, and so on."[11]

Therefore these philosophers believed that the knowing powers were actually the elements of the objects known by them, that these powers were able to know things because they consisted somehow of these objects. Because of this, they said that knowing was a case of like being acted upon by like, or that sensing was such, for they did not distinguish between sensing and understanding.[12]

In analyzing this view of the early philosophers, Aristotle arrives at the conclusion that the sense powers are in potency in their objects, a truth that has many ramifications in his theory of knowledge. Thus, we find this principle at the beginning of his doctrine on intellectual knowing. Aquinas, commenting on this passage, says:

> First of all then, as a preliminary to the statement of his own theory, he suggests that the acts of understanding and of sensing are similar, in that, just as sensing is a kind of knowing, and as it may be either *potential or actual*, so understanding is a kind of knowing which may be either potential or actual.[13]

Again, in arriving at the necessity of the agent intellect, Aristotle is building upon the original foundation laid when he saw the flaws in the position of the early philosophers. Aquinas's elaboration here is as follows:

> Having examined the potential intellect, the Philosopher now turns his attention to the agent intellect.... The argument he uses is this. In any nature which alternates between *potency and actuality* we must posit (1) a factor akin to matter which, in any given class of things, is potentially all the particulars included in the class; and (2) another factor which operates as an active and productive cause, like art with respect to its material. Since then the intellectual part of the soul alternates between *potency and act*, it must include these two distinct principles.[14]

Having pointed out the importance of the principle that the sense powers are in potency to their objects, let us note the reasoning that forces Aristotle to come to this conclusion. He sees that, if he accepts the opposing position that the sense powers are actually their objects, two insolvable problems will arise. They are as follows: "Why do we not perceive the senses themselves as well as the external objects of sense, or why without the stimulation of external objects do they not produce sensation, seeing that they contain in themselves fire, earth, and all the other elements which are the direct or indirect objects of sense."[15]

In other words, Aristotle realizes that, if the senses are actually their sense objects and these can be sensed, then the powers of sensation should be sensed too. But obviously this is false, for who ever sensed his power (not his organ) to see or hear? Then again, if the senses are composed of their objects, sensation should occur without any external object being present, for it is already present in the faculty itself. But Aristotle sees from observation that such is not the case, for he knows that hearing, for example, takes place only when there are sounds which can be heard. Because of these insurmountable difficulties, Aristotle concludes that the sense powers are only potentially their sense objects, such as color, sound, and flavor.[16]

The early thinkers' theory, therefore, that sensation is a case of like being acted upon by like, is false; for everything potential is acted upon by some active agent different from the thing acted upon at the beginning of movement.[17] Thus the heat of the stove is different from the coolness of the water to be heated. At the end of the action, however, they are similar, "for the agent, in acting, assimilates the patient."[18] Nevertheless, in the beginning that which is acted upon, that which is potential, is unlike the agent acting upon it. Since the sense powers are potentially their objects, they cannot be like the sense objects acting upon them. The power of sight, for example, is unlike the color impressed upon it. In a word, sensation cannot be a case of like being acted upon by like.

Therefore, neither the theory of the early philosophers nor that of Plato is an adequate explanation of knowing, for the knower is not in actual possession of the objects known. On the contrary, he is only in potency to the things that he knows. How then does he become assimilated to them?

3. Aristotle's Solution

We shall now proceed with Aristotle's answer to the way that knowing occurs, an answer that must take into account both the sense and the intellectual orders. Because he realizes that sensation is more obvious than intellection, Aristotle will work out his solution in the sensitive order first. Then he will apply his findings to the intellectual order, an application which he can make only after he has established the existence of a higher power than sensation.

In giving his solution in the sense order, Aristotle will not hesitate, however, to call upon his experience in the intellectual order to help clarify a point. Thus he will use an example of intellectual knowing to clarify the different degrees or stages that potency has and also to decide whether or not sense knowing is a case of physical alteration. This does not mean that he has settled the question of the existence of an intellectual power but only that the things of which he speaks (such as the capacity to know grammar and the acquisition of knowledge by teaching) are matters of common experience.

Aristotle begins his analysis of the way in which sense knowing occurs with two general observations: (1) The senses are in potency to their objects. (2) In sensation the senses are moved or acted upon in some way when the assimilation proper to knowing occurs.[19] This is a good beginning for "what is to us plain and obvious at first is rather confused masses, the elements and principles of which become known to us later by analysis. Thus we must advance from generalities to particulars."[20]

To arrive at these opening principles, Aristotle draws upon his own experience and that of his predecessors, as we have already seen in our discussion of the first of these principles. Without the theories of the early philosophers and of Plato to think through, Aristotle might not have been able to see his own position so clearly. Their ideas represent a certain level of refinement in philosophical thought, and one might not reach even this level if one did not have the good sense to utilize their experience in the matter at hand. Aristotle realized this very clearly, as the historical section found in many of his works indicates. He notes the value of this procedure when he says that "it is necessary, while formulating the problems of which in our further advance we are to find the solutions, to call into council the views of those of our predecessors who have declared any opinion on this subject, in order that we may profit by whatever is sound in their suggestions and avoid their errors."[21]

From these opening principles, Aristotle will finally conclude that, although the senses are in potency and are acted upon when the assimilation needed for knowledge takes place, they are not acted upon, moved, or changed as a thing is when it is altered physically. (Why this is so will be evident as we proceed.) With this possibility eliminated, he can then draw the further conclusion that the assimilation occurs in an immaterial way. Thus he says that "by a 'sense' is meant what has the power of receiving into itself the sensible forms of things without the matter."[22] How he arrives at this conclusion we will now investigate.

a. Senses in Potency

When Aristotle says that the sense powers are in potency to their objects, he is emphasizing the fact that they lack these objects and are receptive to them. For this reason potency, as used in this context, denotes a lacking and a consequent receptivity. We can see this from the following quotation:

> For even sensing, as we have seen, is not strictly a being passive to anything—for this, strictly, involves an object of a nature contrary to the passive subject. Yet sensing resembles a passion inasmuch as the sense is potential with respect to its object; for it receives sensible impressions. So far then as understanding resembles sensation the intellect too will be impassible (taking passivity in the strict sense), yet will it show some likeness to what is passive, in its receptivity to intelligible ideas; for these it possesses only potentially, not actually. Thus, as sensitive life is to sensible objects, so is the intellect to intelligible objects, each being potential with respect to its object and able to receive that object.[23]

As the above quotation also points out, it is the potential condition of these sense powers that enables them to be acted upon in some way, that enables them to be assimilated to their objects. If they were actually their objects, such action upon them could not occur. We mention this before proceeding because, following our present treatment of potency, we shall discuss that the senses are acted upon in some way.

Having seen that the potential condition of the sense powers means that they are able to receive their objects and are thus capable of being acted upon in some way, we must now explain that these powers have both a remote and proximate potency (and a corresponding actuality). This is possible, for potency can admit of varying degrees as it moves closer to perfect actuality, and can be considered as actuality in relation to a remote stage. Thus a boy and a man are both in potency to being a soldier, but the former is only remotely so, while the latter is in proximate potency to this condition. When we say, therefore, that the senses are in potency to their objects, we must consider that this potency can be both remote and proximate.

In order to clarify that potency can admit of both remote and proximate degrees, Aristotle uses the various ways in which *potency*, or *capacity*, is employed when speaking of intellectual knowing. As mentioned above, Aristotle does this because the stages of potency are more evident in this type of knowing.

In terms of intellectual knowing, then, Aristotle notes that the remote type of potency is exemplified when we call the human being a knower and mean his natural capacity for knowledge. "Man, we say, is one of that class of beings that know or have knowledge, meaning that his nature *can* know and form habits of knowing."[24] Then the proximate level of potency is indicated when we call the human being a knower, meaning here that he knows certain definite things, such as the science of grammar. In both of these cases, potency or capacity is indicated, but there is a difference. In the first, one has a capacity to know because of his rational nature; in the second, the one with an intellectual habit has a capacity in the sense that when he wishes he can reflect on his habit, unless circumstances such as work prevent him.

There is still another way in which we call the human being a knower, meaning here that he is actually thinking about something.

> He it is who most properly and perfectly is a knower in any field.... Of the three, then, the third is simply in act; the first is simply in potency; while the second is in act compared with the first and in potency as compared with the third. Clearly, then potentiality is taken in two senses (the first and second man); and actuality also in two senses (the second and third man).[25]

Just as intellectual knowing admits of stages moving from natural capacity through an intellectual habit to actual thinking, so too in sensation there are various levels of potency and act. These are respectively the capacity to have a sense faculty (before its organic formation in the fetus), the capacity to sense, and the state of actually sensing.

> For what so far possesses no sense-faculty but is due by nature to have one, is in potency to sensation; and what has the sense-faculty, but does not yet sense, is in potency to actual sensation in the same way as we have in the case of acquired intellectual knowledge.... And when it actually senses it corresponds to the man who actually exercises his knowledge by thinking.[26]

As can be seen from this enumeration, there is not a perfect parallel here between sensing and intellection, for

> whereas a sense-faculty is natural to every animal,—so that in the act of being generated it acquires a sense-faculty along with its own specific nature—the case is not the same with intellectual knowledge; this is not naturally inborn in man; it has to be acquired through application and discipline.[27]

Since it is not inborn, the potency preceding it (the capacity for knowledge) is more evident than the same stage in sense knowing, which is actualized into the second stage when the sense is organically formed. It is of this second stage, that of proximate potentiality, that Aristotle will be speaking throughout his treatment of the way in which sensation occurs. If it is associated with the corresponding state in intellection, that of the person possessing an intellectual habit, what he says will be more understandable.

b. Senses as Acted Upon

Having seen why the senses are in potency to their objects and what is meant by this, let us examine Aristotle's second opening principle, keeping in mind the material just explained. This principle, which states that in sensation the senses are moved or acted upon in some way when the assimilation proper to knowing occurs, has much evidence to support it. For this reason, we find Aquinas saying that it is an "admitted fact that sensation and knowledge are a sort of being acted upon."[28]

In what does this evidence consist? First of all, it is clear to any one who observes sensation carefully that at least some of the organs of sensation are changed or acted upon. Thus "in the case of touching and tasting (which is a kind of touching) it is clear that a material change occurs: the organ itself grows hot or cold by contact with a hot or cold object."[29] Secondly, as we have just explained, the senses are in potency to their objects, which impress themselves upon these powers in some fashion. We know that "a man cannot sense whatever he pleases; not possessing sense-objects inwardly, he is forced to receive them from outside."[30]

Given this evidence, why then do Aristotle and Aquinas say that sensing is only a sort of being acted upon, attribute being acted upon to sensation in only a qualified way? To understand this, we must define *being acted upon*, a definition that will do much to answer the basic problem of this section about the way in which the knower and the known are assimilated.

If we were asked the meaning of the phrase *to be acted upon* or *to be passive*, we might respond that it denotes to be moved or changed. Thus, when we say that a chemical has been acted upon by a catalyst, we imply that it has been changed in some way. Without too much difficulty we can see that to be acted upon means to undergo a change.[31]

Aristotle points out, however, that to undergo a change can include a change either for the worse or for the better. Thus we could call both the apple's rotting and the student's acquiring knowledge changes. It is the change for the worse, however, that is a change in the strict sense. Here there is implied a loss of what is natural to the thing and the imposition of a contrary form. Such changes are found in physical alteration, as exemplified by the rotting of an apple. Here there is the loss of the fresh quality and reception of the rotten one. We can see that there is an assimilation here, but an assimilation with a loss.

> That which receives along with a change in itself something other than what is natural to it is said in a proper sense to undergo a change. Hence such undergoing is also said to be a removing of something from a substance. But this can come about only by way of some contrary. Therefore, when a thing is acted upon in a way contrary to its own nature or condition, it is said in a proper sense to undergo a change or to be passive.[32]

Aristotle notes, however, that only in a broad sense does undergoing a change refer to a change for the better. Thus, when we think of a person's gaining knowledge, we more readily associate the word *perfecting*, rather than the word *change*, with what has taken place. "Whatever receives a perfection from something else is said in an improper sense to undergo a change; and it is in this sense that to understand is said to be a kind of undergoing."[33] Here there is a reception of something, such as an intellectual habit, but no loss. Since this broad meaning of undergoing a change implies a reception without a loss, it is not found in things changed materially, in cases of physical alteration. We can conclude, therefore, that it must refer to those changes or developments that come about in an immaterial way. In this kind of change there is also assimilation, but it is an assimilation without a loss.

We can see, therefore, that being acted upon has both a strict and a broad meaning. Strictly, it means a loss of something proper to the thing acted upon and the imposition of a contrary form, as found in physical alteration; broadly, it denotes a reception of something perfecting the thing without any loss, as found in an assimilation in an immaterial way.[34]

Why is Aristotle able to make the above distinctions? Simply because observation reveals that such is the case. Aristotle sees that being acted upon is used most properly in cases where a loss occurs, as in the rotting of an apple. He also notes, however, that it is used where there is no loss, but rather a perfecting, as in knowing. Naturally, presupposed to such word usage is the fact that there are changes for the worse or for the better.

Now one of the reasons that a thing can be changed or acted upon is that "it lacks something which could resist the change."[35] Thus the lack of heat in the water makes it possible for a change in temperature to take place. We wish to emphasize that this factor is needed for a thing to be acted upon, because it is this characteristic that we note in the senses. They are in potency to their objects. In other words, they lack these objects and are receptive to them. For this reason they are capable of being acted upon, if only in the broad sense.

Having seen that *being acted upon* has two meanings and that this condition requires that the thing lack what will be received, let us return to Aristotle's opening principle that in sensation the senses are acted upon in some way when the assimilation proper to knowing occurs. Is *acted upon* used here with the strict or the broad meaning? Is there an assimilation with or without a loss? To help us to understand this, Aristotle employs intellectual knowing as an example, since the senses are involved in a bodily organ, which does undergo change in the strict sense. Let us then look at what occurs when the two potential stages in intellectual knowing (stages capable of being acted upon because of their potential quality) are acted upon, or actualized.

The actualization of the remote type of potency, of that belonging to the person with only the capacity for knowing, occurs when one is brought from his potential state to the possession of new knowledge either by means of an instructor or by his own efforts. In both of these cases the potential of the person is actualized by something actual. Thus the instructor, whose work is to cause science in another, must actually possess the knowledge that he hopes to bring about in the person being helped. Within the person himself, who is in potency to new knowledge, there is also something actual, for he possesses the light of reason by means of which he obtains immediate actual knowledge of the first principles.[36] "In virtue of this actual knowing he is led to actual knowledge of conclusions previously known by him only potentially."[37]

Is such actualization an example of strict passivity (of physical alteration), a case of the destruction of something proper to the patient and the imposition of something contrary? When one acquires new knowledge, he does not lose something proper to him and acquire something contrary to his nature. Rather, this actualization is the developing and perfecting of a power by the acquisition of an intellectual habit, such as grammar. "A certain preservation and perfection of a thing in potency is received from a thing in act."[38] This, then, is a case of the broad meaning of *being acted upon*, in which there is a reception without a loss. The one acquiring new knowledge is not altered physically, for both the knower and the known remain. Thus neither the one knowing the nature of a tree nor the tree so known loses its identity. This, then, is an assimilation in an immaterial way.

The proximate type of potency, of that belonging to the scientist who can reflect on his habit when he wishes, is actualized when one simply moves from inactive possession to active exercise of his habit. This he does by himself unless he is impeded by accidental circumstances. This actualization cannot be a case of strict passivity (of physical alteration), for it is the development of what is already possessed; there is no loss so that something contrary may be received. Rather it is a case of the broad meaning of *being acted upon*, for it is "a development into its [the knower's] true self or actuality."[39] Here, again, in the use of an intellectual habit Aristotle notes that there is a perfecting without a loss. The assimilation taking place does not occur in a physical, but in an immaterial, way. Neither the knower nor the known suffers a loss.

From the above we can see that in neither level of intellectual potency is there a *being acted upon* in the strict sense of passivity. In other words, the actualization of intellectual potency, bringing about the assimilation of the knower and the known, is not a case of physical alteration. Rather, in intellectual knowing the power is acted upon only in the broad sense of the term, only to the extent that there is a reception and a perfecting, only in the sense that there is an assimilation in an immaterial way. How does Aristotle know this? It is based on the observation that in intellectual knowing there is not a loss, but a perfecting.

Having reached such a conclusion about intellectual knowing, Aristotle sees that this is also true for the proximate potency found in sense knowing, since the movement from capacity to sense to the act of sensing is also a developing or perfecting. Sensing, in which the knower and the known are assimilated, is not a case of physical alteration, in which there is a loss of something natural to the sense and the imposition of something contrary to it. Thus one who sees a range of mountains does not suffer any loss. As Aristotle expresses it: "In the case of sense clearly the sensitive faculty already was potentially what the object makes it to be actually; the faculty is not affected or altered."[40] Rather the sense is perfected in the reception of its object, in the assimilation occurring. For this reason we have an assimilation in an immaterial, not in a material, way. Therefore, when Aristotle says that the senses are acted upon in some way, he means this only in a broad sense.

One might object at this point that the organ is physically altered, as, for example, the organ of touch becomes hot when it contacts a hot object. This is true, but the organ is only the subject of the power of sense, and we are speaking of the sense itself.[41] In sensation proper there is passivity only to the extent that there is a receptivity and a subsequent perfecting. In the action of sensing there is an assimilation of the sense to its object without any loss, an assimilation that can occur only in an immaterial way.

Before explaining what Aristotle means when he says that the knower and the known are assimilated, not by physical alteration, but in an immaterial way, let us briefly review the material that we have thus far covered:

1. The problem of this section is the way in which Aristotle says that knowing occurs.
2. We began by positing the following definition: Knowing is a disposition caused by an assimilation of the knower to the known.
3. This definition of knowing refines our problem to the following: How do the knower and the known become assimilated?
4. They are not already assimilated, as Plato and the early philosophers maintained.
5. On the contrary, Aristotle shows that the sense powers are in potency to their objects. For this reason they are able to be acted upon in some way, are able to be assimilated to their objects.
6. *To be acted upon* includes both a strict and a broad meaning. Strictly, it means the loss of something natural to the thing and the imposition of a contrary form, as found in physical alteration; broadly, it denotes a reception of something perfecting the thing without any loss, as found in an assimilation in an immaterial way.
7. The sense powers are perfected when they are acted upon. (This point is made clear by the example of intellectual knowing.)
8. Therefore the assimilation of the sense power to its object occurs, not by physical alteration, but in an immaterial way.

c. Senses Receive Form without Matter

When we say that the sense power is assimilated to its object in an immaterial way, we do know the way in which sense knowing occurs, but we need to refine this knowledge. In order to help our understanding, let us first recall briefly the way Aristotle describes physical alteration. We have mentioned already that there is a loss and a reception of a contrary form. We see, for example, that the coolness of water is lost and that a certain degree of warmth is gained. This new form exists in a material thing (the water), for we are speaking here of physical change. In this change, an assimilation occurs, namely, the form of warmth actualizes the water, but there is also a loss, that is to say, of the coolness.

The assimilation occurring in an immaterial way, however, not being physical alteration, is not the educing of a form from matter. Rather here a form is received without matter. In other words, in the assimilation occurring a form does not actualize matter; instead it is assimilated to a recipient only in respect to form. Thus the form of a sense object, the principle by which it is knowable, is received into the sense power of a human soul. Here the form exists in an immaterial way, exists as abstracted from matter. Aquinas expresses this as follows:

> The form is taken into the recipient 'without matter', the recipient being assimilated to the agent in respect of form and not in respect of matter. And it is thus that a sense receives form without matter, the form having, in the sense, a different mode of being from that which it has in the object sensed. In the latter it has a material mode of being, but in the sense, a cognitional and spiritual mode.[42]

In order to clarify this immaterial mode of receiving form, Aristotle uses the example of the way that wax receives the impress from a metal ring. Here the wax receives the form or image without the form thus received actualizing gold or bronze. Instead the form received exists in the wax without the metal or matter. Aristotle's text here is as follows:

> By a 'sense' is meant what has the power of receiving into itself the sensible forms of things without the matter. This must be conceived of as taking place in the way in which a piece of wax takes on the impress of a signet-ring without the iron or gold; we say that what produces the impression is a signet of bronze or gold, but its particular metallic constitution makes no difference; in a similar way the sense is affected by what is coloured or flavoured or sounding.[43]

Therefore, when we say that the sense is assimilated to its object in an immaterial way, we mean that this power in knowing receives forms without matter. Only in this way can knowing occur. It does not happen, as Plato thought, by a process of remembering or, as the early philosophers believed, by like being acted upon by like. Rather the sense power is in potency to its objects, and it "has the power of receiving into itself the sensible forms of things without the matter."[44]

Why is it that knowing occurs when the sense powers receive the forms of things without matter? We know that this is so, but let us now examine the reasoning behind the truth. To explain it we must first recall Aristotle's position that "all knowing is produced by an assimilation of the knower to the thing known."[45] In this assimilation or in this being acted upon, however, there is not a loss and the imposition of a contrary form. Rather, there is "a development into its [the knower's] true self or actuality."[46] In other words, there is not the loss of either the knower or the known, but there is a perfecting of the knower in the assimilation of the two.

Such a state, however, that in which the known is in the possession of the knower without any loss on either side, is not possible insofar as each is an individual, particular thing. In other words, the knower and the known cannot become assimilated without any loss by that which limits them to being only themselves, to being the particular individual things that they are. Obviously a thing cannot be in another or be another by that which limits or determines it to being only itself. Thus a tree cannot be known, cannot be in the knower, by means of that which confines it to its own individuality. If this is so, then we can conclude that knowing, requiring such an assimilation, does not occur according to that which limits a thing to being a particular individual.

In the previous chapter we explained what it is that limits a thing to being a particular individual. There we pointed out that "in so far as a thing is *material*, it is restricted by its matter to being this particular thing and nothing else, e.g. a stone."[47] In other words, the form of a thing is limited by its matter to actualizing just this particular thing. Form of itself, however, "is naturally disposed to exist in many things."[48] Thus the form of a given species is naturally disposed to exist in the many individuals possible to that species.

If, then, a thing is determined by its matter to being a particular individual, and knowing can occur only if a thing is not so determined, then we can conclude that knowing can occur only if a thing is separated from matter. For this reason Aristotle says that "by a 'sense' is meant what has the power of receiving into itself the sensible forms of things without the matter."[49]

d. Why Things Know and Are Knowable

It is this separation from matter that both makes things knowable and also gives things the power to know. Aquinas explains this as follows:

> Moreover, the perfection of one thing cannot be in another according to the determined act of existence which it has in the thing itself. Hence, if we wish to consider it in so far as it can be in another, we must consider it apart from those things which determine it by their very nature. Now, since forms and perfections of things are made determinate by matter, a thing is knowable in so far as it is separated from matter. For this reason, the subject in which these perfections are received must be immaterial; for if it were material, the perfection would be received in it according to a determinate act of existence. It would, accordingly, not be in the intellect in a state in which it is knowable, that is, in the way in which the perfection of one thing can be in another....

For this reason, we observe, a nature capable of knowing is found in things in proportion to their degree of immateriality. Plants and things inferior to plants can receive nothing in an immaterial way. Accordingly, they are entirely lacking in the power of knowing, as is clear from *The Soul*. A sense, however, can receive species without matter although still under the conditions of matter; but the intellect receives its species entirely purified of such conditions.[50]

From the above quotation we can see that a thing is knowable insofar as it is separated from matter. In other words, as we stated in the previous chapter, the thing is knowable by means of its form. To be knowable, however, is not the same as being known. Thus, the fact that a sunset can be sensed does not mean that it is actually sensed. For this it is necessary that there be a power which can actually sense. This means that it must be freed from materiality, must be immaterial in nature.[51] Otherwise, in spite of the fact that things have a knowability about them, no knowing will take place. It is only when something is so freed from matter as to be able to receive forms in an immaterial way that knowing can occur.

If, contrariwise, the thing is material in nature, the form actualizing it will be a form in matter, not a form received in an immaterial way. In such a circumstance knowing cannot occur, for the form is determined by the matter to being one particular thing. Thus the accidental form of rottenness actualizes a particular material thing, this apple. Since here a form actualizes matter, knowing cannot occur.

On the other hand, however, when something because of its immaterial nature is able to receive form in an immaterial way, then knowing can occur. As we mentioned before, Aristotle's example to clarify this immaterial reception is the way that wax receives the imprint of a seal. It is in this way, as we have already shown, that the sense receives the forms of its various objects, such as color, sound, and so forth. Since this power resides in an organ, such as that of touch, there is, to be sure, a physical alteration, but there is also a spiritual alteration, an immaterial reception. Thus a change of temperature occurs in the organ of touch, but, in addition, the form of this warmth is received into the power of touch in an immaterial way. Aquinas expresses this as follows:

. Now, immutation is of two kinds, one natural, the other spiritual. Natural immutation takes place by the form of the immuter being received, according to its natural existence, into the thing immuted, as heat is received into the thing heated. Whereas spiritual immutation takes place by the form of the immuter being received, according to a spiritual mode of existence, into the thing immuted, as the form of color is received into the pupil which does not thereby become colored. Now, for the operation of the senses, a spiritual immutation is required, whereby an intention of the sensible form is effected in the sensible organ. Otherwise, if a natural immutation alone sufficed for the sense's action, all material bodies would feel when they undergo alteration.[52]

e. Knower in Act/Known in Act

In this spiritual immutation a true assimilation occurs, for the power is informed or determined by the given sensible form. Therefore it is correct to say that there is effected an assimilation of the knower and the known. In knowing, the knower and the known are one in the respect that "the one who sees [for example] is assimilated to the object, so that his act of seeing is the same being as the actuality of the object."[53] The actuality of the knower and the actuality of the known are one thing. Therefore "knowledge is in a way what is knowable, and sensation is in a way what is sensible."[54] In knowledge there is a true identity caused by the assimilation of the knower to the thing known.

Let us elaborate on the fact that the act of the knowing power is identical in being with the act of the known object. What does Aristotle mean by this? This principle can be clarified if we remember that both the power and the object can be considered as in potency or as in act. Thus the power of hearing is either in the state of being capable of hearing or of actually hearing. In like manner a given audible object, such as the sound of a bell, is either capable of sounding or actually sounding.

If the above is true, then we can better understand what Aristotle means when he says that the act of the power and of the object are one in being. By this he means, using the same example, that the actualized sense of hearing and the bell actually sounding and being heard are one thing. He does not mean that this sense as capable of hearing and the sound not actually heard are one thing. If we realize that there is a distinction between the power and the object as in potency and as in act, we can better understand the kind of identity he is positing. It is an assimilation in which the actualized sense and the actualized object are one thing. In knowing, the knower truly possesses the object known.

Aristotle's text on this doctrine is as follows:

> The activity of the sensible object and that of the percipient sense is one and the same activity, and yet the distinction between their being remains. Take as illustration actual sound and actual hearing: a man may have hearing and yet not be hearing, and that which has a sound is not always sounding. But when that which can hear is actively hearing and that which can sound is sounding, then the actual hearing and the actual sound are merged in one (these one might call respectively hearkening and sounding).[55]

Because of this assimilation Aristotle will say that "the soul is in a way all existing things."[56] By this he does not mean that the soul is

> simply identical with the things it knows; for not stone itself, but its formal likeness exists in the soul. And this enables us to see how intellect in act *is* what it understands; the form of the object is the form of the mind in act.... [Thus] the soul in man takes the place of all the forms of being, so that through his soul a

man is, in a way, all being or everything; his soul being able to assimilate all the forms of being—the intellect intelligible forms and the sense sensible forms.[57]

f. Knowing as Oneness of Knower and Known

As assimilated to the form of its object, the given power knows this object. In other words, this power, actualized by a sensible or intelligible form, responds to such actualization by knowing that which actualizes or assimilates itself to the power. When we say this, we do not mean to imply that any temporal sequence is involved. Rather the actualization and the knowing are two ways of looking at what occurs. It is possible for us to consider the sense of sight, for example, as actualized and also as in act. To say that sight is in act is to say that it sees. This is "the response of a sense-faculty already actualized by its object. Only the senses in act can have sensations."[58]

With good reason, then, we posited in the beginning of this chapter Aristotle's position that knowing is the assimilation of the knower to the known. Now we see how such assimilation occurs. Not by being physically altered, but by receiving forms without matter, does the knowing power become one with its object. Truly the power in act and the object in act are one thing, for

> action and passion are one single actuality of the same subject, though they differ in thought.... [Therefore] the sensible object and sentient subject are actually identified in one subject, though they differ to thought. Hence the act of sound or of the sounding thing is the sensation of sound, while that of the hearer is hearing.[59]

It is this assimilation that causes knowing.

4. Value of This Insight for Teacher

We have completed the explanation of the way in which Aristotle says that knowing occurs, of the way in which he says that the knower and the known are assimilated. Therefore we must now return to the question asked at the beginning of this explanation: How is this knowledge of benefit to the teacher? Since the purpose of the teacher is that his students advance in knowledge or in intellectual virtue, he can gain from this discussion an additional understanding of that which he hopes to achieve. In other words, he can consider his purpose in teaching not only as the student's growth in intellectual virtue but also as the student's assimilation to that which he knows.

Such an assimilation, as we have already pointed out, is not a physical alteration, but a perfecting of the student's intellectual power. In this union neither his power nor the object known undergoes a loss. Rather the student, in the assimilation proper to knowing, finds the perfection of his intellect. Indeed, it can be said that this assimilation, by uniting the knower to the known, perfects the knower by permitting him to have within himself the excellence of all that he knows.

Although the human being of himself is only a part of the perfection of the entire universe, he can, by the assimilation proper to knowing, possess the perfection of all the objects known to him. Since these objects extend to the essences of all material things, each person's knowledge enables him to have within himself the excellence of the whole material cosmos. In other words, one's power of knowledge, by which "the soul is in a way all existing things,"[60] enables him to possess the perfection of the entire universe.

The teacher who has studied the nature of the assimilation proper to knowing will understand this. He will realize that, as a teacher, he can help his students to attain to a perfection not possible to them by any other natural means. He will see that, to the degree that his students advance in knowledge, he helps them to become one with all the perfections of the universe. Such an insight is not to be minimized, for it gives the teacher a better understanding of the purpose of his work. He begins to realize that, in helping his students to know, he is assisting the process whereby "it is possible for the perfection of the entire universe to exist in one thing."[61]

C. Way Intellectual Knowing Occurs

Having pointed out the value for the teacher of an understanding of the knowing process, we must now make this understanding more complete. We say this because our explanation thus far has been focused chiefly on the sense order. Therefore, utilizing what we have learned from Aristotle, we shall now direct our explanation into the intellectual order. Perhaps the most valuable principle for this present purpose is the one basic to the sense order also, namely, that the knowing power is in potency to its object and that, as such, it is acted upon in some way. With an awareness of this principle, we shall be much better equipped to understand the chief point of this section, which is that the intellectual power admits of both a potential and an active principle.

Aristotle, according to the exposition of Aquinas, begins his understanding of the intellectual part of the soul by suggesting "that the acts of understanding and of sensing are similar, in that, just as sensing is a kind of knowing, and as it may be either potential or actual, so understanding is a kind of knowing which may be either potential or actual."[62] Aristotle draws upon observation and experience here, for he knows that, in relation to a particular truth, at first a person is only capable of knowing it and that later he actually knows it.

1. The Possible Intellect

Precisely because the intellect is initially in potency to its objects, Aristotle posits that principle in this power called the possible intellect. This intellect is that principle in the intellectual power which is open to the whole of sensible nature. In other words, it is that principle which lacks, until it knows them, those objects which it understands. That this is the nature of the possible intellect stems from the truth that

> anything that is in potency with respect to an object, and able to receive it into itself, is, as such, without that object; thus the pupil of the eye, being potential to colours and able to receive them, is itself colourless. But our intellect is so related to the objects it understands that it is in potency with respect to them, and capable of being affected by them (as sense is related to sensible objects). Therefore it must itself lack all those things which of its nature it understands.[63]

Since the possible intellect is lacking in all bodily natures, we can say that it is receptive to them or that it is capable of being acted upon by them. Thus this intellect, lacking the whatness of an elephant, is capable of receiving it or is passive to it. This is only a broad usage of passivity or of being acted upon, however, for no physical alteration occurs when the possible intellect receives any intelligible object. In this change there is no loss of something proper to the intellect and a reception of a contrary form. Rather there is "a certain preservation and perfection of a thing in potency,"[64] namely, the possible intellect.

Because of this, the possible intellect is considered passive or capable of being acted upon only in the broad sense of the term, only in the respect that there is a reception and a subsequent perfecting of the thing involved. In the words of Aquinas: "The mind...is called passive just in so far as it is in potency, somehow, to intelligible objects which are not actual in it until understood by it. It is like a sheet of paper on which no word is yet written, but many can be written."[65]

The awareness that the possible intellect has an "intrinsic distinction from all the corporeal natures that it knows,"[66] leads Aristotle also to the conclusion that the intellect has no bodily organ. He is able to reason thus, for he knows that, if the intellect did have a bodily organ, "it would necessarily be just one particular sensible nature among many."[67] In other words, it would be a form (the intellect) existing in matter (the physical organ). When we say this, we are simply indicating that the intellect would be a particular sensible thing with the sensible nature proper to it. But this is impossible, for the nature of the possible intellect is to be open to all sensible natures. Therefore Aristotle can conclude that it has no bodily organ.

Knowing that the intellect has no bodily organ, Aristotle is then able to infer that the soul's intellectual part is immortal and perpetual.[68] This conclusion will be clear if we remember the principle that "whatever can operate on its own can exist on its own."[69] Since the intellect, having no bodily organ, does so operate, then we can see why it is immortal. This conclusion is of no small import, for it is "the answer to a question that everyone asks very eagerly about the soul: whether it can be separated from the body."[70] In fact, this question could easily be classed as the most important to anyone who attempts a serious study of the

soul. Granted the significance of this question, then we have a deeper understanding of the importance of Aristotle's doctrine that the powers of the soul are
in potency to their objects, for it is this doctrine that helps to clarify the question
about the immortality of the soul.

2. The Agent Intellect

Having seen the nature of the possible intellect and noted the conclusion
concerning the immortality of the human intellect which can be drawn from its
nature, we must now approach an understanding of the agent intellect. Aristotle
realizes the necessity of such a principle in the intellect, for he knows that

> in any nature which alternates between potency and actuality we must posit (1) a
> factor akin to the matter which, in any given class of things, is potentially all the
> particulars included in the class; and (2) another factor which operates as an ac-
> tive and productive cause, like art with respect to its material.[71]

In other words, such a nature demands both a potential and an active principle,
as art demands both the artist and the materials with which he works. Since the
intellect does alternate between being in potency to its objects and actually understanding them (as Aristotle sees from introspection), then it must include
these two principles: the possible and the agent intellect.

What do we mean by the agent intellect? It is that principle in the intellect
which is "the primary source, for us, of the actual intelligibility of anything."[72]
In other words, it is the "light of reason...[which] is implanted in us by God as a
kind of reflected likeness in us of the uncreated truth."[73] As such, it precedes, in
priority of nature at least, the presence in the mind of the first principles upon
which all reasoned knowledge is based. This must be so, for these principles
(the first of which is that it is impossible for a thing both to be and not be at the
same time) can be understood only if certain objects, such as that of being, are
actually intelligible to the mind.[74]

Since to define the agent intellect as the primary source of a thing's intelligibility may not be too revealing, let us elaborate upon this definition. From the
material which we have already treated in this chapter, we know that a thing is
knowable or intelligible if it is separated from matter. Therefore we can immediately say that the agent intellect is that principle in the intellectual power
which, because it makes its object intelligible, separates or abstracts this object
from matter. The agent intellect is the abstractive principle of the mind.

Aristotle saw that there must be such a principle in the intellect, for he rejected

> Plato's theory that the essences of sensible things existed apart from matter, in a
> state of actual intelligibility. For Plato there was clearly no need to posit an agent
> intellect. But Aristotle, who regarded the essences of sensible things as existing

in matter with only a potential intelligibility, had to invoke some abstractive principle in the mind itself to render these essences actually intelligible.[75]

Thus we see that Aristotle arrives at the presence of this abstractive principle in the mind because of the nature of the material world. Aware of the fact that the essences of material things are only potentially intelligible, he saw that the mind, knowing such things, must be capable of making them intelligible, of abstracting them from matter.

As the active principle in the intellect, the agent intellect possesses all those qualities proper to the possible intellect, for "what acts is nobler than what is acted on, an active principle is nobler than its material. Now the agent intellect...is to the potential intellect as an active principle is to its material; therefore it is the nobler of the two."[76] In connection with this, we have already pointed out that the possible intellect does not undergo a change in the strict sense of the term and that, being free from all sensible natures, it has no bodily organ. If the possible intellect, the passive principle, has these qualities, then they are found to a greater degree in the agent intellect, the active principle. In like manner, we say that art exists to a greater degree in the mind of the artist than in the material with which he works.

In addition to being unsusceptible to physical alteration and to being "neither made up of bodily natures nor conjoined with a bodily organ,"[77] the agent intellect possesses a quality not found in the possible intellect. It is essentially actual or in act. This is the very nature of an agent or active cause, for it is that which brings a thing from potentiality to actuality. But "the potential is actualized only by something already in act."[78]

> Hence what is potentially a man becomes actually a man as a result of the man who generates him, who is an actual being; and similarly one who is potentially musical becomes actually musical by learning from a teacher who is actually musical. And thus in the case of anything potential there is always some first thing which moves it, and this mover is actual.[79]

Therefore it is clear that it is the nature of the agent to be in act, and, correspondingly, that the agent intellect be in act.

When we say that the agent intellect is in act, we do not mean that it has always possessed the forms of the objects known, as Plato thought, "for if the agent intellect as such included the definite forms of all intelligible objects, the potential intellect would not depend upon phantasms; it would be actualized simply and solely by the agent intellect."[80] Aristotle knows, however, that the human being must depend upon phantasms, for, as we showed in the preceding chapter, he realizes that the objects of the human intellect "have their beings *in* the objects of sense."[81] Therefore the agent intellect, although the active principle, has not always possessed the forms known.

Rather, in saying that the agent intellect is in act, we mean that "it is an active immaterial force able to assimilate other things to itself, i.e. to immaterialise them."[82] As Aristotle puts it, this intellect "is what it is by virtue of making all things."[83] His meaning here is that this intellect makes things immaterial. To illustrate this, he compares the agent intellect to light, which, without making a certain color to be red or green, makes it visible by illuminating the atmosphere in which it is. In like manner, the agent intellect, without making the intelligible object to be the particular thing that it is, makes it actually intelligible by abstracting it from its individuating material principles.

These, then, are the natures of both the possible and the agent intellects, principles found in the intellectual power because it alternates between potency and act. By means of the possible intellect we are open to all sensible natures, while through the agent intellect we can abstract these natures from matter and thus render them actually intelligible.

3. Value of This Insight for Teacher

To be aware of the possible and agent principles in the intellect is of great import for the teacher. This becomes clear to us when we realize first that the possible intellect, as being open to all sensible natures, makes learning (and its counterpart, teaching) more than Plato's process of remembering. Learning is thus the acquisition of knowledge, not the removing of impediments to permit the remembrance of knowledge once possessed, as the filing of rust from iron would permit its brightness to shine forth. Since the mind of the student is open to all material natures and thus is able to be acted upon, there is a real reception of knowledge on the part of the student and a correspondingly real causality exercised on the part of the teacher.

The instructor is more than an accidental cause, as would be the case if learning and teaching were just a process of remembering, a process of removing impediments.

> For, since a thing which removes an obstruction is a mover only accidentally, as is said in the *Physics*, if lower agents [as contrasted to the First Cause] do nothing but bring things from concealment into the open, taking away the obstructions which concealed the forms and habits of the virtues and sciences, it follows that all lower agents act only accidentally.[84]

Since the teacher, working with the potential state of the student, does more than remove impediments to the pupil's remembering, he is more than an accidental cause in the learning process.

Even though the teacher is a real cause of the knowledge received by the student, he is only an instrumental one, because the student has within his intellectual power that principle called the agent intellect. As an active immaterial force able to abstract sensible natures from matter, it constitutes (together with the first principles obtained by this intellect's immaterialization of sense data at hand when reason begins to function) that active potency which enables one to acquire knowledge by himself. In other words, the agent intellect, together with the first principles, is the student's basic potential enabling him to learn on his own without a teacher.

When, however, something is able to actualize itself (as the sick man is able to bring himself to health), the external agent is a cause only by helping the internal agent and by giving it the means whereby it can become actual. For example, the doctor assists the natural forces in the sick person by strengthening these vital powers and by prescribing medicines, which these powers use as instruments for the recovery of health.[85] From this we can see that the teacher, as the external agent, is only an instrumental cause. As such he can only assist the development of the minds of his students.

The knowledge that the teacher is a real cause, if only an instrumental one, of the intellectual growth of his students is obtained from the truth that the intellect, being a power that goes from potency to act, has two principles called the possible and the agent intellect. If the teacher considers it worthwhile to know that he exercises a real causality, then this section on the nature of the student's intellectual power has a true importance for him.

4. Way Intellectual Knowing Occurs

Thus far in our discussion of the acquisition of intellectual knowledge, we have brought out the nature of the intellectual power and the value of such an understanding for the teacher. Now we must set forth Aristotle's doctrine on the way that the assimilation found in intellectual knowing occurs. In order to facilitate this purpose we already have at hand much of the needed knowledge, such as our understanding of the objects of knowledge, of the fact that the knower and the known are assimilated, and of the nature of the agent and possible intellects.

a. Origin in Sense Order

First of all, then, we must recall that "the proper object of the human intellect, which is united to a body, is a quiddity or nature existing in corporeal matter."[86] We do not properly know immaterial substances, as the angels do; for we, unlike these separated spirits, are a body-soul composite. Therefore it is proper for us to know the essences of material things. But, since essence has a real existence only in the individual,[87] the essences of material things exist in a singular thing and therefore not apart from corporeal matter.[88] Thus the nature of a dog exists only in this or that dog living in a particular place at a particular time.

Since, therefore, the natures of material things have a real existence only in individual material things, the intellect, in attaining these objects, must depend on the senses. The intellect must depend on these powers, for individual things, such as this red flower and that sounding bell, are known only by means of the senses.   Therefore the beginnings of the assimilation found in intellectual knowing must be traced back to the sense order.

In this order the imagination "is as it were a storehouse of forms received through the senses."[89] This power, moved by the external senses acted upon by their proper objects, forms for itself images derived from these external things.[90] As sensible forms derived from the individuals wherein exist the natures of material things, these images are the material upon which our intellects are dependent.[91]

More concretely, it is upon an image of an individual human being, such as Tom Jones, that the intellect must depend in a material way to obtain an understanding of the nature of human being. These images, however, are not proportionate to the intellect, for they are sensible forms, or forms subject to material conditions. The intellect, on the other hand, is an immaterial power open to all sensible natures and without a bodily organ.[92] Therefore, from these sensible forms, such as that of this color, the nature or essence must be abstracted.[93] This task is the work of the agent intellect.

b. Process of Abstraction

What do we mean when we say that the agent intellect abstracts the nature from its individuating material principles? For Aristotle, the work of abstraction as performed by this intellect is simply an apprehension of one or more aspects of the knowable thing without a consideration of the remaining aspects. Thus the intellect apprehends from the phantasm of Tom Jones his rational nature without any consideration of the particular accidents which characterize his individuality, such as a certain height and weight. In doing this the intellect in no way posits that these exist separately. Rather it apprehends the one without considering the other. To do this involves no deception, as we can see from the following words of Aquinas:

> There is no deception when the mind apprehends a common nature apart from its individuating principles; for in this apprehension the mind does not judge *that* the nature exists apart; it merely apprehends this nature without apprehending the individuating principles; and in this there is no falsehood. The alternative would indeed be false—as though I were so to discriminate whiteness from a white man as to understand him *not* to be white. This would be false; but not if I discriminate the two in such wise as to think of the man without giving a thought to his whiteness. For the truth of our conceptions does not require that, merely apprehending anything, we apprehend everything in it.[94]

Without any deception, then, the agent intellect may, in its process of abstraction, consider one aspect of a thing without any consideration of its other aspects, provided that the aspect considered does not depend for its understanding on the other aspects. This is precisely what this intellect does when it abstracts the nature from its individuating principles, an activity necessary in order to render the phantasm knowable in the intellectual order.

c. Abstracted Nature as Universal

As so abstracted, this nature can be predicated of many things and thus is classified as a universal notion.[95] In other words, this nature is considered as a universal notion predicable of many things when it is abstracted from its individuating material conditions. Thus the nature *human being* can be said of many individual persons when it is abstracted from all individuating accidents such as a certain height, weight, and complexion proper to a particular one. Only then do we predicate the nature of many things and classify it as a universal notion. We cannot do this in terms of the nature as it exists in the individual thing, as it is not abstracted; for here, being individuated by its matter, it is not predicable of many. From this we see that the nature as existing in the individual is not classified as a universal notion, while, as abstracted from such individuality, it is. Aquinas expresses this as follows:

> It is clear, then, that universality can be predicated of a common nature only in so far as it exists in the mind: for a unity to be predicable of many things it must first be conceived apart from the principles by which it is divided into many things. Universals as such exist only in the soul; but the natures themselves, which are conceivable universally, exist in things. That is why the common names that denote these natures are predicated of individuals; but not the names that denote abstract ideas. Socrates is a 'man,' not a 'species'—although 'man' is a 'species.'[96]

It is important to note that universality is predicated of a nature only as it is abstracted from its individuating material principles, for later we shall be speaking of the movement of the mind from the singular to the universal level. Then, from the insight gained here, we will be aware of the fact that the universal is not a thing separated from material reality, as Plato thought. Rather Aristotle holds that it is an attribute meaning that which is predicated of many; it is a notion applicable to a nature abstracted from its individuating material principles. This nature, nevertheless, has its real existence only in singular things. As abstracted from its individuating principles and thus called a universal, it exists only in the mind of the one knowing.

d. Actualized Possible Intellect as Knowing

After the agent intellect abstracts the nature from its individuating principles, this nature is now intelligible in act. Before, only intelligible in potency, this nature is now actually capable of being understood. This understanding takes place when the agent intellect impresses upon the possible intellect the form that it has abstracted. In doing so, the agent intellect actualizes the possible intellect.[97] To say that the possible intellect is actualized is equivalent to saying that this intellect is in act. But to say that the possible intellect is in act is to say that it knows.

Thus we see that the agent intellect's actualization of the possible intellect calls forth the actual understanding by this latter intellect of what has been impressed upon it. No temporal sequence occurs here. In the actualization brought about by the active intellect, the possible intellect knows. "The imprinting of the species or image of the sensible thing, first immaterialized by the active or agent intellect, upon the possible or receptive intellect, is intellectual knowledge."[98]

e. Formation in Possible Intellect

When informed by the species or form abstracted by the agent intellect, the possible intellect knows or has a concept of the given object in reality. In other words, in being actualized by the species, it has an idea of the thing. Possessing this idea, it then "forms a definition, or a division, or a composition, expressed by a word."[99] Thus, the possible intellect, possessing the idea *human being*, gradually forms within itself the definition *rational animal.*

The possible intellect forms within itself an intention of that species impressed upon it by the agent intellect, for it is able to understand a given intellectual object whether it is present or absent. In addition, it knows its object as abstracted from material conditions. Now this could occur only if, from that species impressed upon the possible intellect, some likeness would be formed and retained, just as the imagination forms and retains a likeness of that impressed upon it by the activated external senses. We can note this truth in the following words of Aquinas:

> We must further consider that the intellect, having been informed by the species of the thing, by an act of understanding forms within itself a certain intention of the thing understood, that is to say, its notion, which the definition signifies. This is a necessary point, because the intellect understands a present and an absent thing indifferently. In this imagination agrees with the intellect. But the intellect has this characteristic in addition, namely, that it understands a thing as separated from material conditions, without which a thing does not exist in reality. But this could not take place unless the intellect formed the above mentioned intention for itself.[100]

This formation by the possible intellect of an intention of the thing understood represents the term of the process in which intellectual knowing occurs. We have seen that this is a process which began in the sense order, which required on the part of the agent intellect an abstraction from the individuating elements of this sense order, and which reached its term in the actualization and formation proper to the possible intellect. Now we must comment briefly on

Aristotle's doctrine that in this process the species actualizing the possible intellect is not that which is known, but that by which this intellect knows.

f. Intelligible Species as Vehicle

The intelligible species is not that which is known, for, if the species itself were the object of the intellect, we would know ideas, not the things themselves. Thus we would fall into the Platonic error of thinking that we know, not the rational nature existing in this person, but a universal existing apart from things. This is not the object of the intellect, for, as we saw in the previous chapter, Aristotle emphasizes that its object is the essence of material things. We can also see the falsity of this by reflecting on what occurs in the sense order. "For, as with sight the image in the eye is not what is seen, but what gives rise to the act of sight (for what is seen is colour which exists in an exterior body), so also what the intellect understands is the essence existing in things."[101] The species actualizing the possible intellect is that by which it understands.[102]

We have pointed out that the intelligible species is no more than that by which the intellect understands, for this fact will lend credence to the principle that the intellect is dependent on the senses. Why do we say this? We make this statement because, if the intelligible species were the intellect's object, this species, as existing apart from sensible things, would not require an initial perception on the part of the senses. The intelligible species, however, is not the intellect's object; rather this power knows the essences of material things, essences which have their real existence only in these objects of sense.

It follows then that without some use of the senses we can neither learn anything new, as it were for the first time; nor bring before our understanding any intellectual knowledge already possessed. Whenever the intellect actually regards anything there must at the same time be formed in us a phantasm, that is, a likeness of something sensible.[103]

5. Threefold Activity of Intellect

Having seen that the intelligible species is that by which the intellect knows, we must point out that, although the possible intellect knows when it is actualized by the agent intellect, it does not have immediately a complete and perfect knowledge of the given intellectual object. Rather, Aristotle holds that in the beginning the intellect's understanding of an object is very general and confused. Thus at first one knows only the most obvious characteristics of a given species of animal. The reason that one begins with such an elementary knowledge of a thing is that,

since the intellect passes from potentiality to act, it has a likeness to things which are generated, which do not attain to perfection all at once but acquire it by degrees [such as the growth to maturity of any animal generated by the parent animals]: so likewise the human intellect does not acquire perfect knowledge by the first act of apprehension.[104]

Since the human intellect does not immediately have perfect knowledge of a thing, its activity admits of more than simple apprehension of this thing, such as the angelic intellect has. In the process of clarifying its initial understanding, it arrives first at a definition of the thing. Thus, from a confused notion of the nature of human being such as little children have, the mind is finally able to define the human being as a rational animal. One's simple apprehension of a nature (such as human being), which culminates in the definition of it, is much more limited, however, than the apprehension of the angelic intellect.

There is still much about the thing, such as its properties, that the human intellect must discover. To do this, the mind compares or divides notions from its experience in its effort to arrive at a further understanding. Thus it may judge, in relation to the human being, that he can laugh and that he is not colorless. Finally, utilizing the definitions and propositions possessed, the intellect may further refine its knowledge by the process of reasoning. Thus, knowing that the human being is a rational animal and that those beings which are reasonable can develop the art of grammar, the intellect can conclude that the human being is grammatical.

From this short description we can see that the activity of the intellect in knowing is threefold: that of simple apprehension, of composition and division, and of reasoning. Aristotle maintains that this process is so complex because he realizes that the intellect in its activity goes from potency to act, goes from general to more particular notions about a thing. If, on the other hand, it arrived at clear and perfect knowledge about a thing immediately, this threefold activity would not be necessary.[105]

This concludes our section on knowing in the intellectual order, in which we have attempted to clarify the nature of the active and potential principles in the intellect and the way in which intellectual knowing occurs. Our ultimate purpose in doing this is to give the teacher an understanding of the nature of human knowing, so that he can then construct his art. This is necessary, for "natural learning by discovery is the model for the art of education.... The teacher must study how the mind functions in the natural, unaided discovery and acquisition of science, in order to "streamline" and polish that process in the art of teaching."[106]

6. Value of This Insight for Teacher

We have already answered to some extent the value for the teacher of an understanding of the nature of knowing. Thinking now in terms of intellectual knowing specifically, we can see that, through an awareness of the potential principle in the intellect, the teacher is able to know that the student can be acted upon, is teachable. Is this of import to the instructor? It indicates no less than that there can be a profession of teaching, that the teacher can proceed to construct his art.

With an understanding of the nature of the active principle in the intellect, the teacher can realize that the student is able by his own efforts to abstract the essences of material things. In other words, the pupil is able to arrive at the universal level in knowing, a level which must take its rise from the sense order. This gives the teacher a definite insight into the movement of the mind from the sensible to the universal level, into the inductive movement basic both in intellectual knowing and in the art of teaching imitating such knowing.

In addition, we saw that there is a threefold activity of the mind because of its movement from potency to act. Knowing first only very general notions about the nature of a thing, the intellect, by a process of defining, judging, and reasoning, arrives at a more particular understanding of a given subject, an understanding which comes to rest only when the causes for the conclusions are known. This knowledge forms the basis for the deductive method of teaching, since this procedure is built upon the principle that the mind moves from the general to the particular in its acquisition of knowledge.

Thus we see that, from an understanding of the nature of knowing, the teacher is able to realize the following:

1. The nature of the possible intellect initiates the possibility of a profession of teaching.
2. The movement from the sensible to the universal level, made possible by the agent intellect, forms the basis for the inductive method of teaching.
3. The movement from general to particular universal knowledge, caused by the intellect's movement from potency to act, lays the foundation for the deductive method of teaching.

To enable the teacher to obtain the above principles, we have treated the natural acquisition of knowledge from a psychological viewpoint. In other words, we have studied this process in terms of the human knowing powers, their activities, and their objects. Therefore, in order to have a better foundation for the art of teaching, we must now approach the nature of knowing from a logical viewpoint. In doing this, we will emphasize the fact that the acquisition of knowledge is a movement from the known to the unknown. More specifically, we will show that knowing moves from the sensible to the universal, and then, on this level, from the general to the particular.

Chapter 4

Natural Order in Knowing

A. A movement from potency to act
B. Nature of basic potency
   1. Existence of basic potency
   2. The agent intellect
   3. The first known object
     a. That which is known to us
     b. The first concept
     c. The first principle
C. A movement from sense to universal
   1. Steps to the universal
   2. Needed number of examples
D. A movement from general to particular
   1. Nature of this movement
     a. A movement from known to unknown
     b. Need for a middle term
   2. Stages of this movement
     a. Statement of the problem
     b. The goal sought
     c. The foreknowledge
     d. Order in the foreknowledge

Natural Order in Knowing

A. A movement from potency to act
B. Nature of basic potency
C. A movement from sense to universal
D. A movement from general to particular

Following the principle that all art imitates nature, we examined in the two preceding chapters the Aristotelian doctrine concerning the natural acquisition of knowledge, treating first the objects of knowledge and then the manner in which it is obtained. Our purpose in this examination was to understand the nature of knowing so that we might possess the guiding principles for the art of teaching. In order to more fully understand this natural process, we must now consider Aristotle's position on the logical order found in the acquisition of knowledge. This means that we must treat knowledge as a movement from the known to the unknown. In chapter 3 we laid the foundation for this treatment by emphasizing that knowledge is a movement from potency to act. Now let us refine this understanding by examining more closely the order present in this movement. Consequently, we will stress in this chapter that the mind's transition from potency to act is a movement from the known to the unknown.

A. A Movement from Potency to Act

First, let us recall Aristotle's doctrine that the acquisition of knowledge is a movement from potency to act. Whether knowing is on the sense or the intellectual level, there is a similarity, "in that, just as sensing is a kind of knowing, and as it may be either potential or actual, so understanding is a kind of knowing which may be either potential or actual."[1] To put this in another way, the person seeking knowledge at first lacks the understanding which he may later possess. To illustrate this lack, Aristotle explains that

> mind is in a sense potentially whatever is thinkable, though actually it is nothing until it has thought. What it thinks must be in it just as characters may be said to be on a writing-tablet on which as yet nothing actually stands written: this is exactly what happens with the mind.[2]

Because the human being's knowing powers at first lack that knowledge which he seeks, he must move from a state of potential to actual knowledge. This movement is not a direct vision of things, such as God and the angels have, but rather a gradually developing understanding. Thus, in sense knowledge we can note that "when someone is seen at a distance, we perceive him to be a body before we perceive that he is an animal, and animal before we perceive him to be a man, and finally we perceive that he is Socrates."[3]

On the intellectual level this gradual growth in knowledge is a process of apprehending, then judging, and finally reasoning about a given thing. Thus, if a person is studying the nature of human being, he will first possess, by means of a sufficient number of sense experiences, the apprehension of the human being's whatness or quiddity. This initial apprehension, expressed by the words *human being*, he must then refine into a definition, thus arriving at the notion *rational animal*. Although he possesses this definition, the person has yet an imperfect knowledge of human being, for he has not yet compared the notion *rational animal* with other ideas that he possesses.

By the process of judgment, he can combine or separate this notion of human being with other ideas in his fund of experience. Thus he may form the judgment *the human being is a social animal*. In addition to the ability to make such judgments, the person can continue to advance in his knowledge of human being by the process of reasoning. He can conclude, for example, that the human being can laugh, since he can reason that his definition of human being falls under the general principle *whatever is rational has a sense of humor*. In this way the person will gradually perfect his knowledge concerning human being. This gradual procedure is a threefold movement from potency to act, a movement from simple apprehension, through judgment, to reasoning.

This gradual growth in knowledge is explained very succinctly by Aquinas:

> Since the intellect passes from potentiality to act, it has a likeness to things which are generated [such as animals], which do not attain to perfection all at once but acquire it by degrees: so likewise the human intellect does not acquire perfect knowledge by the first act of apprehension; but it first apprehends something about its object, such as its quiddity, and this is its first and proper object; and then it understands the properties, accidents, and the various relations of the essence. Thus it necessarily compares one thing with another by composition or division; and from one composition and division it proceeds to another, which is the process of reasoning.[4]

The human being's way of arriving at knowledge is imperfect in comparison to that found in God and the angels, who "have the entire knowledge of a thing at once and perfectly."[5] Since these separated beings have perfect knowledge immediately, they are called intellectual substances, while the human being is denoted a rational substance. These two kinds of beings are so named because to understand (the meaning for *intelligere*) indicates simple and absolute knowledge, while to reason denotes "a transition from one thing to another by which the human soul reaches or arrives at knowledge of something else."[6]

Since an immediate understanding of a thing far surpasses a gradual movement toward such knowledge, it is not the conclusion of a proof, but rather the immediate principle, which is of superior intellectual quality. In the search for intellectual perfection the human being seeks ultimately, not proofs, but the immediate perception of wholes. Thus, in the beatific vision, God will be seen directly and all else will be seen through him. In searching for knowledge, one tends to unify that which he discovers and to seek for immediate principles, finally resting in God—the most immediate Principle of all.[7]

Although the human being seeks immediate principles, Aristotle holds that the proper human activity is the process of reasoning, the process of moving from one thing to another.[8] Nevertheless, the human being does participate in the type of knowing proper to the angelic substances in the respect that his knowledge both starts and ends in an act of understanding. His way of knowing

> is related to understanding as to its source and its term. It is related to it as its source because the human mind could not move from one thing to another unless the movement started from some simple perception of truth, and this perception is understanding of principles.... This examination proceeds to first principles, the point to which reason pursues its analysis.[9]

In this quotation we note that the human being begins with some perception of the truth, basically the concept of being, and ultimately obtains, by means of his reasoning power and of his experience, the conclusions of the different sciences. These, in turn, must be seen to rest on the self-evident concepts and principles from which they have proceeded. In other words, these conclusions must be capable of being resolved back to their first principles, principles which themselves rest on "the unimpeachable evidence of the senses as to each fact."[10] Human knowing, therefore, both starts and ends in the understanding of principles. In this respect one participates in an imperfect way in the type of intellectual activity proper to God and the angels.

B. Nature of Basic Potency
1. Existence of Basic Potency

Having recalled Aristotle's doctrine that the human being knows by moving from potency to act, let us now examine more closely the nature of this basic potency. Before doing so, however, we must comment briefly on the fact that the human being does have a basic potential for learning, since one might conjecture either that a person has no potential at all or that he has actual possession of all knowledge, a possession now unnoticed or forgotten about. Aristotle confronts this problem in the last chapter of the *Analytica Posteriora*, a work on the demonstrative syllogism. Since the very existence of the syllogism rests on the fact that the human being has a basic potential for learning,[11] Aristotle must treat the alternate possibilities.   His question concerning these possibilities is "whether the developed states of knowledge are not innate but come to be in us, or are innate but at first unnoticed."[12]

In answering this question about the state of the human mind as one begins to know, Aristotle concerns himself solely with the first common principles of demonstration, the chief of which is the principle of contradiction. He does so, for these are the "seeds of knowledge...which by the light of the agent intellect are immediately known through the species abstracted from sensible things."[13] He begins, then, by saying that "it is strange if we possess them [the first principles] from birth; for it means that we possess apprehensions more accurate than demonstration and fail to notice them."[14]   In other words, he reasons that the human being could not always have had an actual, but unnoticed, possession of these principles, since they are even clearer than the knowledge acquired by scientific reasoning.

Now this latter knowledge cannot remain concealed from the person possessing it, for, by its definition, it is a knowledge which is always so, which cannot be otherwise.   Thus the person knowing scientifically that the exterior angle of a triangle is equal to the opposite interior angles possesses a clear knowledge which, because of its certainty, cannot remain hidden from him.   If, then, scientific knowledge, because of its certain nature, should be clear to the person possessing it, "much less is it possible that someone should have the knowledge of immediate principles and that it be hidden from him. [But] this is the unfitting thing which would follow if such habits were in us, and unknown to us."[15] Since it is impossible for the knowledge of immediate principles to be hidden from the person possessing them, then Aristotle concludes that the human being could not always have had an actual, but unnoticed, possession of these principles.

Having rejected the possibility of an innate possession of the knowledge of first principles, Aristotle then objects to the notion that such principles "be generated in us as absolutely new, with complete previous ignorance, with no other habit being had."[16] Since "all instruction given or received by way of argument proceeds from pre-existent knowledge,"[17] the knowledge of the first principles also must proceed from some preexisting potential. Just exactly what this pre-existing potential is, he will have to investigate. This question poses somewhat of a problem, for "preexisting knowledge is more certain, since it is the cause of certitude in those things which are made known through it. But no knowledge is more certain than the knowledge of these principles."[18] If the first principles are the most certain of all knowledge, what will be the potential from which they proceed?

Nevertheless, Aristotle maintains that there must be some preexisting potential for the knowledge of first principles, since any other position is untenable. He sees that the human being does not possess all knowledge from the beginning and yet that he does not depend completely on external agents in the acquisition of it. The student can learn just by his own efforts, just by his own potential. This potential may not be of the best quality, for, as Aristotle says, just "as the eyes of bats are to the blaze of day, so is the reason in our soul to the things which are by nature most evident of all."[19] Nevertheless, the student has a basic potential for learning.

Corresponding with this basic potential for learning, the human being has the desire to possess all knowledge, to actualize his potential. As Aristotle expresses it, "all men by nature desire to know."[20] Why is this so? Aquinas's commentary points out three reasons, the first of which is particularly applicable to the present discussion:

> The first [reason] is that each thing naturally desires its own perfection. Hence matter is also said to desire form as any imperfect thing desires its perfection. Therefore, since the intellect, by which man is what he is, considered in itself is all things potentially, and becomes them actually only through knowledge, because the intellect is none of the things that exist before it understands them, as is stated in Book III of *The Soul*; so each man naturally desires knowledge just as matter desires form.[21]

This desire to know will never cease until it rests in the First Cause of all things. This is so, for only there can the human being find the answer to all things. For this reason Aristotle says that

> the scanty conceptions to which we can attain of celestial things give us, from their excellence, more pleasure than all our knowledge of the world in which we live; just as a half glimpse of persons that we love is more delightful than a leisurely view of other things, whatever their number and dimensions.[22]

We find this natural desire to know the Ultimate Cause of all reality in one's tendency to generalize, to make universal statements, such as that all adolescents are irresponsible, that all old people live in the past. Even in statements such as these, the human being reveals his desire for the universal, and finally for the Ultimate Universal Cause.

2. The Agent Intellect

Having shown that the human being does have a basic potency for knowledge and that this potency will be completely actualized only in the First Cause of all things, let us examine what this potency is. It is first of all the agent intellect, which is, "as Aristotle...maintains, the primary source, for us, of the actual intelligibility of anything."[23] This intellect, as we explained in chapter 3, "is an active immaterial force able to assimilate other things to itself, i.e. to immaterialise them."[24] In other words, the agent intellect performs the function of abstraction. By means of this power the human being is able to abstract the natures of things from their individuating principles. Thus, by means of the agent intellect, the human being is able to arrive at the nature *rational animal* from the many individual people that he encounters. Without this power, this basic active potential, he would be restricted to the level of sense knowledge, a level which knows the individual accidents of sensible things, but not their essences.

Because of its particular function of abstraction, the agent intellect is compared to a light and is called the light of reason. Therefore Aristotle says that this power "is a sort of positive state like light; for in a sense light makes potential colours into actual colours."[25] In other words, just as light, by illuminating the atmosphere, makes it possible for the various colors to be seen, so the "agent intellect...actualizes the intelligible notions themselves, abstracting them from matter, i.e. bringing them from potential to actual intelligibility."[26]

This power, "implanted in us by God as a kind of reflected likeness in us of the uncreated truth,"[27] is the human being's basic active potential. We may speak of it today as native intelligence, but, whatever the phrase used for it, it is that power in the intellect by which one is able to arrive at the natures of sensible things and to know ultimately that there is a First Cause. The highest human power, it "is a certain participation in the intellectual light of separated substances."[28] By this power the human being shares in the divine, just as brute animals participate in reason inasmuch as they have a kind of natural prudence or instinct.[29]

The agent intellect, in its work of abstraction, performs the vital function of providing the human person his first concepts and truths, his first knowledge of a universal order. Aquinas speaks of these insights as "certain seeds of knowledge...which by the light of the agent intellect are immediately known through the species abstracted from sensible things."[30] With good reason he can call them such, for from these beginnings all other knowledge flows. This first knowledge, obtainable directly from sense experience by the agent intellect, stands as the basis upon which all truth depends. The human being arrives at these seeds of knowledge by the power of the agent intellect.

3. The First Known Object

Having seen that the agent intellect is "the primary source, for us, of the actual intelligibility of anything,"[31] let us now examine what are the first concepts and principles abstracted by the agent intellect. Then we shall investigate the natural procedure for obtaining these seeds of knowledge. Aristotle holds that the discussion of first what a thing is and then how it is produced is the way to think through a problem. On this point he says that

> the causes concerned in the generation of the works of nature are, as we see, more than one. There is the final cause and there is the motor cause. Now we must decide which of these two causes comes first, which second. Plainly, however, that cause is the first which we call the final one. For this is the Reason, and the Reason forms the starting-point, alike in the works of art and in works of nature. For consider how the physician or how the builder sets about his work. He starts by forming for himself a definite picture, in the one case perceptible to mind, in the other to sense, of his end—the physician of health, the builder of a house—and

this he holds forward as the reason and explanation of each subsequent step that he takes, and of his acting in this or that way as the case may be.[32]

Because the final cause precedes the motor cause in any generative process, we shall first discuss Aristotle's doctrine on the nature of the first concepts and principles and then his position on the procedure for obtaining them. Before we see what these seeds of knowledge are, however, we must point out that our first knowledge is always the known to us.

a. *That Which Is Known to Us*

Aristotle holds that we must always begin with that which is known to us, for "all instruction given or received by way of argument proceeds from preexistent knowledge."[33] It is impossible for a person to proceed to the unknown except by means of that which he knows. Thus anyone with a problem searches through previous knowns to find a solution for the present unknown. The reason for such a procedure from the known to the unknown is that "no potency would ever be actualised unless something were already in act."[34] "Hence what is potentially a man becomes actually a man as a result of the man who generates him, who is an actual being; and similarly one who is potentially musical becomes actually musical by learning from a teacher who is actually musical."[35]

In like manner, the student, attempting to actualize his state of potential knowledge, must proceed from that which is actual. If he is studying by himself, this actual principle will be first his abstractive intellectual power, the agent intellect, and then the knowledge in his experience. If he is being helped by a teacher, the actual knowledge the teacher possesses will assist his active potential.

Because the potential can be actualized only by that which is in act, the student must proceed from the known to the unknown. This known, however, is the known to us, as Aristotle is very careful to specify. Thus he says in the opening book of the *Ethica Nicomachea*: "Presumably, then, *we* must begin with the things known to *us*."[36] This seems like an unnecessary qualification, since naturally "all learning proceeds from those things which are more knowable to the learner, who must have some prior knowledge in order to learn."[37] Why, then, does Aristotle say this?

Aristotle speaks in this fashion, for that which is knowable to us and that which is knowable by its very nature are not necessarily the same. To clarify this statement, we must distinguish these two types of objects of knowledge. We shall begin with that which is known to us. Since all of our knowledge takes its rise from the senses, the known to us will be those things which are close to the senses. Thus the outer effects of things—such as their colors, textures, sounds, shapes, and actions—will be more evident to us than their inner natures or essences. We are much more familiar, for example, with the shape and color of a polar bear than with his inner nature.

In contrast to the known to us, that which is more knowable in itself or by its very nature is that which has "more being, because each thing is knowable insofar as it is being. However, those beings are greater which are greater in act. Whence these are the most knowable by nature."[38] In other words, that which is most knowable is that which is most actual and is therefore a being to the greatest degree. The most knowable object, therefore, is God himself, and after him, the other immaterial substances.

That which is knowable to us, therefore, and that which is knowable by its very nature are not necessarily the same. Thus the things available to our senses, although most known to us, are less knowable by nature, because "they have little or nothing of being."[39] In other words, material things are less knowable by nature precisely because they are material and not pure actuality. On the other hand, immaterial substances, although most knowable in themselves, are less knowable to us, because they are not available to our senses. Thus that which is knowable to us and that which is knowable in itself do not necessarily coincide.[40]

In order to acquire knowledge, however, we must always proceed from that which is best known to us. This means that we will almost always (the exception is the subject of mathematics) be proceeding from that which is less knowable by nature. We will be proceeding from the things of sense to that which does not fall under sensory perception, the immaterial world. This is a monumental, but also a noble, task, namely, to "attempt to know the things which are 'wholly,' i.e., universally and perfectly, knowable, by advancing to a knowledge of such things by way of those which are only slightly knowable by nature."[41]

b. The First Concept

Having seen that our first knowledge is always the known to us, let us now investigate Aristotle's position on what this first known is. Since human intellectual activity moves from concepts through judgments to conclusions, the first known will be a concept. Because of the intellect's movement from potency to act, this first concept will be the most vague and most confused idea of all, for the confused stands between pure potency to knowledge and distinct, actual knowledge. In Aquinas's words:

> Because to know something indistinctly is a mean between pure potency and perfect act, so it is that while our intellect proceeds from potency to act, it knows the confused before it knows the distinct. But it has complete science in act when it arrives, through resolution, at a distinct knowledge of the principles and elements. And this is the reason why the confused is known by us before the distinct.[42]

This most confused concept of the mind will be a universal or general notion, for the fact that universals are confused is clear. For universals contain in themselves their species in potency. And whoever knows something in the universal knows it indistinctly. The knowledge, however, becomes distinct when each of the things which are contained in potency in the universal is known in act.[43]

Thus the universal concept *animal* is confused, since it contains under it potentially all the species and subspecies proper to it.

What is this most confused, this most universal concept? It is the apprehension of things in their simplest form, the apprehension of them as things or beings. Thus the first concept achieved in the process of knowing is that of being. Little children exemplify the fact that being is the first concept by their manner of describing and categorizing objects. Not knowing much about them except that they are things, they ask, "What is that thing?" Thus, "being is the first thing that comes into the intellect."[44]

c. The First Principle

Having seen that being is the first thing that the intellect knows in the act of simple apprehension, let us now approach the Aristotelian doctrine on what the intellect first knows when it combines or separates whatever it apprehends. In this second act of the mind, in which the intellect arrives at principles, what is the first one of all? To know this principle is most important, for it is the foundation of all subsequent knowledge. This first principle, abstracted from sense experience by the agent intellect, constitutes the basic judgment for the student acquiring knowledge.

From the fact that being is the first concept of the mind, we can receive much help in pointing out this first principle. Since the concept first apprehended is the vague notion *being*, then the first judgment will be on the same plane of confused knowledge. As the starting point of all other principles, it will be the most universal of them all. Since the first concept is being, then Aristotle holds that the first judgment will be that being is not nonbeing.

Having apprehended being, the mind can instantly judge that being is not the opposite of being, namely, nonbeing. This opposition set up between being and all-that-is-not-being is the first judgment made and underlies all subsequent affirmations or negations. This principle of contradiction is the first knowledge of the second act of the mind, for this judgment can be made as soon as the mind knows being, the first knowledge of all.

Stated more precisely, this principle of contradiction is that the same thing cannot both be and not be, at the same time and under the same respect. Aquinas explains the fundamental nature of this principle as follows:

In the first operation the first thing that the intellect conceives is *being*, and in this operation nothing else can be conceived unless being is understood. And because this principle—it is impossible for a thing both to be and not be at the same time—depends on the understanding of being (just as the principle, every whole is greater than one of its parts, depends on the understanding of whole and part), then this principle is by nature also the first in the second operation of the intellect, i.e., in the act of combining and separating. And no one can understand anything by this intellectual operation unless this principle is understood.[45]

As the first principle of knowledge, this principle of contradiction must be the firmest and most certain of all. For this reason it must be impossible for a person to be in error concerning it. "This is evident because, since men make mistakes only about those things which they do not know, then that principle about which no one can be mistaken must be the one which is best known."[46]

In addition to this, the first principle must not be based on any other one, must not be an assumption. This is understandable because, as the first principle, it is used for understanding all other knowledge and must therefore be self-evident.

Lastly, such a principle must be naturally known and not acquired by any process of scientific reasoning. This is so,

> for first principles become known through the natural light of the agent intellect, and they are not acquired by any process of reasoning but by having their terms become known. This comes about by reason of the fact that memory is derived from sensible things, experience from memory, and knowledge of those terms from experience. And when they are known, common propositions of this kind, which are the principles of the arts and sciences, become known.[47]

All these characteristics—that the most certain principle can have no error concerning it, that it is not based on an assumption, and that it is obtained spontaneously and naturally—are true of the principle of contradiction. It is impossible for anyone to be in error about this principle, thinking that the same thing both is and is not at the same time. One may say that such is the condition of a given thing—that, for example, the coffee is both hot and nonhot—but one cannot err in his mind like this. For, if one did so, "he would have contrary opinions at the same time,"[48] and for one subject to possess contraries at the same time is impossible.[49]

In addition to being unable to err mentally about the principle of contradiction, one cannot consider it as an assumption or acquire it by any complex process of scientific reasoning, because this principle is the first which flows from the basic concept of being. As the starting point of all principles, it is not based on an assumption or acquired by any reasoning process. "Indeed, insofar as it is by nature a starting point, it clearly comes unsought to the one having it and is not acquired by his own efforts."[50]

Aristotle's doctrine, then, is that the principle of contradiction is the first of all principles. As abstracted from sense experience by the agent intellect, this principle, as well as the first concepts, forms the basic potential that one has in acquiring knowledge. For this reason Aquinas says that certain seeds of knowledge pre-exist in us, namely, the concepts of understanding, which by the light of the agent intellect are immediately known through the species abstracted from sensible things. These are either complex, as axioms, or simple, as the notions of being, of the one, and so on, which the understanding grasps immediately. In these general principles, however, all the consequences are included as in certain seminal principles.[51]

We must now show how this principle of contradiction is acquired. To know this will be especially important for the teacher, since all art is interested in procedure. Before we examine the Aristotelian doctrine on the way that the first principles are acquired, however, let us discuss briefly the fact that these self-evident principles are of two kinds: those self-evident to all, and those self-evident to the wise. In order to do this, let us first state what we mean by self-evident.

Those propositions are self-evident "which are known as soon as their terms are known."[52] More specifically, self-evident propositions are those in which one term is in the definition of the other. Thus, in the proposition *the human being is an animal*, the word in the predicate is part of the definition of the subject, for human being is defined as a rational animal. In the proposition *every number is either odd or even*, we again have a self-evident proposition, but this time the subject is part of the definition of the predicate. We say this because odd is the property of number which has no middle, while even is the property of a number which has a middle. As these examples illustrate, self-evident propositions are those in which one term is in the definition of the other.

Those propositions in which one term is in the other's definition are rightly called self-evident, for they are clear as soon as their terms are defined. Thus the truth of the proposition *the human being is an animal* is evident as soon as the definition of human being is given.

Aristotle lays down a distinction, however, in these self-evident propositions; for he maintains that some are evident to all, but some, only to the wise.[53] "Now those are self-evident to all whose terms are comprehended by all. And common principles are of this kind, because our knowledge proceeds from common principles to proper ones, as is said in Book I of the *Physics*."[54] Hence propositions such as *being is not nonbeing* or *every whole is greater than the part* are self-evident to all, because their terms are known to all.

The second kind of self-evident principle, that which is evident to only the learned or wise, is still a proposition in which one term is in the definition of the other; but it is not self-evident to all, because its terms are more specialized than the common terminology.

For example, this proposition: *All right angles are equal*, is of itself self-evident or immediate, since equality enters into the definition of a right angle. For a right angle is one which a straight line makes falling upon another straight line, in such a way that on both sides the angles are made equal.[55]

Because propositions such as this example have one term in the definition of the other, they are self-evident, if only to those learned in such terminology. They will be self-evident to all as soon as their terms are explained, but they are not so immediately. The prerogative of being immediately self-evident to all belongs only to the common axioms, such as the principle of contradiction.

These common axioms, abstracted from sense experience by the agent intellect, form the basic human potential for knowledge. From such principles the human being advances to knowledge of the various arts and sciences. Aristotle holds, however, that these principles are used only in a restricted fashion in the particular sciences, in a way that is proportioned to the given subject matter. Thus the axiom *a thing cannot both be and not be at the same time and in the same respect* is contracted in natural science to such a principle as *every human being is an animal*. This natural principle, since it automatically implies that the human being is not a nonanimal, is truly a contraction of the principle of contradiction.

These first principles are so restricted in the particular sciences because these subject matters

> do not use the foregoing principles insofar as they are common principles, i.e., as extending to all beings, but insofar as they have need of them; that is, insofar as they extend to the things contained in the class of beings which constitutes the subject of a particular science, about which it makes demonstrations. For example, the philosophy of nature uses them insofar as they extend to changeable beings and no further.[56]

Having said that the first principles are used in a restricted manner in the particular arts and sciences, we must add that one does not automatically deduce such restricted principles from those which are first in the mind. Given the first principles, one must also build up a fund of experience about a given subject matter, such as natural science. Thus, in order to know the principle *the human being is an animal*, one must encounter sufficient individual persons. This experience with human beings, as well as the understanding of the first principles, is needed before this particular natural principle is known. Since the first principles are abstracted by the agent intellect, we can see that this active power, the understanding of the first principles, and the experience with a given thing are all needed before a particular principle is understood.

C. A Movement from Sense to Universal

Having clarified the two types of self-evident principles, let us examine Aristotle's doctrine on the way the human being arrives at the universal level found in every concept or principle. An understanding of this natural way is particularly valuable for the teacher, for it presents the basic technique used in all human knowing. Since the human being's natural way of knowing is the guide for the art of teaching, this basic technique gives the blueprint for the fundamental process in pedagogy. These natural steps lay out carefully the initial, bedrock method for instruction. Since "the beginning is thought to be more than half of the whole, and many of the questions we ask are cleared up by it,"[57] the study of the human movement from the sense to the universal level of knowledge is an essential for the teaching profession.

1. Steps to the Universal

To discover the human sequence from sensation to universal concepts and principles, Aristotle, working always with the reality around him, observes that there are three levels of knowing in animals. He notes, first of all, that all animals have the obvious characteristic of possessing "a congenital discriminative capacity which is called sense-perception."[58] Here Aristotle is focusing on the lowest level of knowing, the general ability to sense, which may be nothing more than the possession of the sense of touch.

Among the animals which are capable of sense impressions, however, there are those which cannot move and those which can do so. In the stationary animals, such as the shellfish, the impressions simply come and go, but there is a higher level of knowing in those which can move. This is so, for, to guide themselves in their movements, these self-moving animals must retain the sense impressions which they have received from the external world. Thus the dog, having once sighted a pheasant, must be able to remember what it is that he is chasing. For this reason the animals which can move have, in addition to the ability to receive sense impressions, the power of memory.

> For if the anticipated goal by which they are induced to move did not remain in them through memory, they could not continue to move toward the intended goal which they pursue. But in the case of immobile animals the reception of a present sensible quality is sufficient for them to perform their characteristic operations, since they do not move toward anything at a distance.[59]

There is, moreover, a third level of knowing in animals, for, among those that can remember there are those which have "reasoning concerning those things which remain in the memory, as in men; in certain others not, as in the brutes."[60]

According to Aristotle, then, the animals possess three levels in their capacity to know: the ability to receive sense impressions, the ability to remember, and the ability to reason. Why is Aristotle able to say this? He is simply reporting on his observations, on his experience in the matter, as the following sentence indicates: "And this at least is an obvious characteristic of all animals, for they possess a congenital discriminative capacity which is called sense-perception."[61]

Having noted that there are three levels in knowing, Aristotle then shows how the first principles are acquired by the human being, who, as the superior animal, possesses all three cognitional levels.[62] First of all, one must have some sense experience with the thing (or with its elements) about which a principle is to be obtained. In addition to having these sensations, one must be able to remember what he has sensed, so that he will have some singulars to compare as he seeks a principle about what is studied.

To remember sense experiences, one requires not only his memory but also his cogitative power because the singulars remembered are those with a beneficial or harmful quality. Thus an individual can easily recall any traumatic experience, such as an automobile accident. Since awareness of this value quality is the work of the cogitative power, the person striving to remember requires the assistance of his cogitative faculty. For the retention of sense experiences, then, the powers of cogitation and memory work hand in hand, since "for the apprehension of intentions which are not received through the senses [such as the thing's value], the *estimative* power is appointed: and for the preservation thereof, the *memorative* power, which is a storehouse of such-like intentions."[63]

With these two powers working together in such a fashion, a person, as he remembers many encounters with a given thing, gradually builds up experience, which is a refined sense knowledge resulting from the comparison of many memories.[64] To obtain experiential knowledge is most important for the person seeking a principle about a given object, for experience is the proximate material for any universal insight.

How, then, does one obtain this refinement of sense knowledge from the many singulars that he remembers? To secure experiential knowledge, the person will compare the many singulars retained by the memory. Utilizing the first value impression as a stable unit for comparison, one will gradually group around this initial impression other memories of the same type until he is experienced with the thing about which a principle is sought.

Let us now illustrate this natural process of arriving at experience, a procedure which the art of teaching will imitate. On a given occasion, a man with a cold took some aspirin, went to bed, and later got up feeling better. Because of the relief that he felt, this singular occurrence made an impression. Later he tried the same remedy on different members of his family and on his circle of friends. Gradually he built up in this way experience of a satisfactory way to take care of a cold.

Such experience is nothing more than the sum of all the individual encounters that he has had with treating colds, a summation which includes the comparison of each of these, however, by the cogitative power. For "experience is seen to be nothing other than to receive something from many things retained in the memory. But nevertheless experience requires some ratiocination about particulars, through which one is related to the other."[65] Thus this man now knows, by means of his cogitative power, that such-and-such a remedy has helped many individual people with colds. His own first encounter, received into the memory from the cogitative power, was the stable unit with which this same cogitative faculty compared later contacts with the remedy.

Because of this gradual build-up from a first memorable encounter, Aquinas, commenting on Aristotle, compares the process of obtaining experience to a situation which occurs in battle:

> And he [Aristotle] gives an example in battles which are brought about by the turning back of an army overcome and put to flight. For when one of them will have made a stand, i.e., will have begun to stand immovably and not flee, another stands, adding himself to him, and afterwards another, until enough are congregated to bring about the beginning of a fight. Thus also from sense and memory of one particular, and again of another and another, one sometimes arrives at that which is the principle of art and science.[66]

This quotation not only illustrates the process of obtaining experience but also points out that experiential knowledge can lead to principles. From this refined sense knowledge a person may arrive at universal principles because his intellectual power is capable of abstracting the universal from what his senses present to him. By means of his agent intellect (as abstracting) and of his possible intellect (as receptive), one can see a universal principle in all the encounters woven together in a given experience. The human being's

> reason does not come to rest in the experience of particulars, but from many particulars of which one has had experience, it grasps one common thing, which is confirmed in the soul, and considers it without the consideration of any of the singulars; and this common thing it takes as the principle of art and science.[67]

Thus, continuing the previous example, we see that the reason knows, not just that aspirin and sleep will help a cold in certain individuals, but that this remedy will help in all cases of colds. When it has attained such a universal notion, the reason is beyond that type of knowledge proper to experience, which is concerned with singular cases. For the intellect "considers some nature, e.g., that of man, without considering Socrates and Plato."[68] For this reason Aristotle says that the universal comes to rest in the soul, meaning by this that it is considered apart from the singulars, in which there is mobility and change.

From the above explanation, we can see that the human being is able to obtain universal principles from his experience because of his intellective power. Already in the first stable experience mentioned above, the intellect begins to perceive the universal, if only very dimly. This is the very nature of the active power in the intellect: to penetrate into the sensible singular and to abstract the nature therefrom. It is true that the intellect's first insight will be very obscure because of this power's movement from potency to act; nevertheless the first outlines of the universal are there.

Thus far we have seen that Aristotle's doctrine on the process toward universal principles admits of the following steps:

1. One must have sense experiences of a given thing. When we say this, we do not mean that a person must have direct experience of every single situation. Rather we mean that one must have sensed the given thing or at least such elements as are necessary to imagine the thing at hand. Thus, in reference to the latter case, if one has had sense experiences of houses and fires, one could imagine what a burning house would be like without having actually seen one.

2. In such sense experiences, those with value (which intentions are apprehended by the cogitative power) are retained in the memory.

3. The cogitative power also compares the many particulars retained in the memory, thus gradually building up a unified sense knowledge called experience in the full sense of the word.

4. Out of this experience, the human being is able, by means of his reason, to arrive at a universal principle. With the active power of his agent intellect, he is able to penetrate into that which is common to all that he has experienced.

2. Needed Number of Examples

We have now explained Aristotle's doctrine on the procedure for arriving at universal principles. Since the use of individual cases or experiences is a vital part of this process, our next problem is concerned with the number of cases needed before the universal is perceived. Aristotle holds that it cannot be every single instance of the principle in question (in the above illustration, of everyone who has had, has, or will have a cold), for the number of such cases is potentially infinite.[69]

If every instance were needed, how could one ever arrive at the concept of being in a single lifetime? Yet people continue to arrive at the universal, to make inductions. That such inductions are sound is demonstrated by their actions. Thus Salk vaccine has not been tried on all potential victims of polio, but the principle concerning its usefulness for this disease is now accepted. Plainly, then, one does not need every single case to arrive at the universal.

In order to point out that the process of making inductions is not based on every single case, Aristotle utilizes the way that a person states his principles, his premises. He says that "no premiss is ever couched in the form 'every number which you know to be such', or 'every rectilinear figure which you know to be such': the predicate is always construed as applicable to any and every instance of the thing."[70] Thus people do not say that Salk vaccine is a good preventive against polio for all the cases in which it has been tried, but that it is a good preventive against polio for all potential victims.

Consequently, the ability to arrive at the universal does not require the consideration of every single case. Instead it rests with the power of the intellect to abstract the universal nature of a given thing from the sensible singulars which are part of the individual's experience. This power will vary from individual to individual, and thus, because of differences in the ability to penetrate to the essence of the material thing, a greater or fewer number of examples will be needed. Thus one student, by means of the examples used in a single class, will understand the decimal number base, while another will need the illustrations of several classes.

The variation in the knowability of the principles will also cause a difference in the number of examples needed. Thus one particular case of the principle *being is not nonbeing* could easily cause a firm assent of the mind. For example, at the outset of the use of reason, one may understand that one's pet is an animal. With this knowledge, one implicitly understands that one's pet is none of the nonanimals, thus assenting to the validity of the principle of contradiction. On the contrary, however, if the principle involved is only probable or quite abstract in character, it will require many examples. Thus the principle *all Democrats are progressive* may require many examples of democratic political activity. For this reason Aquinas says that "one self-evident proposition convinces the intellect, so that it gives a firm assent to the conclusion, but a probable proposition cannot do this."[71]

The number of examples needed to arrive at the universal, therefore, is not every instance of the principle involved, but only a number sufficient to permit the intellect of the individual to arrive at the universal. In other words, the number of examples needed for a universal must be enough to satisfy the mind of the individual. One has the universal when one sees that such is the case, when one can assent or accede to a given fact. The inductive process is an intuitive, not a syllogistic, one. Because induction rests on assent, not proof, Aquinas says

that the one proceeding inductively, having made the induction that Socrates runs and also Plato and Cicero, cannot with necessity conclude that every man runs, unless it is conceded to him by the one answering that nothing other is contained under man than those things which have been induced.[72]

One does not have to search for proof when a sufficient number of sense examples reveal the nature of the case. In this process one needs both some type of experience with a given thing and the power to arrive at the universal from a sufficient number of examples. Thus, if one were on the moon and could sense the cause of its eclipse (namely, the interposition of the earth between it and the sun) a sufficient number of times, one would have the experience needed to arrive at the universal principle concerning this phenomenon. One would not have to arrive at the principle by an indirect procedure because one could sense the occurrence directly and could abstract from a sufficient number of sensations the cause of the moon's eclipse.

If one sees a principle such as the above, and yet maintains that he does not, perhaps he belongs to the school of those who doubt the validity of sense knowledge—the foundation of all that the human being ever knows. Aristotle says that such a person is lacking in education, for not to know of what things one should demand demonstration, and of what one should not, argues want of education. For it is impossible that there should be demonstration of absolutely everything (there would be an infinite regress, so that there would still be no demonstration).[73]

D. A Movement from General to Particular
1. Nature of This Movement

Having explained how the human being moves from sense knowledge .to universal principles and how much sense experience is required, let us now discuss Aristotle's doctrine concerning the movement of the human mind from the general to the particular. At the beginning of this chapter, we pointed out that the primary emphasis throughout this section would be, not on the activity of the knowing powers, but on what is known. In other words, this chapter will treat the fact that the human being moves from the known to the unknown. In this process he moves first from sense to universal knowledge, and then, on this level, he moves from general knowledge to particular applications thereof. Having covered the movement from sense to universal knowledge, let us now treat the movement from the general to the particular.

The human being moves from general knowledge to particular applications contained therein because his knowing moves from potency to act. In the beginning "the mind...is in potency, somehow to intelligible objects which are not actual in it until understood by it. It is like a sheet of paper on which no word is yet written, but many can be written."[74] At the outset of learning, the human intellect does not actually understand that which it desires to know. Rather the truths a person seeks are

> known *in potency* or *virtually* in the foreknown universal principles [in the general known knowledge], but unknown in act, according to proper knowledge. And this is to learn, to be reduced from potential, or virtual, or universal knowledge, to proper and actual knowledge.[75]

In the reason's movement from potency to act, it advances discursively, i.e., from one thing to another, from what is known to what is unknown. Thus, the scientist, seeking the origin of the universe, uses what he knows of the world around him to arrive at a knowledge of the world's beginnings. This procedure is proper to the human being, namely, "to come to an understanding of intelligible truth by way of rational enquiry; whereas the immaterial substances, which are in a higher degree intellectual, apprehend truth immediately without having to reason about it."[76] In fact, the human "intellect is called 'reason' in so far as it comes to intelligible truths by a process of enquiry."[77]

The human being encounters the general or universal principle first in this process of inquiry, and from this he moves to particular applications contained therein. The general precedes the particular in human knowing because the knowledge of the general principle contains potentially all the particular applications proper to it. Thus, when one knows the general principle *every triangle has its three angles equal to two right angles*, he knows potentially the same truth about all the particular kinds of triangles to which it can be applied. For this reason, when Aristotle makes a reference to the particular applications under a universal, he describes "the particulars actually falling under the universal...[as] already virtually known."[78]

a. A Movement from Known to Unknown

When one advances from general knowledge to particular truths contained under it, he must naturally rely on that which he knows first. As Aristotle puts it, "all instruction given or received by way of argument proceeds from pre-existent knowledge."[79] Thus, let us suppose that a person knows the following general principle: A wound without an angle has parts which "do not approach each other in such a way as to be easily joined."[80] In other words, a wound without an angle is one that heals more slowly than other wounds.

In addition to this, one knows that a circular wound is the type of wound without any angle. Then relying on the knowledge of the general principle and of the specific case involved, he can immediately conclude that a circular wound is one that heals more slowly than other wounds. Here the person has reached a specific insight about the circular wound by means of his knowledge of the general principle and of the nature of such wounds. He has relied on what he knows to arrive at what was previously unknown.

This procedure of moving from the known to the unknown is the reasoning, syllogistic, or deductive process. Aristotle defines it as follows: "Now reasoning is an argument in which, certain things being laid down, something other than these necessarily comes about through them."[81] In other words, it is a process in which, certain known truths being laid down, that which is unknown follows necessarily from these truths. More simply, reasoning is a process of moving from known truths to those which are unknown.

This reliance on known truths is not found in the inductive process, in the movement from sense to the universal. Here the mind simply abstracts the universal from sense experience; no other universal need be part of the process. Thus, from several sense experiences such as rubbing one's hands together, touching used roller skates, and rubbing sticks together to build a fire, the student can arrive at the principle *friction produces heat.*

Therefore Aristotle says that "induction is the starting-point which knowledge even of the universal presupposes, while syllogism proceeds *from* universals. There are therefore starting points from which syllogism proceeds, which are not reached by syllogism; it is therefore by induction that they are acquired."[82] This independence from other universal truths proper to the inductive method is not found in the syllogistic process, in which the student can arrive at a new truth only if he possesses other universal truths. This is the very nature of the reasoning process: to move from universals to special applications contained therein.

b. Need for a Middle Term

This movement from general knowledge to particular cases contained under it does not happen in any manner whatsoever. Rather it is possible because a common element or link exists between the general principle and the particular case. Only by means of such a connection can one actually utilize his known truths in order to find out the unknown. If no such connection existed, he would not have the possibility of building on the universal knowledge he possesses, but he would be forced to start at the beginning, at that which his senses tell him. Granted such a connection, however, one can arrive at new knowledge by means of the universal truths that he knows. The following example makes this evident:

Whatever has parts	(B)	is corruptible.	(A)
Material things	(C)	have parts.	(B)
∴ Material things	(C)	are corruptible.	(A)

As is evident from the above example, the application of corruptibility to material things is possible only by means of the link that exists between them, namely, whatever has parts. This link, or middle term, is the bridge between one's general knowledge and the specific new truth to which he is able to conclude.

Aristotle calls the above mentioned link in knowledge a middle term because of its position among the terms present in the known truths. Referring to the above example to make this clear, we can see that there are two known truths, in which something is predicated of something else. Thus corruptible is predicated of whatever has parts. As can also be seen, there are only three terms: *corruptible, whatever has parts,* and *material things.*

In addition to this, a little reflection will reveal that all of **B** is contained in **A**, while all of **C** is contained in **B**. Thus, starting with **A** and moving down through **B** and finally to **C**, we can think of these terms as circles becoming ever smaller. Thus the extension or universality of **A** is greatest, while that of **C** is smallest. **B**, on the contrary, has the middle position in extension or universality. It is contained in **A**, while **C** is contained in it. For this reason it is the middle term. In Aristotle's words: "I call that middle which is itself contained in another and contains another in itself: in position also this comes in the middle."[83] As such, it is truly a bridge between **A** and **C**. Because of it, **A** can be said of **C**, or we can conclude that material things are corruptible.

We have just seen that the human mind is able to apply its universal knowledge to a particular case contained under it by means of a middle term that exists between them. Such a link exists because the particular case is part of the general principle and is defined as falling under such a principle. Thus material things are a case of the principle *whatever has parts is corruptible.* In addition material things are defined as falling under such a principle, namely, are defined as things which have parts.

Such a definition may not be a complete outlining of the thing's essence, but it must be true of at least some aspect of the thing and it must place the particular case under the general principle. In performing such a function, the definition of the subject acts as a middle term between the general principle and the particular case. There is a middle term because the subject is defined as falling under the general principle.[84]

Granted that the reasoning process rests on the fact that the subject is defined as falling under the general principle, we must still realize that such a process rests ultimately on the nature of reality. By this we mean that it would be impossible for us to reason from general principles to particular applications of them, unless there existed a real connection between the things about which one is reasoning.[85]

If all the things in the world had no connection with each other, how could one reason about them, since argumentation presumes such connections? On the contrary, however, Aristotle holds that "all things are ordered together somehow, but not all alike—both fishes and fowls and plants; and the world is not such that one thing has nothing to do with another, but they are connected. For all are ordered together to one end."[86]

Because the things of the universe are so ordered to each other, the human person is able to speculate about them in his own particular way: by reasoning from one thing to another. "Instead of being a movement of the body, it [reasoning] is a movement of the mind along the converging tracks of reality towards a single ultimate Answer, both the Cause of the things in reality and the final Goal of the mind, the Fountain-head of Being."[87]

2. Stages of This Movement

Thus far we have seen that the movement of the mind from the general to the particular is nothing other than the reasoning process, which rests on the connection existing between known truths—a connection which is founded ultimately on the reality of things. Now we must explain Aristotle's position on the stages in this process, so that the teacher can work in like manner. What, then, is the beginning of the procedure from the general to the particular?

a. Statement of the Problem

In general, the reasoning process begins in wonder. Thus, precisely because the human being sees things vaguely, or sees only the outer effects of them, he wonders about their specific natures or the causes of them. Since the human intellect moves from potency to act, the human person knows only the general outlines of things at first, and he wonders what makes these outer effects as they are. If the human being had angelic penetration, he would see both the effects and the causes of these effects instantaneously. Thus he would both hear the bell on the front door and know instantly who was ringing it. The human person is not endowed with such penetration, however, and must reason to the causes of the effects that he sees. Because of this, Aristotle says

> all men begin, as we said, by wondering that things are as they are, as they do about self-moving marionettes, or about the solstices or the incommensurability of the diagonal of a square with the side; for it seems wonderful to all who have not yet seen the reason, that there is a thing which cannot be measured even by the smallest unit.[88]

To say, however, that the mind, in moving from the general to the particular, begins with wonder, is to say that the first step in the process is a problem to be solved. To put this in another way, the mind does not wonder about that which is self-evident, the general outline of the thing; but it wonders about that which presents a problem to it, i.e., the specific nature of the given thing. Thus the intellect will not linger on that which is immediately clear or that which presents no problem, such as the fact that the whole is greater than the part. The mind, in the reasoning process, begins with problems, not with the self-evident.

The statement of the problem, then, is the beginning of the process from the general to the particular.

> This is true for this reason, that, just as the terminus of a journey is the goal intended by one who travels on foot, in a similar way the solution of a problem is the goal intended by one who is seeking the truth. But it is evident that one who does not know where he is going cannot go there directly, except by chance. Therefore, neither can one seek the truth directly unless he first sees the problem.[89]

Granted that the perception of the problem is the first stage in solving it, we must also recognize that this is an ability not given in equal measure to everyone. Not everyone stops to ask if there might be a connection between smoking and lung cancer, if there might be a relation between the exterior angle of a triangle and its opposite interior angles. This ability to wonder about things and to ask about them is not found in the same degree in each individual, but the use of such ability, nevertheless, is at the beginning of every reasoning process. Expressed in current terminology, the statement of the problem must precede the hypothesis and the verification of such a hypothesis.

The neglect of this first stage of the reasoning process is seen in many situations. Thus the speaker who fails to tell his audience in the beginning the points that he intends to cover condemns his listeners to the lot of "those who do not know where they have to go."[90] In like manner, the teacher who does not state at the outset the objectives of the day's lesson will hinder the student from knowing "whether he has at any given time found what he is looking for or not."[91] As is evident, if the problem is not stated in the beginning, one is handicapped in the natural desire to arrive at a clearer knowledge of things.

b. The Goal Sought

Having formulated the problem, the mind must then begin to solve it, must move from the general knowledge that it owns to the solution of the specific problem at hand. In order to see how the mind goes about this, let us state Aristotle's position on what the human being is seeking in this movement from the general to the particular, in this reasoning process.

Aristotle holds that the human being, in the reasoning process, seeks to apply his general principle to a specific case falling under that principle. Since the human intellect moves from potency to act, it first possesses general knowledge and then it arrives at specific applications of that knowledge. Thus a human being might first know the general principle *all things having parts are corruptible* and later, by the reasoning process, reach the conclusion *all material things are corruptible*. This conclusion is simply the application of what is known about things having parts (namely, corruptibility) to material things, a particular case falling under the general principle. This illustration indicates that the conclusion is the application of the general principle to the subject falling under it. In other words, that which is new or unknown in the reasoning process is the application for the first time of the general knowledge to a particular subject under it.

In the process of reasoning, the human being is not searching for the knowledge of the general principle or even for a definition of the particular case, but rather for the application of the general principle to the given case. Why is this so? Since the human person reaches the unknown by means of what he knows, he should expect to use his general knowledge, to apply it to new and more specific cases. This reasoning movement is not an independent process, but one which uses or applies the general principle to other subjects which must also be known before the principle can be applied. Therefore, that which is unknown is the application of the general knowledge to a particular subject falling under it. Aristotle points this out in the following quotation:

> Then too we hold that it is by *demonstration* that the being of everything must be proved.... The being of anything as fact is matter for demonstration; and this is the actual procedure of the sciences, for the geometer assumes the meaning of the word triangle, but that it is possessed of some attribute he proves.[92]

c. The Foreknowledge

Granted that in the reasoning process the human being seeks the application of his general knowledge to the particular case falling under it, we must now state what knowledge is necessary in order to arrive at such a goal. Then we shall point out the sequence or order for using this knowledge. In stating the knowledge needed for this movement from the general to the particular, we shall utilize Aristotle's doctrine on the foreknowledge necessary for demonstration, the strictest or ideal type of reasoning. We use this doctrine deliberately, for it gives the standard or ideal, which can then be adapted as circumstances make it necessary. A similar procedure can be found in Aristotle's *Politica*, where he proposes to ascertain the nature of the ideal state. Thus he says that his "purpose is to consider what form of political community is best of all for those who are most able to realize their ideal of life."[93]

In Aristotle's doctrine on demonstration, he points out that the foreknowledge needed for this particular reasoning process is threefold: knowledge of the general principle, of the particular case, and of the property to be applied to the given case. Thus, if a student wishes to arrive at the conclusion *all material things are corruptible*, he must have the following foreknowledge: (1) He must know the principle *all things having parts are corruptible*. (2) He must understand that material things (the subject) are things with parts. (3) He must have at least a nominal meaning of corruptibility (the property) in relation to these same material things.

The student requires this threefold knowledge in order to demonstrate because of the relationship which exists between these three and the conclusion sought. First of all, the parts of the conclusion are the subject and the property; secondly, the knowledge of the conclusion flows from the knowledge of the principle. Because of this dependence of the conclusion upon the subject, the property, and the principle, these three must be foreknown if the student wishes to reach a given conclusion. Aquinas, commenting on Aristotle, expresses this as follows:

> Since the knowledge of simple things precedes the knowledge of composite things it is necessary that, before the knowledge of the conclusion is had, in some way the subject and the passion [property] should be known. And likewise it is necessary that the principle be foreknown, since from the knowledge of the principle, the conclusion is made known.[94]

This quotation states that the person who would demonstrate must know the subject, the property, and the principle. Since these three parts of the foreknowledge are not all known by the same act of the mind,[95] they will be known in different ways. Before we distinguish just how one knows each of these three, however, we must point out that it is possible to know both that a thing is and what it is. Thus a person can ask and answer both whether a human being exists and, if so, what is his nature.

This possibility exists, for in every created thing its essence is other than its existence. Thus the nature of a human being is different from the fact that he is or exists. This is so, "for only in the first Principle of being, which is essentially being, are its being and quiddity one and the same. But in all other things, which are beings by participation, it is necessary that *being* and *quiddity* of being be other."[96] In other words, only in God do we find that *to be* is his nature; in all other things their nature and being are distinct.

With this realization that we can know about a thing both that it is and what it is, let us examine Aristotle's doctrine on how a person knows the principle, subject, and property, the three parts of the foreknowledge needed to reason to a demonstrative conclusion. Concerning the principle, one will not know what it is, i.e., its definition, because "it is characteristic of the notion of definition that it should signify one thing."[97] Thus *human being*, as signifying one definite thing, is definable.

Since the principle, in which one thing is predicated of another thing, is not something simple but complex, the person will not have a definition of it, will not know what the principle is. Rather he will know whether the predicate of the principle can be affirmed or denied of the subject. Thus it is possible for him to know that corruptibility can be affirmed of things having parts. Expressed in another way, the human being can know that the principle is true. "Since a principle is a certain enunciation [which is something complex], one cannot foreknow of it *what it is*, but only *that* it is true."[98]

Of the subject or specific case, however, one must know both that it is and what it is. First, he must know the existence of the subject, for, since he intends to apply his general knowledge (specifically, the property) to it, he must know that there is such a subject to which the property can be applied. Thus a person cannot apply corruptibility to material things, if no such things exist.

Secondly, one must know what the subject is, i.e., its definition, since by means of such knowledge he sees that the subject has a relation to the general principle. Thus, when a person defines material things as things having parts, he can see that material things fall under the general principle *all things having parts are corruptible*. If he did not know the definition of material things, the person could not make this connection with his general knowledge. The definition of material things, therefore, is the connecting link or middle term in the movement from the general to the particular.[99] For this reason Aquinas says that "of the subject it is necessary to foreknow both *what it is* and *that it is*, especially since it is from the definition of the subject and passion that the middle of demonstration is taken."[100]

Having seen what knowledge one must have of the principle and of the subject, let us point out Aristotle's position on how the property is known. Since the purpose of the reasoning process is to show that the property belongs or exists in the specific case, the person will not know that it exists in the particular subject. In other words, the knowledge of the property prior to the conclusion is not that it is in the particular subject, for this must be proved. Thus the human being will not know that corruptibility belongs to material things.[101]

Since one does not know of the property that it is, neither can he have a real definition of it, i.e., know what it is in the strict sense of the term. The reason for this is that "before it is known of something whether it is, it is not possible properly to know of it what it is; for there are no definitions of non-beings.

Whence the question, *whether it is*, precedes the question, *what it is.*"[102] Thus, before one can understand the essential nature of something, one must know first whether there is such a nature to be understood. For example, "he who knows what human—or any other—nature is, must know also that man exists; for no one knows the nature of what does not exist—one can know the meaning of the phrase or name 'goat-stag' but not what the essential nature of a goat-stag is."[103]

If one knows neither the existence nor the essential nature of the property, what kind of knowledge does he have of it? In Aristotle's example of the goat-stag, we already have the answer. The person will have simply a nominal description or definition of the property. He will know only what is meant by the word or phrase being used. This is even a more elementary knowledge than knowing whether a thing is (which precedes knowing what it is), since "it cannot be shown of something whether it is, unless it is first understood what is signified by the word."[104]

Thus, suppose that the person wished to prove that a certain excavated skull was the Missing Link, that this property could be predicated of this particular subject. Then, of the property, Missing Link, the person would have only a nominal description, would know only what should be the requisites for such an attribute. He would know, for example, that the Missing Link would have to possess physical characteristics neither wholly human nor wholly nonhuman. Rather its qualities would be a combination of both species—whether such a creature ever existed or not. To possess such a nominal description of a given property is indeed an elementary knowledge; yet in a mind that knows by moving from potency to act, one should not expect too much at the start.

Let us now summarize what knowledge one needs in order to move from the general to the particular in demonstrative reasoning. We shall do so by utilizing our previous example:

All things having parts are corruptible.
   The person knows that the principle is true.
corruptible
   The person knows the nominal definition of the property in relation to the
   subject. Thus he knows only a nominal meaning of corruptible in relation
   to material things.
All material things are things having parts.
   The person knows both the existence of the subject and its nature. Thus he
   knows both that material things exist and that they are things having parts.
∴ All material things are corruptible.
   Because of the above kinds of foreknowledge, the person is able to arrive
   at new knowledge, namely, that the property belongs to the subject.

This, then, is the knowledge required in order that one may move from the known to the unknown in the demonstrative process of reasoning. Aristotle states this requirement as follows:

> The pre-existent knowledge required is of two kinds. In some cases admission of the fact must be assumed, in others comprehension of the meaning of the term used, and sometimes both assumptions are essential. Thus, we assume that every predicate can be either truly affirmed or truly denied of any subject, and that 'triangle' means so and so; as regards 'unit' we have to make the double assumption of the meaning of the word and the existence of the thing. The reason is that these several objects are not equally obvious to us.[105]

Before we indicate the order in which one uses the knowledge that he possesses, we must point out that what we have been saying about the person's foreknowledge represents the ideal situation. If possible, one must know that the principle is true at all times and in all cases. Sometimes, however, he must work with principles that are only probable, that are true only for the most part, such as the principle *all young people are impetuous*. If this is the nature of the principles used, the person's foreknowledge is still that the principle is true, but he possesses a truth which is only probable. Since his principle is only a matter of opinion, his conclusion can possess only the same degree of certitude.

Concerning the subject, one should know not only that it exists but also its essential nature. Many times, however, this is not possible, and he must utilize a definition taken from the external characteristics of an object, such as the definition of an elephant as an animal with a long trunk, flappy ears, and wrinkled skin. To the extent that the person does not know the object's essential nature, he must employ external descriptions. Such definitions, of course, will weaken the force of the conclusion; the ideal, naturally, would be to know the existence and the essential nature of the subject.[106]

d. Order in the Foreknowledge

Having seen what knowledge of the principle, the subject, and the property one needs to move from the general to the particular in demonstrative reasoning, let us now state Aristotle's position on the order in which the human being uses this knowledge. To know this order is important for the teacher, for he must know not only the materials with which he will work, but also the order in which he will use them. He must proceed as the builder of a house would do,

> for if a house or other such final object is to be realized, it is necessary that such and such material shall exist; and it is necessary that first this and then that shall be produced, and first this and then that set in motion, and so on in continuous succession, until the end and final result is reached, for the sake of which each prior thing is produced and exists.[107]

In what order, then, does one utilize his knowledge as he moves from the general to the particular? As stated in the beginning of this section, he must first of all see the problem to be solved. Thus, if he has encountered a man who is severely bleeding from an accident, a person may immediately formulate a question such as the following: In what way can this bleeding be stopped?

To solve this particular problem, one must know both some universal principles about handling severely bleeding wounds and also the nature of the case at hand. In other words, he must know that certain universal principles about bleeding are true and also the definition of the particular subject. (The nominal description of the property, i.e., of the remedy to be applied, will be in the general principle selected for the case.) How then shall the person proceed? Shall he search through his stock of universal principles first, or shall he identify the case?

Since the person cannot apply principles or rules about bleeding, such as those about direct pressure, digital pressure, or the tourniquet, until he has identified the case, he must move from the statement of the problem to the identification of the subject. After the person knows, for example, that this is a severely bleeding wound in the injured man's back, then he will know that this is a case in which to apply the principle about direct pressure. It is after the identification of the subject that the person's store of principles becomes useful. Identification of the case, therefore, precedes application of the general principle.

The following, then, is Aristotle's thinking on the order of using the foreknowledge in the movement from the general to the particular: (1) statement of the problem, (2) identification of the particular case or subject, (3) application of the universal principle helpful for the case at hand. An indication of the priority of the definition of the particular subject is found in the following quotation:

> Beginning from the whatness itself of a thing, which has been made known either by the senses or by assuming it from some other science, these sciences demonstrate the proper attributes which belong essentially to the subject-genus with which they deal; for a definition is the middle term in a causal demonstration.[108]

We have just described how one uses his knowledge to move from general principles to particular applications contained therein. Preceding this movement, however, is the process of abstracting universal principles from sense knowledge. This latter movement is the basic process of acquiring knowledge, for, in his efforts to arrive at the unknown, the human being must rely first of all on sense experiences. Then, utilizing the universal abstracted from what his senses tell him, a person can move gradually into the unknown. Such intellectual advance is part of the very nature of the human being, for it is his way of attempting to unite himself to the source of his being, a union supremely natural,

> since it is in this that the perfection of each thing consists.... [But] it is only by means of his intellect that man is united to the separate substances, which are the source of the human intellect and that to which the human intellect is related as

something imperfect to something perfect. It is for this reason, too, that the ultimate happiness of man consists in this union. Therefore man naturally desires to know.[109]

This quotation explains why it is natural for the human being to desire to advance intellectually. In addition to this realization about the human desire for knowledge, it must not be forgotten that the human person can fulfill this natural desire only if he employs the two procedures discussed in this chapter, namely, the movement from sense to universal knowledge and the movement from universal principles to particular applications contained therein.

Throughout this chapter, as well as the two preceding ones, we have been discussing Aristotle's position on the nature of knowing: first, its objects; then, its psychological procedure; and finally, the logical order in knowing. We have attempted to explain very carefully the nature of this process, for the art of teaching must build upon this foundation. Only after careful observation of the way in which the mind moves naturally can the teacher construct his art. Having studied the natural acquisition of knowledge, let us now examine the Aristotelian doctrine relevant for teaching, remembering that the material we have thus far treated will form the basic principles for this art.

Chapter 5

Inductive Process of Teaching

A. Summary of knowing process
   1. Knowing's objects
   2. Knowing's process
      a. The process in general
      b. The process in intellectual knowing
B. Induction's purpose
   1. The definition
      a. Statement of genus and specific difference
      b. Statement of causes
   2. The proposition
      a. The immediate proposition
      b. The mediate proposition
C. Induction's materials
   1. Objects of sense perception
   2. Object of cogitative power
      a. Its importance for memory
      b. Its importance for students
   3. Rules for memorizing
D. Induction's procedure
   1. For universal propositions
   2. For definitions
      a. Method of division
      b. Method of composition

Inductive Process of Teaching

A. Summary of knowing process
B. Induction's purpose
C. Induction's materials
D. Induction's procedure

In the three chapters preceding this one, we examined Aristotle's position on the natural acquisition of knowledge in order that we might have the guiding principles for the art of teaching. This examination must precede the discussion of teaching because the activity of instruction, as an art, is primarily interested in doing or production. But "the end of the science [such as teaching] concerned with practicable matters is not to know and investigate individual things, as in the speculative sciences, but rather to do them."[1] Thus the purpose of the teacher of geometry is not simply to speculate about geometry, but to produce students learned in this subject matter. In like manner, the primary purpose of all teaching is the actual production of intellectually virtuous students.

Aristotle holds that the basic principle of production in all the arts, however, is that they should follow the principles and example that nature sets for them. To be productive of fruitful results, every art must imitate nature, a nature which "does not perfect those things which are of art, but only prepares certain principles and furnishes an exemplar for the work in a certain way to the artisans. Art, for its part, is able to look at the things which are of nature, and use them to bring about its own work."[2] This principle *art imitates nature* can be found in all human artistic productions. Thus the doctor, if he wishes to heal someone, first observes how nature does her healing and then, utilizing the chemicals furnished by nature, proceeds to practice his art.

In order to imitate nature in a profitable way, the artist must first observe the pattern or exemplar presented by nature. Thus the rocket technician, desirous of producing a serviceable weapon, must first study the natural laws of gravity and friction. Since every artist must first observe nature, the teacher, whose principal art consists in helping the student move from the known to the unknown, must first understand the natural acquisition of knowledge. Since we have examined the natural way of knowing in the preceding chapters of this book, we can now approach the Aristotelian doctrine relevant to the art of teaching.

A. Summary of Knowing Process

Before we examine Aristotle's doctrine useful for teaching, let us summarize his position on the natural acquisition of knowledge. In this summarization, we shall point out first the principles concerning the objects of knowing and then those related to the process of knowing. Expressed more simply, our summarization shall move from what to how. The soundness of this order can be seen, for example, in the activities of the doctor or the builder.

> For consider how the physician or how the builder sets about his work. He starts by forming for himself a definite picture, in the one case perceptible to mind, in the other to sense, of his end—the physician of health, the builder of a house—and this he holds forward as the reason and explanation of each subsequent step that he takes, and of his acting in this or that way as the case may be.[3]

Both the physician and the builder move from the understanding of the end desired to the procedure needed to accomplish this end because "the *type* of every act or operation is determined by an object."[4] These individuals move from object to procedure, since any activity is determined by the object connected with it. Thus the builder moves from the study of the blueprint of the house to the actual construction of the building, because all of his work is determined by the object in which it terminates, namely, the finished dwelling. Since the order of all activity is from the end desired to the process needed to accomplish this end, we shall summarize Aristotle's doctrine on the natural activity of knowing by treating first the objects of knowledge and then its procedure.

1. Knowing's Objects

Aristotle has two major principles concerning the objects of the human being's natural activity of knowing. The first is that human knowledge begins with the sense objects, "since all of the objects of our understanding are included within the range of sensible things existing in space, that is to say, that none seems to have that sort of distinct existence apart from things of sense which particular things of sense have apart from one another."[5] Without the knowledge of his senses, one could not begin the pursuit of truth, since the proper object of his knowing is the material thing—a material thing knowable by the senses in relation to its individuating principles and knowable by the intellect in relation to its essence. Thus without the knowledge of the sense objects, such as color, sound, and the tangible, one could not begin to move from the known to the unknown. In acquiring knowledge, the human being must begin with the sense objects.

Can the human being trust the sense knowledge with which he begins? Aristotle responds most emphatically in the affirmative. He says that "each sense has one kind of object which it discerns, and never errs in reporting that what is before it is colour or sound (though it may err as to what it is that is coloured or where that is, or what it is that is sounding or where that is)."[6] Since a natural power usually does not fail in its proper activity, the human senses can be trusted in relation to their proper objects.

Thus the human being can believe that the red reported by his power of sight is actually red, "unless there is an impediment in the organ or in the medium [through which the color of red is being sensed]."[7] Although such trust in the senses has been open to dispute at different times,[8] one demonstrates by his actions that he believes the reports of his senses concerning their proper objects. Thus a person who steps back after touching a hot stove demonstrates that he trusts the message given to him by his sense of touch.

The reports given the human being by his senses are the beginning of all of his knowledge. As we have already pointed out, this observation about sense knowledge is Aristotle's first principle about the activity of knowing in relation to its object. The Philosopher's second principle is that the human being, as a rational animal, seeks not just sense knowledge, but that which is proper to his intellect, namely, the essence of the material thing. Although the beginning of human knowledge is in the sense order, each person seeks to know the very essences of things, a type of knowledge not possible to the brute animals. Thus one is not satisfied with sense knowledge about the human being; he wants to know such a person as a rational animal. For this reason Aquinas says that "the intellect attains perfection, in so far as it knows the essence of a thing."[9]

The intellect's desire to know the essence of a thing is most natural, for the thing's essence, namely, that which makes the given object what it is, can be found in the causes of the thing. The thing's essence lies in its causes, for "those things are called causes upon which things depend for their existence or their coming to be."[10] Thus, if a house had an essence in the strict sense of the term, it would consist of the causes of the house, primarily its formal structure as existing in a certain kind of material.

The human desire to know the thing's essence, therefore, is actually wonder about the causes of the thing. This state of wonder began with lesser problems about the things of the universe, but gradually advanced to a desire to know about its origin, i.e., to know the Ultimate Cause of all reality. In the words of Aquinas:

> Those who first philosophized and who now philosophize did so from wonder about some cause, although they did this at first differently than now. For at first they wondered about less important problems, which were more obvious, in order that they might know their cause; but later on, progressing little by little from the knowledge of more evident matters to the investigation of obscure ones, they began to raise questions about more important and hidden matters, such as...the origin of the whole universe, which some said was produced by chance, others by an intelligence, and others by love.[11]

Since the human desire to know the essences or causes of things leads ultimately to wonder about the First Cause of the universe, it is truly a most natural
desire, for the knowledge of the Ultimate Cause constitutes human perfection.
Since "each thing naturally desires its own perfection,"[12] this eagerness of the
human being to know the essences or causes of things is most natural to him.

This principle concerning the human desire to know the essences of things
points out the goal of the human mind, while Aristotle's first principle about the
fundamental quality of the sense order clarifies the beginnings of the natural
process of knowing. When planning his methodology, the teacher must carefully remember both of these principles concerning the objects of human knowledge. If he ignores either, he cannot hope to be successful.

Thus, if he omits the use of examples and forgets that "the objects of perception are better known, to most people if not invariably,"[13] he will not provide
any firm sense foundation on which his students can build their knowledge. On
the other hand, if the teacher limits his students to the observation of facts and
forgets that they have a natural desire to know the nature and causes of these
facts, he will hinder them from attaining their intellectual perfection, namely, a
knowledge of the causes of things and ultimately of the First Cause.

2. Knowing's Process

Having pointed out Aristotle's basic principles concerning the objects of
human knowing, let us now recall his major principles about the human procedure in acquiring knowledge. As we do so, we shall speak first of the process of
knowing in general and then we shall discuss intellectual knowing.

a. The Process in General

The following are the two general principles that Aristotle stresses about the
process of knowing: (1) The knowing powers are in potency to their objects.
(2) When the assimilation proper to knowing occurs, the knowing power receives, without the matter, the form of the thing known. In discussing the sense
powers, the Philosopher expresses these principles as follows: (1) "It is clear
that what is sensitive is so only potentially, not actually."[14] (2) "By a 'sense' is
meant what has the power of receiving into itself the sensible forms of things
without the matter."[15] These two principles form the general framework within
which the process of knowing takes place, for the first one points out the condition of the knowing powers at the beginning of the process, and the second, the
condition permitting the assimilation proper to knowing.

A simple illustration of these principles can be given in relation to the power
of sight. In the beginning of the process of seeing a color, such as green, the
power of sight is without that color; while, when knowing occurs, this power
receives the form of green without the matter, but subject to the individuating
conditions of matter. More briefly, the power of sight is at first without its sense
object, green; while, when it knows this color, this power receives the form of

this green with its peculiar hue, but not in the way that this green exists materially.

The foregoing principles form Aristotle's general framework for the process of knowing. Any specific statement that he makes about this activity will agree with these truths concerning the initially potential state of the knowing powers and concerning these powers' reception of form without matter. What importance do these general principles have for the teacher?

The first indicates to the instructor that it is possible for the art of teaching to exist. If the student at first only potentially knows, he can advance in knowledge through the teacher's instruction, because he does not actually know all things. If the student were in a state of actuality, there would be no need for the art of teaching. Since the teacher knows, however, that the pupil has an initial potency to knowledge, he can conclude that the art of teaching is possible. Thus it is evident that this first principle should be a fundamental part of the teacher's knowledge.

In addition, the teacher must also know the second principle about the condition that makes knowing possible (namely, that knowing is a reception of form without matter), for his art is one that leads the student from the known to the unknown. Since this is the purpose of his work, the instructor must understand the nature of knowing. For this reason he must understand the second principle that knowing, whether with or without the help of a teacher, is an assimilation of the knower to the known, made possible by the reception of form without matter. More briefly expressed, the teacher must be able to define what knowing is.

b. *The Process in Intellectual Knowing*

Both the definition of knowing and the principle about the initially potential state of the knower, however, are principles at the general level of this process. Therefore, let us now recall Aristotle's doctrine concerning intellectual knowing specifically. For this process he sees the need, not only of the external and internal senses, but also of the active and possible principles of the intellect. He points out that such principles exist in the mind when he says that "in fact mind as we have described it is what it is by virtue of becoming all things [the possible intellect], while there is another which is what it is by virtue of making all things [the agent intellect]."[16]

Equipped with both the sense and the intellectual powers, the human being is capable of a type of knowing not possible to the brute animal. Because of these powers, the human person can arrive at universal knowledge, at a knowledge of the arts and sciences, at a knowledge of the causes of things.

The human procedure for moving from sense to universal knowledge is described by Aristotle as follows:

> Out of sense-perception comes to be what we call memory, and out of frequently repeated memories of the same thing develops experience; for a number of memories constitute a single experience. From experience again—i.e. from the univer-

sal now stabilized in its entirety within the soul, the one beside the many which is a single identity within them all—originate the skill of the craftsman and the knowledge of the man of science.[17]

In this quotation Aristotle states the way that the human being, beginning with sense knowledge, arrives at the universal level of knowing, a level which reaches its perfection in causal knowledge. Briefly, this method (called induction) is one in which a person first coalesces his memories into experience by organizing them around an initial, stable memory. Following this, the human being, utilizing his agent intellect, abstracts from such experience a universal concept or principle. This inductive method, demanding both the sense and intellectual powers, begins in sense knowledge, which must be remembered and organized into experience, and ends, because of the abstractive power of the agent intellect, in a knowledge of the essence of the material thing.

By means of this inductive method, one is able to move from sense knowledge to the universal level. On this level the human being advances from the known to the unknown by means of the reasoning or deductive process. This reasoning procedure, in Aristotle's words, "is an argument in which, certain things being laid down, something other than these necessarily comes about through them."[18]

Having reached the universal level, one reasons to the unknown by means of certain things which he lays down, by means of what he knows. By means of his knowledge of general principles and of particular cases under these principles, the human being is able to apply his principles to these cases, is able to advance to what he did not actually know before. To do so, one needs the knowledge just mentioned and the correct syllogistic order of procedure.

This deductive method, anchored to a firm sense foundation by means of the inductive method, constitutes the natural procedure that the human being follows when he acquires intellectual knowledge. According to Aristotle, these two methods are the human being's way of never neglecting sense knowledge and of arriving ultimately at the causes of things. The Philosopher shows that these two methods are the human way of acquiring knowledge when he says that "every belief comes either through syllogism or from induction."[19]

This discussion of the way that the human being acquires intellectual knowledge completes our summary of Aristotle's principles about knowing's natural process which are pertinent for the teacher. These principles are outlined as follows:

A. Knowing's objects
    1. The objects of the senses are the beginning of all of human knowledge.
    2. The object of the human intellect is the essence of the material thing.
B. Knowing's process
    1. In general
        a. The knowing powers are in potency to their objects.

b. When the assimilation proper to knowing occurs, the knowing power receives, without the matter, the form of the thing known.
2. In relation to intellectual knowing
   a. The inductive method is one in which the human being first coalesces his memories into experience by organizing them around an initial, stable memory. Following this, the human being, utilizing his agent intellect, abstracts from such experience a universal concept or principle.
   b. The deductive method is one in which the human being, by using his knowledge of general principles and of particular cases under these principles and by moving in a correct syllogistic procedure, advances from the known to the unknown.

B. Induction's Purpose

Having seen that induction is the teacher's basic procedure, let us examine more carefully Aristotle's doctrine on this method. We have defined induction as a passage from individuals to universals, as a movement from the level of experience to the level of art and science. In this definition we find both the material utilized by the teacher, namely, singulars, and the purpose for his activity, i.e., the student's grasp of the universal level of knowledge. Since both of these must be understood by the teacher before he can successfully use the inductive method, we shall elaborate upon both its purpose and its material. Then we shall point out how the actual procedure of induction, utilizing such material and aiming at such a purpose, takes place.

The teacher's purpose in using the inductive method is that the student may arrive at the universal level of knowledge, may arrive at the level of knowledge proper to him as a rational being. The human being, gifted with the power of intellect, is capable of more than a knowledge of singular sense experiences. Unlike the brute animals, who "live by appearances and memories, and have but little of connected experience,...the human race lives...by art and reasonings."[20] Thus the human being is capable of more than sense knowledge of the many individual trees that he encounters; he can also arrive at the knowledge of the nature or essence of these trees. It is by the inductive method that a person has his first contact with the universal nature of things and, correspondingly, that the teacher helps the student to obtain such a contact.

In helping the student to arrive at the universal level of knowledge, the teacher must assist him in the understanding of both definitions and universal propositions. The instructor must achieve both of these purposes, because the human intellect moves from potentiality to actuality in its acquisition of knowledge. Because of this movement,

it [the human intellect] has a likeness to things which are generated, which do not attain to perfection all at once, but acquire it by degrees: so likewise the human intellect does not acquire perfect knowledge by the first act of apprehension; but it first apprehends something about its object, such as its quiddity, and this is its first and proper object; and then it understands the properties, accidents, and the various relations of the essence. Thus it necessarily compares one thing with another by composition or division; and from one composition and division it proceeds to another, which is the process of reasoning.[21]

In the foregoing quotation we can note that the human intellect, because of its movement from potency to act, performs the activities of apprehension, judgment, and reasoning. The mental formation resulting from apprehension is the definition, while that which is proper to judgment is the proposition. Therefore it is evident that the human being, in attempting to reach a perfect understanding of reality, needs both definitions and propositions.[22] In correspondence with this requirement of the human mind, the teacher, as he assists the student to acquire universal knowledge by the inductive process, will help him to arrive at both definitions and universal propositions.

1. The Definition

Aristotle holds that definition, the first of the mental formations sought in learning and teaching, is simply the mind's notion of what a thing is. In other words, "the whatness of a thing is what its definition signifies."[23] Thus each time that one finds himself trying to answer what a thing is, he is in the realm of definition. If he is attempting to understand the nature of a particular type of natural phenomenon, for example, he is attempting to define it. Thus, if one explains an eclipse of the moon as the interposition of the earth between it and the sun, he has given its definition. To seek such knowledge is proper to the human being, for the object of his intellect is "a quiddity or nature existing in corporeal matter."[24]

a. Statement of Genus and Specific Difference

In arriving at a definition, the mind, again because of its movement from potency to act, gradually reaches clarification of the essence that it seeks, and in some cases must be content with only approximations of such an essence. Thus, in seeking to know what a thing is, the mind first grasps only its most general characteristics and then gradually discovers its more specific or distinguishing aspects. The small child in its attempts to understand the human being, for example, will be aware of this type of being first as something that moves, sees, hears, and touches things—in short, as an animal. Only later will the child begin to discern the distinguishing trait, rationality, proper to the type of animal that the human being is. This gradual focusing on the whatness of a given thing is the process of defining, a process which, because of the dimness of the human mind, moves from the general outlines of a thing to its more specific traits.

Aristotle notes this tendency of the mind to focus gradually on the knowledge that is sought when he says that "what is to us plain and obvious at first is rather confused masses, the elements and principles of which become known to us later by analysis. Thus we must advance from generalities to particulars."[25] As a sign that this is true, he takes an example from the sense order. Thus, according to the exposition of Aquinas, Aristotle holds that

> the more common sensible is first known to us according to sense, for example, we know this animal before we know this man.
>
> And I say first according to sense both with reference to place and with reference to time. This is true according to place because, when someone is seen at a distance, we perceive him to be a body before we perceive that he is an animal, and animal before we perceive him to be a man, and finally we perceive that he is Socrates. And in the same way with reference to time, a boy apprehends this individual as some man before he apprehends this man, Plato, who is his father.[26]

Since the human person moves from the confused to the distinct in the sense order, Aristotle takes this as an indication that the human being only gradually reaches clarification in the intellectual order.

Because of the movement of the human mind from the confused to the distinct, the definitions of things, as containing this process of delineation, will consist of both general and specific elements, will comprise both genus and specific difference. Although the nature of a thing, such as human being, is not so divided, the human person will define this entity as a rational animal because of his gradual way of seeing things. Such a definition, consisting of both genus and specific difference, will be expressed in words, which, strictly speaking, are not the definition, but only the expression of the definition. The definition is the concept of the mind as refined into the notions of genus and specific difference. Thus the definition *rational animal* is the refinement in the mind of the original, blurred concept that one has of human being.[27]

Frequently, however, in his search for the nature or essence of things, one cannot obtain an exact notion of what it is. Without too much difficulty he can detect the general kind of thing that he is studying, the general category into which it falls, but it is much harder to find the characteristic that makes the thing specifically different from all other things. Thus one could easily classify an elephant as an animal, but he would be hard pressed to state that specific part of its essence which makes it different from all other animals.

For this reason one would be forced to define the elephant in terms of its genus and only some external signs or accidents of its specific difference. Thus he might say that an elephant is an animal with large flappy ears and a long trunk. Because of the obscurity of the specific difference, this definition includes the genus and some accidental differences. Aquinas says that we will define in this way whenever "necessity compels us to use accidental differences in place of essential differences inasmuch as accidental differences are the signs of certain essential differences unknown to us."[28]

Aristotle has many excellent examples of definitions employing the genus and accidental differences. The following is one of these:

[The bison] is the size of a bull, but stouter in build, and not long in the body; its skin, stretched tight on a frame, would give sitting room for seven people. In general it resembles the ox in appearance, except that it has a mane that reaches down to the point of the shoulder, as that of the horse reaches down to its withers.... The colour of the body is half red, half ashen-grey.... It has the bellow of a bull. Its horns are crooked, turned inwards towards each other and useless for purposes of self-defence.[29]

b. *Statement of Causes*

Since the definition, consisting ideally of genus and specific differences, expresses what a given thing is, it will be a statement of the causes of the thing. This is understandable, for the question *what is this thing* can be restated as *what makes this thing to be what it is*. Thus we can ask, "What is a human being?" or "What makes a human being to be what he is?" But that which makes a thing to be what it is, is called the cause of that thing. Accordingly, Aquinas says that "those things are called causes upon which things depend for their existence or their coming to be."[30] Therefore, the definition, giving the whatness of the thing, will be a statement of its causes. Thus, if we define a house as "*a covering made from...[stones, cement, and wood], protecting from rain, cold and heat*,"[31] we are showing what it is by means of its causes.[32]

Of the four causes possible to a definition, Aristotle holds that the formal cause is the one which is most natural to the process of defining.[33] In the definition of a house, for example, one could possibly omit the agent and final causes, which are extrinsic to the thing. Hence these causes do not necessarily contribute the needed information about what the thing is. Thus, if the agent that built the house, such as a certain construction company, were to go out of existence after the structure was finished, the house could still be defined without a knowledge of the given company. As for the final cause, if it is fulfilled, this cause is expressed in the form that the house has; if the end is unfulfilled, it does not tell what the house is, but rather what the house is supposed to become. "The two causes outside the thing, then, the purpose and the execution, are not always of prime importance in ascertaining what a thing is."[34]

Of the two remaining causes, the material exists for the formal cause. Thus, in the same example, the bricks exist that a certain formation may be produced, such as a Georgian house. Because the matter exists for the form, it is possible to define a house as a certain type of structure without mentioning the material, but the converse would not be adequate. To define a house, for example, as a certain quantity of bricks with no mention of its form, will do little to tell what a house is. Since the material of the thing exists for the form educed from it, it is natural for one to define things in terms of the formal cause.

One emphasizes the formal cause in his definitions of things because the form is the thing's ultimate actualization in its process of coming into being. In a certain sense, the form stands as the terminal point of a thing, as that to which everything else leads. Thus the original intention or purpose, if it is realized, is fulfilled in a given form, such as a house. In addition, the agent, keeping in mind the given purpose, works to educe the form from the potentialities of the matter, i.e., to create a Georgian house from a given quantity of bricks. Finally, the material is important only that a particular form may be brought about from it. Truly, then, the form is the actualization, the terminal point, of the other causes.

Since the form is the actualization of the other causes, it is the cause most frequently used in definitions, for Aristotle holds that it is the actual thing, not the thing in a potential state, that is knowable.[35] Thus the human being who is actually mature, not the child in the process of becoming an adult, is the source of one's best knowledge about such a nature. Therefore, the form, as the actualization of the given thing, is that by which the thing is knowable. Since one's knowledge is the source of his definitions of things, then the formal cause of an object constitutes the principal part of its definition.

Thus far in this section we have seen that definition is a mental notion telling us what a thing is. Because of the mind's movement from potency to act, this mental formation will be expressed in terms of genus and specific difference. In addition to this, we saw that the definition gives us the causes of a thing, of which the one most frequently used is the formal cause. If we link both of these insights together, we can see that the definition gives us usually the formal cause, expressed in terms of genus and specific difference. A common example of this is the definition of the human being as a rational animal.

2. The Proposition

We have explained the nature of definition because it is one kind of universal knowledge which the teacher helps the student to acquire by the inductive method. Let us now discuss the universal proposition, the other type of knowledge possible by the same procedure. Aristotle defines the proposition as "either part of an enunciation, i.e. it predicates a single attribute of a single subject."[36] In other words, the proposition is an enunciation that has been determined into either an affirmation or a negation, in which a single predicate is said of a single subject.[37] Thus the following are examples of propositions: (1) All human beings are mortal. (2) The young are not pessimistic. In both of these illustrations, there is either affirmation or negation, and "one thing is predicated of one thing."[38]

The universal proposition can admit of several kinds of division, but the one most pertinent to our present discussion is that of immediate and mediate. The reason is that this particular division, based on whether or not the propositions have a middle term, indicates the procedure by which the proposition may be obtained. Since we are concerned with the inductive procedure of the teacher, we shall treat the universal proposition as it is divided into immediate and mediate.

a. The Immediate Proposition

Aristotle holds that "an immediate proposition is one which has no other proposition prior to it."[39] This proposition is one which stands first in the process of proof or demonstration; there is no other one prior to it by which it can be proved. Consequently, not being obtained by a deductive or demonstrative process, such a proposition can be secured only by induction. The reason that an immediate proposition is prior in the demonstrative order is that its "predicate is of the nature of the subject [and thus it] is *immediate* and *self-evident* in itself."[40]

To be immediate or self-evident, the proposition must fulfill one of the following: (1) The predicate is in the definition of the subject. (2) The predicate is identical with the subject. (3) The subject enters into the definition of the predicate. These three conditions are illustrated by the following statements respectively: (1) The human being is an animal. (2) The human being is a rational animal. (3) Every number is either odd or even.[41]

Immediate propositions themselves can be divided in a twofold manner, for there are those which are self-evident to all and those which are self-evident just to the wise. Thus the proposition *the whole is greater than its part* is an example of the former, while the proposition *all right angles are equal* illustrates the latter. This first proposition is self-evident to all, for its terms, *whole* and *part*, belong to the common terminology of all and thus are commonly known. The second proposition is self-evident just to those learned in such terminology; for, although its predicate enters into the definition of its subject, its terms are more specialized than common human speech. The following quotation points out the self-evident quality of this second proposition:

> This proposition: *All right angles are equal*, is of itself self-evident or immediate, since equality enters into the definition of a right angle. For a right angle is one which a straight line makes falling upon another straight line, in such a way that on both sides the angles are made equal.[42]

Since self-evident propositions have one term in the definition of the other or have the predicate identical with the subject, they are understandable as soon as their terms are known. But to explain the meanings of terms or to arrive at definitions is proper ultimately to the inductive procedure.[43] Therefore the immediate proposition is known by the inductive method. In the words of Aquinas:

> The philosopher [Aristotle] does not establish the truth of these [first] principles by way of demonstration, but by considering the meaning of their terms. For example, he considers what a whole is and what a part is; and the same applies to the rest. And when the meaning of these terms becomes known, it follows that the truth of the above-mentioned principles becomes evident.[44]

b. The Mediate Proposition

Having defined the immediate proposition and noted that it is obtained only by induction, let us turn now to the mediate proposition. Unlike the immediate proposition, its predicate is not of the nature of its subject. Rather the mediate proposition is one which has "a *middle* through which is demonstrated the predicate of the subject."[45] Expressed in another way, the mediate proposition is one in which the predicate inheres in the subject because of some intervening term. Thus the proposition *all material things are corruptible* is a mediate proposition, since the predicate inheres in the subject because of the definition *all material things have parts*. The mediate proposition, therefore, is not prior in the process of demonstration, for it presupposes other propositions by which its truth can be demonstrated. Because this proposition presupposes other truths to make it known, it is by nature the conclusion of a syllogism.

Mediate propositions can be established, however, not only by the deductive process but also by the method of induction. A simple process of inspection will indicate this, for one can arrive at the truth of the above proposition *all material things are corruptible* by means of singular cases. Thus the decay of plants and animals and the erosion of rocks are sufficient to help one establish this principle about material things. That mediate propositions can be obtained also by the inductive method can be seen in the fact that Aristotle employs such principles to illustrate this method. Thus he says that "induction is a passage from individuals to universals, e.g. the argument that supposing the skilled pilot is the most effective, and likewise the skilled charioteer, then in general the skilled man is the best at his particular task."[46]

Although mediate propositions can be obtained both by induction and deduction, the immediate principle is established only by the former process. Aristotle notes this when he says that "we must get to know the primary premisses by induction; for the method by which even sense-perception implants the universal is inductive."[47] Since the immediate principles are the basis from which demonstration proceeds, they cannot be known by any other process.

At this point we have described Aristotle's doctrine on both the definition and the universal proposition, two kinds of universal knowledge to which the teacher may lead the student by the inductive process. Before discussing the material with which the teacher will work in order to achieve such a goal, let us summarize what we have treated thus far. By the inductive method the teacher hopes to guide the student from sense to universal knowledge, a universal knowledge which includes both definitions and propositions. The definition to which the teacher can lead the student usually gives the formal cause of the thing being defined, expressed ideally in terms of genus and specific differences. Often, however, the definition will include the genus and only accidental differences because of the weakness of the human intellect.

In addition to the definition, the teacher by the process of induction can help the student acquire the universal proposition, whether it is immediate or mediate. The first of these propositions, which includes those self-evident to all and those self-evident just to the wise, is defined as that type of proposition in which one term is in the definition of the other or in which the predicate is identical with the subject. The mediate proposition, on the other hand, is one in which the predicate inheres in the subject because of a middle term. Both of these types of propositions, as well as the definition, are the goal of the teacher as he works with the student by means of the inductive process.

C. Induction's Materials

Having seen the goal at which the teacher aims in the inductive process, let us now examine the materials with which he can work in order to achieve this purpose. From Aristotle we have a general statement concerning the nature of these materials, for he says that "induction is a passage from individuals to universals."[48] In other words, one attains to the universal level of knowledge by means of individual sense experiences. Let us, then, look more carefully at the sense order upon which induction relies ultimately for its material.

In our examination of the sense order we will be guided by the following sentence, which states more specifically the nature of the material needed for the inductive process: "So out of sense-perception comes to be what we call memory, and out of frequently repeated memories of the same thing develops experience; for a number of memories constitute a single experience."[49]

In this statement Aristotle first emphasizes the need of sense perception, which includes the awareness of the proper, common, and incidental sense objects. He then draws our attention to the work of memory, which stores that which is perceived by the cogitative power, and to the need for repeated memories, which are compared with each other by this same cogitative power. Lastly he points out that from such remembered and compared sense perceptions one arrives at experience, which is the proximate raw material for the universal.

Since in this statement about the material for the inductive process, Aristotle points out the need not only for sense perception but also for memories frequently repeated and compared, we shall treat this section as follows: (1) We shall speak of the objects of sense perception in general. (2) We shall discuss in particular those sense objects which are perceived by the cogitative power and stored in the memory.

1. Objects of Sense Perception

As we begin our general discussion of the sense objects, we must point out that one perceives the more common qualities of the sensible thing first. This is true both in relation to place and to time. Thus, if we consider place first, we know that

when someone is seen at a distance, we perceive him to be a body before we perceive that he is an animal, and animal before we perceive him to be a man, and finally we perceive that he is Socrates. And in the same way with reference to time, a boy apprehends this individual as some man before he apprehends this man, Plato, who is his father.[50]

These illustrations show that the sense order is perceived first in a general way and later with more discrimination. Thus, if a person encounters a new invention, he may be aware of it as a gadget, rather than as a machine for speed reading. The teacher, working with the inductive process, must realize that this is the way one first perceives the sensible thing and must therefore not be too demanding at the beginning. Rather he must begin at the student's level of general sensible knowledge and lead him gradually to more refinement.

Granted that "it is a whole that is best known to sense-perception,"[51] what are the aspects of the material thing that are perceived in this composite fashion? From chapter 2 we know that a sense experience includes the proper, common, and incidental sense objects. In the sense order one does not arrive at the nature of the thing. Rather, in a sense experience, such as that of this tree, the human being apprehends such sense objects as its greenness, the texture and rustling sound of its leaves, its size and shape, its movement in the wind, its beneficial quality, and its being this individual tree. "The object *per se* of sense is not substance and what a thing is, but some sensible quality, e.g., hot, cold, white, black and other such things."[52]

The material, then, of the teacher working with the inductive process is the proper, common, and incidental sense objects. These are those aspects of the sensible thing which form the foundation of all human knowing and of the teacher's basic methodology. Sometimes, however, Aristotle does not refer to them in terms of this threefold classification. Instead he may speak of human knowledge as originating in the effects of things, in their outer signs, or in their operations. In every case, however, he is referring ultimately to these sensible objects. In order that we may realize this, we shall cite several of these passages.

In explaining the material needed for scientific knowledge, Aristotle points out that often, in relation to a given conclusion, one is able to know only that it is so, rather than why it is so. He might know, for example, only that the planets are near, instead of knowing the cause of this given fact. The reason for this is that he is demonstrating such a conclusion, not through its cause, but through its immediate and proper effects. Thus a person might demonstrate in the following way:

Every nontwinkling thing is near.
The planets are nontwinkling.
∴ The planets are near.[53]

In this demonstration the person is arriving at the conclusion, not through its causes, but through a knowledge of the immediate and convertible effects of this conclusion. "For it is not because they do not twinkle that the planets are near, but because they are near, that they do not twinkle."[54] Hence one knows that the planets are near through the effects of such nearness, namely, their nontwinkling.

We often demonstrate with a definition through effects, for in every case but mathematics the effect is better known to us than the cause. As Aquinas expresses it, "the effect is sometimes better known than the cause as to us and according to sense, although the cause is always better known absolutely and according to nature."[55] In this passage, we are given the material from which we must proceed ultimately in our knowing, namely, the objects of sense. They are not designated in this fashion, however; rather they are called the outer effects of an inner cause. Nevertheless, as the argument employing the middle term *nontwinkling* illustrates, these effects are ultimately the sense objects.

Not only are the sense objects called effects of an inner cause but also they may be designated as signs of the essence of the thing. We see this denomination in Aristotle's discussion of the material used in the enthymeme, i.e., the truncated syllogism. Here he defines a sign as "a demonstrative proposition necessary or generally approved: for anything such that when it is another thing is, or when it has come into being the other has come into being before or after, is a sign of the other's being or having come into being."[56] The parts of this definition could be illustrated as follows: "a fluttering flag as a sign of wind, as to the presence of one indicating the presence of the other: yellow skin as a sign of jaundice preceding; a falling barometer as a sign of a storm following."[57]

Although Aristotle designates the whole proposition as a sign, he also points out in his definition that one part of the proposition stands as a sign of the other. This fact we can see from his examples, which are chosen to illustrate that signs can be both infallible and fallible respectively: "The fact that he has a fever is a sign that he is ill;...the fact that he breathes fast is a sign that he has a fever."[58] Here again, although they are called signs, we have examples of the sense objects, specifically one of the proper objects of touch and the common sensible classified as movement. From such sense objects as these, particularly if they are external manifestations peculiar to the given thing, we can approach the inner nature of the sensible thing.

In our last illustration of the different ways in which Aristotle refers to the fact that the sense objects are basic to all knowing and all teaching, we shall quote his passage explaining the manner in which one arrives at an understanding of the powers of the soul. He says that,

> if we are to express what each is, viz. what the thinking power is, or the perceptive, or the nutritive, we must go farther back and first give an account of thinking or perceiving, for in the order of investigation the question of what an agent does precedes the question, what enables it to do what it does. If this is correct, we must on the same ground go yet another step farther back and have some clear view of the objects of each; thus we must *start* with these objects, e.g. with food, with what is perceptible, or with what is intelligible.[59]

In this quotation Aristotle points out that one can understand the powers of the soul by means of their operations, which in turn can be comprehended through their objects. Although the Philosopher does not use the term *sense object* in this statement, the operations and objects of which he speaks are either such objects or rely upon them in a material way. This is true even of the activity of thinking and of its object, the essence of the material thing, for the "intelligible objects have their beings *in* the objects of sense."[60] Therefore, when Aristotle speaks of a person's knowing a thing such as a power of the soul by its operations and objects, he is showing in this context that the basic human material for acquiring knowledge is the sense object, classified as proper, common, and incidental.

Thus far, in this general discussion of sense perception, we have seen that a sense experience includes the awareness of the proper, common, and incidental sense objects, objects which one knows first in a general way and then with more discrimination. We then pointed out that these objects, which are the basic material for all knowledge, may be designated by Aristotle in different ways. He may speak of human knowledge as originating in the effects of things, in their outer signs, or in their operations and objects.

Nevertheless, as our citations illustrate, he is referring ultimately to the objects of sense. We have made this reference to the common note existing in all this terminology so that the pervading character of these sense objects at the beginning of human knowledge would be more apparent. Let us now treat the object of the cogitative power more specifically, since it perceives that which the memory stores, and without memory a person would find it extremely difficult to obtain the universal level of knowledge.

2. Object of Cogitative Power
a. Its Importance for Memory

Although all of the human being's knowledge originates in sense perception, some of his sense experiences do not encompass all the sense objects. Rather, there are times when a person may indeed have a sensation of the material thing, but this awareness may make little impression upon him. In this experience one can assert that he has sensed the proper and common sensibles (such as color, sound, size, and shape), but he has not reacted to the thing as valuable or harmful. Thus one may sense that there are flowers in a garden, but he does not necessarily apprehend them as something good or bad for himself.

To the degree that sensation is so minimal, one does not remember such experiences, for "the principle of memory in animals is found in some such intention, for instance, that something is harmful or otherwise."[61] In contrast, one remembers those sense experiences in which he has sensed not only the proper and common sensibles but also that incidental sense object, namely, the thing's harmful or beneficial quality. Thus a person can easily recall the sense experience of having been in a flood because of the violent reaction that he experienced.

If one wishes to arrive at the universal, however, not only must he be aware of his surroundings but also he must remember that which he has sensed. The reason is that the thing remembered forms a stable unit, so to speak, around which later memories can be linked by the comparative process proper to the cogitative power. In this fashion one gradually builds up experience with a given thing, which experience is the proximate raw material for the universal. This process is illustrated by Aristotle (as commented on by Aquinas) as follows:

> He [Aristotle] gives an example in battles which are brought about by the turning back of an army overcome and put to flight. For when one of them will have made a stand, i.e., will have begun to stand immovably and not flee, another stands, adding himself to him, and afterwards another, until enough are congregated to bring about the beginning of a fight. Thus also from sense and memory of one particular, and again of another and another, one sometimes arrives at that which is the principle of art and science.[62]

To summarize this quotation, out of memory grows experience, by means of which one arrives at the universal. Since this is so, it is vital that one remember the things he senses. In relation to teaching, if the instructor hopes to lead the student to the universal, the material that he presents must be remembered.

Having seen the importance of memory in the inductive process, we can immediately conclude that the material for this procedure must include not only a simple awareness of the thing but also an awareness of the thing as harmful or helpful. Every teacher who sees the need for motivation in the learning process has some degree of understanding of this principle. The material of induction must be so perceived because perception with a value quality is remembered, an activity most important for the subsequent intuition of the universal. Therefore the teacher must present the sense objects of the inductive process to the student in such a way that the pupil will apprehend them as beneficial to himself.

b. Its Importance for Students

How will the student apprehend the sense objects of induction as beneficial to himself? In order to answer this, we shall first point out that the more a student values learning in general, the more attentive he will be to the materials associated with the learning process, such as the singulars used for the inductive method. To value the singulars of induction, however, the student needs more than the general attitude that learning is a good thing for him. He must also apprehend the particular examples of a given lesson as useful for the topic being explained. Therefore, after clarifying ways to help the student value learning in general, we shall indicate what will help the pupil apprehend the material of a given inductive procedure as something beneficial for the particular lesson.

First, let us discuss the need for the student to esteem learning in general if he wishes to value the singulars of induction. Since the examples that the teacher presents to the student are ordered to the acquisition of knowledge, the pupil will value them if he sees the importance of learning the truth about things. In other words, the student will be attentive to the material that the instructor uses in the inductive process if he has a love for learning. If the material for induction is to be useful, then, the pupil must desire to know.

The student has a natural interest in acquiring knowledge. As Aristotle expresses it, "to be learning something is the greatest of pleasures not only to the philosopher but also to the rest of mankind, however small their capacity for it."[63] The reason for this is that

> each thing has a natural inclination to perform its proper operation, as something hot is naturally inclined to heat, and something heavy to be moved downwards. Now the proper operation of man as man is to understand, for by reason of this he differs from all other things. Hence the desire of man is naturally inclined to understand, and therefore to possess scientific knowledge.[64]

This natural inclination to know things is more than just the possession of knowledge; rather it is the actual use of the intellectual powers. The human being wants to be actually contemplating the best possible things. This is better than just the habitual possession of such knowledge, for

> the state of mind may exist without producing any good result, as in a man who is asleep or in some other way quite inactive, but the activity cannot; for one who has the activity will of necessity be acting, and acting well. And as in the Olympic Games it is not the most beautiful and the strongest that are crowned but those who compete (for it is some of these that are victorious), so those who act win, and rightly win, the noble and good things in life.[65]

We can note this natural desire of the student to be actually knowing things in the interest that he takes in the use of his senses. Without any prompting, the student employs his senses to find out in what sort of environment he is and to discover ways to adapt himself to it. Especially in the use of his sense of sight does the student display his desire for knowledge, for this power, "most of all the senses, makes us know and brings to light many differences between things."[66] Thus by means of sight we sense not only color but also all of the common sensibles.

The student's desire for knowledge can also be seen in the natural wonder that he exercises concerning the strange things in his environment. This quality of mind is easily apparent in small children, who are fascinated by all the unknowns around them. Wonder reveals the natural human inclination for understanding, because it is defined as "a kind of desire for knowledge; a desire which comes to man when he sees an effect of which the cause either is unknown to him, or surpasses his knowledge or faculty of understanding."[67]

Although the student has a natural tendency to apprehend a particular learning experience as something beneficial to him, there are also several factors
which might lead him to be aware of it as something arduous or difficult. One
of these stems from the kind of material being studied, since some subjects, because of their involvement in the concrete order, cannot be known in any precise
fashion. The subject of moral science, for example, has not the certitude of
mathematics, for it studies human actions, which "admit of much variety and
fluctuation of opinion, so that they may be thought to exist only by convention,
and not by nature."[68] Such a lack of certitude naturally presents a difficulty for
the student and would incline him to apprehend a learning experience as something difficult to accomplish.

The nature of the subject studied, however, is not the chief factor which
might lead the pupil to react to learning in a negative way. Instead, it is the
weakness of the human intellect, which, in relation to the most knowable things,
is like "the eyes of bats...to the blaze of day."[69] Because the student's intellect
is so imperfect, especially in the beginning, he may apprehend a learning experience as something difficult or arduous.

Therefore we can see that, although the student has a natural desire to know,
there are very real difficulties which might cause him to dislike the process of
learning. Because of these obstacles, Aristotle says that "learning is no amuse-
ment, but is accompanied with pain."[70] Therefore it is imperative, if the material
of the inductive process will be apprehended as beneficial, that the pupil's natural inclination for knowledge be fostered from the very beginning, since "the
beginning is thought to be more than half of the whole."[71]

The student's natural love for learning will be fostered if he witnesses other
persons with a love for the truth, if he has a good example of the intellectual life.
This is especially true if the teacher himself furnishes such good example. The
reason is that "men's acts and choices are in reference to singulars."[72] In other
words, people choose and act in the here-and-now, which encompasses the singular events of daily life. Thus a person chooses to perform this action of
walking; he does not desire walking in general. Aristotle describes the involvement of one's desires and choices with the singular as follows:

> Now mind is always right, but appetite and imagination may be either right or
> wrong. That is why, though in any case it is the object of appetite which origi-
> nates movement, this object may be either the real or the apparent good. To pro-
> duce movement the object must be more than this: it must be good that can be
> brought into being by action; and only what can be otherwise than as it is can thus
> be brought into being.[73]

Since the desires and actions of the human being are in terms of the singular,
he tends to desire more easily a good presented to him in a concrete way. In
other words, a person is inclined to be influenced by a good example of the
given thing. For this reason the teacher, wishing to help the student to desire the
intellectual life, will assist him greatly by presenting to him a good example of

this life. This is so, "since, in human actions and passions, wherein experience is of great weight, example moves more than words."[74]

Thus far we have seen that a good example of the intellectual life will aid the student to value the acquisition of knowledge and in turn to apprehend as beneficial the materials used for such acquisition. Although Aristotle's doctrine contains many additional suggestions pertinent to this problem, we shall treat only one other. If the teacher wishes the student to value the activity of learning, he must present the lesson to him on the level of his experience and slowly, but surely, build up additional experiences with it. In other words, thinking now in terms of the inductive process, the instructor must give the student sensible experiences within the range of his background so that he can easily intuit the given universal. As he achieves success in at least one universal, the pupil has a stable unit around which to build later successes. Gradually, then, he obtains experience with the life of learning.

Experience with the intellectual life is most helpful in assisting the student to value the acquisition of knowledge, for "experience is a cause of hope, in so far as it makes him reckon something possible which before his experience he looked upon as impossible."[75] Since hope "is a movement of the appetitive power ensuing from the apprehension of a future good, difficult but possible to obtain; namely, a stretching forth of the appetite to such a good,"[76] it is most necessary for the life of learning. This virtue is needed for a life of study, since, as we have just explained, learning has many difficulties connected with it. Therefore, in order to find such an activity desirable, the student needs hope. Since experience can engender such a virtue, experiencing success in learning is most useful in fostering the pupil's natural desire to know the truth.

We have pointed out that both the good example of the teacher and the pupil's success in learning will help the latter to esteem learning in general, and thus to value the materials connected with its procedures, such as the singulars of induction. Now we must give Aristotle's suggestions relevant for helping the student value the inductive materials because of the very nature of these materials, for the pupil's general interest in learning is not always sufficient to make him attentive to the illustrations of a given lesson.

The very nature of the singulars used must be such that the student will attend to them so that, by remembering these singulars and molding them into experience, he can arrive at the universal. Although the pupil's general interest in learning is helpful, the teacher must choose examples for his inductive procedure that will draw the student's attention, that will be apprehended by the pupil's cogitative power as something beneficial for the topic being learned.

If the teacher wishes to illustrate his inductive procedure with examples that will attract the attention of the student, he must choose those which are both clear and striking. Insofar as his illustrations are clear, they will permit the student to intuit the universal easily. To the degree that the examples are striking, the student's attention will be drawn to them, for he is always "ready to attend to anything that touches himself, and to anything that is important, surprising, or agreeable; and you [the teacher] should accordingly convey to him the impression that what you have to say is of this nature."[77]

If it is possible, then, the teacher must use examples in induction that are both clear and striking. If he cannot fulfill both of these requirements, he must never sacrifice clarity, for the purpose of the teacher is that his students will see the universal. Thus, if the instructor is trying to help his pupils arrive at the definition of the life-principle or the soul, he should use illustrations in which life is evident, such as the human being or the higher species of brute animals, rather than obscure examples of life, such as hydras, amoebae, and so forth.

Remembering that he must always search for clear examples, the teacher should also try to select illustrations that will strike the attention of the student, that will be apprehended by his cogitative power as beneficial for the learning process. Such examples will not be ordinary cases of the topic being taught, for the student's attention is not drawn to the obvious. Rather, these illustrations will be different and outstanding examples of the given lesson, for

> some things delight us when they are new, but later do so less, for the same reason: for at first the mind is in a state of stimulation and intensely active about them, as people are with respect to their vision when they look hard at a thing, but afterwards our activity is not of this kind, but has grown relaxed; for which reason the pleasure also is dulled.[78]

Since the mind is active and wonders about the new and different, the teacher's examples for induction should be original or unusual.

While the examples chosen should be striking in order to be perceived by the cogitative power, these illustrations must not approach the bizarre. If the teacher's choice of examples is extreme, he will succeed only in puzzling the student, and thus he will defeat his purpose of helping the pupil to see the universal. Therefore the illustrations of the inductive process must first of all be clear and then striking, but not bizarre. These materials must be clear so that the student's agent intellect can abstract the universal; they must be striking so that his cogitative power will attend to them. Aristotle points out the necessity of using material which is both clear and striking (a quality which is the mean between the obvious and the puzzling) in the following quotation:

> Style to be good must be clear, as is proved by the fact that speech which fails to convey a plain meaning will fail to do just what speech has to do....
> ...We see, then, that both speech and reasoning are lively in proportion as they make us seize a new idea promptly. For this reason people are not much taken either by obvious arguments (using the word 'obvious' to mean what is plain to everybody and needs no investigation), nor by those which puzzle us when we hear them stated, but only by those which convey their information to us as soon as we hear them, provided we had not the information already; or which the mind only just fails to keep up with.[79]

In the foregoing quotation Aristotle indicates that the type of material useful for any argumentation should be clear and striking. In his doctrine he has many examples of such material. Thus, when the Philosopher is explaining that everything in nature acts for a purpose or end, he illustrates his point with outstanding examples of purposeful behavior in the animals. Accordingly, he says that nature's acting for an end

> is most obvious in the animals other than man: they make things neither by art nor after inquiry or deliberation.... If then it is both by nature and for an end that the swallow makes its nest and the spider its web, and plants grow leaves for the sake of the fruit and send their roots down (not up) for the sake of nourishment, it is plain that this kind of cause [purpose or end] is operative in things which come to be and are by nature.[80]

To explain that nature acts for an end, Aristotle uses examples which are both clear and striking. Thus he illustrates his case with the activities of those animals, such as swallows and spiders, whose purposeful behavior is at once clear and amazing.

Thus far we have shown that examples which will attract the attention of the student must be first clear, and then striking. Before this discussion of the nature of the examples for the inductive process, we explained ways to have the student value learning in general. We have treated both of these sections because not only the pupil's general attitude toward learning but also the kind of examples used in the particular lesson will help the student to apprehend the teaching materials as valuable to himself.

It is most important that the student have such an apprehension, for the awareness of things as helpful or harmful stimulates their being remembered. Since memory leads to experience, out of which one arrives at the universal, the student will be greatly helped in attaining the universal level of knowledge if he apprehends the inductive materials as beneficial. Since the purpose of the teacher is that the pupil should reach the universal, he must know ways to make the student attentive to the lesson. For this reason we have discussed the importance of the teacher's own love of the intellectual life, of the pupil's success in the activity of learning, and of the use of clear and striking examples in the inductive process.

3. Rules for Memorizing

Having pointed out ways to aid the student to apprehend the sense materials of induction as beneficial to himself, let us now treat briefly the rules for memorizing. Not only must the student be attentive to the given materials, but also he must remember what he has apprehended, for "out of frequently repeated memories of the same thing develops experience.... From experience again ... originate the skill of the craftsman and the knowledge of the man of science."[81] The student must carefully remember that to which he has been attentive, for memory develops into experience, which is the proximate raw material for the universal.

Since the universal level of knowledge is the goal of both the teacher and the student in the inductive method, both can profit from a knowledge of the way to use memory most profitably. In other words, both the teacher and the student should know the art of memorizing. Aquinas, utilizing the doctrine of Aristotle, gives four points invaluable for perfecting this faculty. They are as follows:

> There are four things whereby a man perfects his memory. First, when a man wishes to remember a thing, he should take some suitable yet somewhat unwonted illustration of it, since the unwonted strikes us more, and so makes a greater and stronger impression on the mind; and this explains why we remember better what we saw when we were children.... Secondly, whatever a man wishes to retain in his memory he must carefully consider and set in order, so that he may pass easily from one memory to another.... Thirdly, we must be anxious and earnest about the things we wish to remember, because the more a thing is impressed on the mind, the less it is liable to slip out of it.... Fourthly, we should often reflect on the things we wish to remember.... Wherefore when we reflect on a thing frequently, we quickly call it to mind, through passing from one thing to another by a natural order.[82]

Aquinas, following Aristotle, establishes these four points on the art of memorizing because of the nature of the human knowing powers. In these rules he takes cognizance of the human being's reliance on the sense order, of his ability to order and relate, of the importance of desire and motivation, and of the advantages of good habits. Since these points reveal such an insight into the theory of human knowledge in general and into the art of memorizing in particular, they should help the student to retain that which he has received from the cogitative power. If the student remembers his sense perceptions, he can arrive at experience, the raw material for the universal. Since the attainment of this level of knowledge is the purpose of both the teacher and the student in the inductive procedure, the pupil's knowledge of the foregoing rules will be most helpful to him.

At this point we have completed our discussion of the materials for the inductive process. We have stressed that the basic materials for this procedure are the objects of sense perception, which objects must include an awareness of the thing as beneficial or harmful. In this way the sense experience makes an impression upon the memory. We have also indicated four rules whereby the student might perfect his ability to remember. We have treated these three topics because "out of sense-perception comes to be what we call memory, and out of frequently repeated memories of the same thing develops experience; for a number of memories constitute a single experience."[83]

From a solidly developed experience with a given topic, the agent intellect of the student can abstract the universal which is sought. Since the universal is the goal of both the student and the teacher in the inductive process, and since experience is the proximate raw material for such a goal, the teacher must understand the needed ingredients for experience. Since these are the sense objects as valued, remembered, and compared, in this section we have discussed sense perception in general, the object of the cogitative power, and some rules for memorizing.

D. Induction's Procedure
1. For Universal Propositions

Let us now discuss the inductive procedure itself. We have prepared for this section by a consideration of the purpose and material of this process. We have shown that induction leads to both definitions and universal propositions and that its materials are all the sense objects remembered and molded into experience. Let us, then, show the steps that the teacher takes, aiming at such a purpose and utilizing such materials. As we do so, we shall speak first of the teacher's procedure in helping the student to arrive at universal propositions, for induction as leading to principles is more apparent to the human being.

In order to clarify the teacher's procedure in arriving at universal propositions, we shall make use of an illustration. Let us suppose, then, that the teacher wishes to lead the student to know the following proposition: *Plants give off water vapor by a process called transpiration.* What shall he do first? In the beginning the teacher should stimulate wonder about what happens to all the water that enters the plant through its roots. Does it stay inside the plant, or is some of it lost, just as we lose some of the liquids that we absorb? This initial wonder aroused in the student can be summarized in the following question: Do plants give off water vapor?

To assist the student to see the problem and to wonder about it is the very first stage of the inductive procedure, for

> the subsequent study of truth is nothing else than the solution of earlier difficulties.... Therefore, just as one who wishes to loosen a physical knot must first of all inspect the knot and the way in which it is tied, in a similar way one who wants to solve a problem must first survey all the difficulties and the reason for them.[84]

Therefore the teacher must first of all help the student to see the difficulty to be solved. An example of this first step in both the inductive and deductive procedures is found in the objections which Aquinas lists at the beginning of each article of the *Summa Theologica*, objections which highlight the difficulties of the problem being treated.

Having incited the wonder of the student about the problem at hand, the teacher must then proceed to the solution of it. To do this, he will give the pupil some singular cases of the particular principle. These cases must be chosen carefully, for they have an important role to play in the inductive process. In order to do this, the teacher may point out that, since the leaf produces the plant's food, it may be worth observing. Do the leaves have moisture on them, indicating that plants give off water vapor? If the student responds in the affirmative, the teacher must show him that such moisture may come from the atmosphere and not from the inside of the plant.

Because of this outside difficulty, the student must be helped to see that the leaf, although important, is not valuable for the present problem unless it is separated from the atmosphere. The teacher can do this by putting the leaf under glass, placing its stalk in water, and making sure that the water used cannot penetrate under the glass cover. After several hours in the sun, the glass should have water droplets on it. In this carefully chosen singular, the teacher has a sense experience which should form the first stable unit around which the cogitative power can link later sense experiences.

To help the student become experienced in the observation that a particular leaf gives off water vapor, the teacher should present additional cases, using different kinds of leaves. In this way the student, using his cogitative power and memory, will see that his initial observation is true in many instances. Since this knowledge encompasses only these cases, it is still on the singular level.

To help the student further, the teacher may give him some examples, no longer similar to the original case, but different from it. Thus he may set up a glass receptacle identical in every way except that it has no leaf. After several hours in the sun, this particular receptacle will contain no water droplets. Aided by the observation of both similar and opposite cases,[85] the student can become experienced in this problem, can know that this leaf and that leaf give off water vapor. So equipped, he can abstract, by means of his agent intellect, the universal from these cases and arrive at the proposition *plants give off water vapor*.

What has the teacher done to solve the problem at hand? He has presented a sufficient number of cases, both alike and different, so that the student's intellective power can abstract the universal from them.[86] He has chosen these cases carefully so that the student may move easily from his sense knowledge to the universal proposition. The student, in turn, has retained his first observation in his memory, has organized later observations around it by means of his cogitative power, and has abstracted the universal from this experience through the power of his agent intellect. These are the stages of the teacher's inductive procedure, a process precisely outlined in the doctrine of Aristotle.[87]

By means of this inductive procedure the teacher helps the student to arrive at the universal proposition. This principle is something seen by the student, rather than something proved by him. Thus the pupil, because of the clear evidence before him in terms of many particular leaves, sees that all plants give off water vapor. He admits the truth of this principle, not because of any reason, but because he sees its soundness in the singular cases before him. Given this evidence, he is able to have "the universal now stabilized in its entirety within the soul."[88]

In this inductive procedure, as in division, the student does not arrive at the truth by any reasoning process. Rather, "in both cases it is necessary to suppose that all things have been taken which are under something common, otherwise neither could the one inducing conclude the universal from the singulars taken, nor could the one dividing, from the removal of certain parts, conclude the other [part of the division]."[89]

This inductive method, proceeding from sensible observation and resting finally in a universal proposition, is used today in the scientific method. Thus the scientist, trying to decide the value of a particular drug, will observe its reaction on many individual rats, for example. He will also set up a control group of these animals, which will not receive the drug. In these two groups we have the similar and different examples of Aristotle. Gradually, from his experience with these animals, the scientist can arrive at a hypothesis, at a tentative universal. As this is verified in additional cases, the initial hypothesis can reach the status of a scientific theory. To obtain this theory, the scientist has followed the principle that "from many notions gained by experience one universal judgment about a class of objects is produced."[90] Thus we can see that this current procedure employs the inductive method as explained by Aristotle.

2. For Definitions
a. *Method of Division*

Thus far we have shown the nature of the inductive procedure as leading to universal propositions. Let us now look at this process at work in the securing of definitions. Aristotle gives two ways for arriving at the definition of a thing: the methods of division and of composition. In both of these, the inductive procedure is employed constantly, a fact which our description of these methods will clarify. Let us begin with that of division, for this way of finding the whatness of a thing is more in accord with the movement of the human mind.

To define by division is to proceed as follows: (1) We must start with a known general category or genus to which the thing belongs. (2) We must then find the essential differences under that genus. As we follow these two steps, we will proceed inductively and we must note if the differences found can be subdivided. Let us now illustrate these general directives.

If the teacher, using the method of division, wishes to help the student define human being, for example, he will begin by finding a general category which the student can admit is satisfactory. Thus the pupil might easily agree that a human being is something alive, is a living thing. (This admission is based on the student's experience with human persons, built up by the inductive process.)

The teacher must then help the student to divide this genus into its differences. Thus the pupil may be led to see, again because of his experience acquired inductively, that living things include those that can see and hear and those that cannot, i.e., include both animals and plants. Having arrived at these differences of sentient and nonsentient, the student must then be helped, by the inductive process, to make a further division. He must see that sentient things, or animals, include both those that can think and those that cannot, comprise both rational and nonrational animals. At this point the student can see both the genus and the difference of human being. Having such, he is able to define the human being as a rational animal.

In this procedure the teacher is following the method of Aristotle, who (according to the explanation of Aquinas) lays down the following steps:

> After we shall have arrived, by the division of the genus into species, at what the genus is, for example, whether it is in the genus of quality or quantity, it is necessary in order to investigate the differences to consider the proper passions, which...are signs manifesting the proper forms of the species. And this must first be done by certain common things [accidental differences as signs of essential differences]. For if we congregate the accidents from the more common genera...immediately from their definitions those things will be manifest which we seek.[91]

In this quotation Aquinas points out the necessity of finding first the genus and then its differences in order to arrive at a definition. To do this, i.e., to move from the general category to the specific differences contained under it, is most natural to the human person, who proceeds in his knowing from potency to act. In the beginning the human being knows only the general outlines of a thing and then gradually brings into focus the distinctions proper to it. Thus the child moves slowly from the knowledge that a human being is something alive to the fact that he is a rational animal. For this reason Aristotle says that "a child begins by calling all men 'father' and all women 'mother', but later on distinguishes each of them."[92]

b. Method of Composition

Having described the way that the teacher leads the student to a definition by the method of division, let us now treat his second procedure in defining, namely, that of composition. Instead of moving from the genus to its differences, this latter method, always employing induction, begins with the individuals and then proceeds upwards to the differences. The teacher using this method will do the following: (1) He will help the student try to find a common characteristic in the group of individuals possessing that which is being defined. (2) He will repeat this inquiry in a different group of individuals also possessing that which is to be defined. (3) He will then guide the student to compare the two characteristics discovered to see if these have something in common. If so, this common note will be the difference leading to definition; if not, the definition will lie in the characteristics discovered first. Consequently, there will be two kinds of things, entailing two definitions. In order to clarify these three steps taken by the teacher, let us use the example given by Aristotle.

To illustrate definition by composition, Aristotle searches for the meaning of magnanimity or greatness of spirit. To do this, he examines certain individuals considered to be magnanimous, namely, Alcibiades, Achilles, and Ajax. From experience obtained inductively, he knows that all of these men possess the characteristic of being unable to suffer insults. "The sign of which is that Alcibiades, not suffering insults, fought; Achilles fell into insanity because of wrath; and Ajax killed himself."[93]

Having discovered that these magnanimous men are distinguished by being unable to bear insults, Aristotle then examines another group of individuals considered magnanimous. This time, having chosen Lysander and Socrates, he finds inductively that these men are indifferent to good or evil fortune. With this information, Aristotle is then prepared to "take these two results and inquire what common element...[exists between] equanimity amid the vicissitudes of life and impatience of dishonour."[94] Proceeding by induction, he can discover that these two characteristics are found in men because they think themselves worthy of great things. "For from this it occurs both that a man does not suffer insults and that also he contemns the mutability of external goods as of least value."[95]

Therefore magnanimity can be defined as that virtue whereby a person, thinking himself worthy of great things, is indifferent to good or evil fortune and is impatient of dishonour. If the characteristics first noted in the two groups of men could not have been united in a common principle, however, there would be two kinds of magnanimity and, consequently, two definitions.

From this illustration we see that the teacher, helping the student to define by composition, chooses first one group of individuals possessing the quality to be defined and then a different group possessing the same quality. After he helps the pupil to see what each group has in common, his next task is to lead the student to find the source of the two characteristics. If there is such a source, the definition lies here; if not, it is to be found in the characteristics first discovered. If it is the latter case, there is not one definition, but two.

Although it is natural for the student to define by moving from the genus of a thing to its differences, he often finds definition easier by using the method of composition. The reason is that the pupil can begin with the singular, rather than with the class or the universal. Thus he can begin with Socrates and Lysander, rather than with living things. In doing so, he can avoid ambiguity and equivocation, for it is easier to analyze several individuals than to try to do the same with an abstract class. The reason is that the singulars, being more concrete, are more attuned to the nature of the human mind, to a mind relying on sense knowledge.

At this point we have described both of the methods helping the student to arrive at definition, as well as the teacher's procedure leading to the universal proposition. In all of this methodology the teacher relies constantly on induction, the basic means to assist the student to acquire knowledge. In addition to the inductive process, however, the teacher has at his command the syllogistic or deductive method. To complete our discussion of teaching in relation to its procedure, we shall now treat the Aristotelian doctrine relevant to this second part of pedagogy.

Chapter 6

Deductive Process of Teaching

A. Deduction's purpose
　　1. The general purpose
　　2. The formal purpose
　　3. The material purpose
　　　　a. Science
　　　　b. Opinion
B. Deduction's materials
　　1. The universal principle
　　　　a. For science
　　　　b. For opinion
　　2. Definition of subject
　　　　a. For science
　　　　b. For opinion
　　　　c. For quia demonstration
C. Deduction's procedure
　　1. Statement of problem
　　2. Definition of subject
　　3. Needed syllogistic rules

Deductive Process of Teaching

A. Deduction's purpose
B. Deduction's materials
C. Deduction's procedure

In the preceding chapter we treated the inductive method of teaching, which Aristotle defines as "a passage from individuals to universals."[1] By means of this method, the teacher assists the student to move from the singulars of his experience to definitions and universal propositions. Let us now discuss deduction, the teacher's second method, in which the instructor helps the pupil to move from his general knowledge to particular applications thereof. In the words of Aristotle, this deductive procedure "is an argument in which, certain things being laid down, something other than these necessarily comes about through them."[2] This second method of the teacher is one in which the instructor helps the pupil "toward knowledge, leading him step by step from principles he already knows to conclusions hitherto unknown to him."[3] More briefly expressed, deduction is the procedure by which the teacher leads the student from the known to the unknown.

The instructor must employ the deductive method, in addition to the procedure of induction, because the mind of the student moves from potency to act. In the beginning the student's knowing powers are like "a writing-tablet on which as yet nothing actually stands written;"[4] only later does he possess any actual knowledge. Since the pupil moves from potential to actual knowledge, he has "a likeness to things which are generated [such as the brute animals], which do not attain to perfection all at once but acquire it by degrees."[5] Since things moving from potency to act acquire their perfection only gradually, the student, beginning with only potential knowledge, gradually reaches the perfection of knowledge that he desires.

In his gradually growing fund of knowledge, the pupil first knows something of the thing's whatness; then he proceeds to know the thing's attributes, such as its properties and accidents. Thus, having defined the human being as a rational animal (and having a previous possession of the universal proposition *whatever is rational has the power to laugh*), the student can advance to the conclusion *all human beings have the power to laugh*. To obtain an apprehension of the thing's whatness (and ultimately of the universal proposition), the pupil uses the inductive process; the conclusion, on the other hand, requires the deductive procedure. Therefore, since the student's gradually developing knowledge of things includes definitions, propositions, and conclusions, he must employ both the inductive and deductive procedures. In like manner, the teacher's methodology must include both of these techniques.

To discuss the Aristotelian doctrine relevant to the deductive method of teaching, we shall follow the same order used for the inductive procedure. This means that we shall first examine the purpose of deduction, then elaborate upon the materials needed for this process, and finally treat the procedure itself. This order follows that used in the production of any work of art. Thus the builder of a house must first procure a blueprint, then collect the needed materials, and finally undertake the actual work of construction. Since any artist must proceed in this order, we shall examine the method of deduction in relation first to its purpose, then to its materials, and finally to its procedure.

A. Deduction's Purpose
1. The General Purpose

The general purpose of the teacher in the deductive method is to actualize the potential knowledge of the student. In the beginning of a given lesson, the pupil only virtually knows that truth which the teacher intends to explain to him. As Aristotle expresses it: "Before he [the student] was led on to recognition or before he actually drew a conclusion, we should perhaps say that in a manner he knew, in a manner not."[6] By this statement Aristotle means that the student knows the conclusion to be taught in a virtual manner, but not in an absolute or actual sense.

The pupil has a virtual knowledge of the conclusion, because he already possesses general knowledge or universal principles upon which the teacher is relying to teach the new lesson. But "in a universal the particulars exist in potency, as in the whole the parts are in potency."[7] Therefore the student, already possessing this general background, has at least a potential or virtual knowledge of the new conclusion. "For example, if one [the student] knows that the angles of all triangles are equal to two right angles, one knows in a sense —potentially—that the isosceles' angles also are equal to two right angles, even if one does not know that the isosceles is a triangle."[8]

The virtual knowledge of the student is neither actual, but forgotten, knowledge (as Plato maintained) nor totally new knowledge. Rather, it is an understanding known virtually in the sense that the student knows the general principles from which the new knowledge flows, but unknown actually in the respect that the pupil has yet to learn the particular lesson at hand. The student himself demonstrates that he possesses at least a potential or virtual knowledge of the unknown by his ability to comprehend the carefully developed sequence of the lesson. As the class progresses, the pupil might find himself wondering why, for example, the new topic is so understandable and why he had not thought of this particular material before. In his ready understanding of a conclusion stemming from his general background, the student demonstrates that this conclusion is "known *in potency* or *virtually* in the foreknown universal principles, but unknown in act, according to proper knowledge."[9]

The purpose of the teacher in deduction is to render actual this virtual knowledge of the student. To accomplish this purpose, he must show the pupil that the particular lesson is part of the student's general fund of knowledge. Immediately, then, the student will move from potential to actual understanding of the particular topic. Thus, let us suppose that the teacher wishes to explain the following: The sea lion is warmblooded. This conclusion is only potentially understood by the student when he knows the principle *every mammal is warmblooded*. In order to actualize the pupil's potential state, the teacher must show him that the sea lion is a mammal. Immediately the student will have actual knowledge of the particular topic being explained. The teacher has accomplished his purpose in deduction, which is to actualize the potential knowledge of the student, by showing that the particular lesson is part of the pupil's general background.

In attempting to actualize the potential knowledge of the student, the teacher is working in accordance with his pupil's nature. Since the student naturally desires the perfection of his rational nature, he has a natural inclination to advance from his initial state of ignorance to the perfection of knowledge. At first in a state of potential knowledge, the student wonders about the nature or causes of things and is not satisfied until his mind rests in the knowledge of the First Cause of all.

The student's natural wonder about things rests in the knowledge of their Ultimate Cause, for his knowledge is now the very contrary of his initial state of ignorance. But "each motion [such as the movement from up to down] is terminated in the contrary of that from which the motion begins. Hence, since investigation is a kind of movement towards knowledge, it must be terminated in the contrary of that from which it begins."[10] Since the contrary of the student's initial ignorance and wonder about all reality is the knowledge of the First Cause, his mind naturally finds its rest and termination there. Because of this, Aristotle says that "happiness, therefore, must be some form of contemplation."[11]

2. The Formal Purpose

Having pointed out that the general purpose of the teacher's deductive procedure is to actualize the student's potential knowledge, let us state more specifically the purpose of this method. In doing so, we shall clarify the goal of deduction in relation to first its formal structure and then its content or material. In other words, we shall treat the purpose of deduction first from a formal and then from a material standpoint.

The structural purpose of the teacher as he proceeds deductively is the application of the student's general knowledge to the particular case or subject falling under that knowledge. Expressing this purpose in relation to demonstration, Aristotle says that "every demonstration proves a predicate of a subject as attaching or as not attaching to it."[12] Thus, if the teacher explains deductively the conclusion *all human beings have the power to laugh*, he shows that the student's general principle *whatever is rational has the power to laugh* can be applied or proved of the particular subject *all human beings*. In deduction, the instructor seeks to apply the pupil's general background to a particular case pertinent to it. He undertakes to instruct the student in neither the required general principle nor even the meaning of the particular subject treated. Rather, the teacher's formal purpose in deduction is the application of the student's general principle to a particular subject falling under that principle.

The instructor's formal purpose in deduction is one of application, because the deductive or syllogistic process is a "discourse in which, certain things being stated, something other than what is stated follows of necessity from their being so."[13] In deduction the teacher instructs the student by moving from certain stated things to other knowledge following from what is stated, i.e., by moving from the known to the unknown. Thus, when Aristotle teaches deductively the truth that God is life, he employs certain known principles: (1) The actuality of thought is life. (2) God is the actuality of thought.[14]

In order to teach deductively, the teacher must move from known truths to other truths falling under what is known. Since the deductive procedure by nature is one which reaches new knowledge by means of previous knowledge, the purpose of the teacher in this process is precisely the use or application of the known in order to arrive at the unknown.

In making the application proper to the deductive process, the teacher leads the student to a conclusion by showing him that a particular subject falls under a known universal principle. Thus the instructor helps the pupil deduce the conclusion *all human beings have the power to laugh* by showing him that the subject *all human beings* falls under the general principle *whatever is rational has the power to laugh*. In this deductive procedure, the student understands the given conclusion because of his knowledge of the subject and of the general principle. More simply, he knows the conclusion in relation to its reason or cause. Thus he knows that human beings can laugh because they are rational.

Sometimes, however, without a knowledge of the subject's definition and of the general principle, the student has an understanding of the given conclusion, which he has obtained inductively. Thus, from his observation of a sufficient number of individual persons, the student may realize that human beings have the power to laugh. At this stage the student knows that human beings can laugh but not why; he is also unable to deduce this conclusion because he lacks the knowledge of the subject and of the general principle.

If the student wishes to know this same truth deductively, he must search for this needed knowledge. This means that he must seek for the general principle under which this conclusion falls. Only then will the given conclusion be known deductively, as well as inductively. Often, however, the student knows a given truth only in an inductive way because he lacks the general principle under which it falls. This is frequently the case in experimental research, where, for example, one might know that a certain drug has specific healing properties but not the general principle or cause for this fact.

3. The Material Purpose

Having seen that the teacher's purpose in deduction, formally considered, is the application of the general principle to a particular subject falling under that principle, let us now examine the purpose of the deductive method from a material viewpoint. In this examination of the teacher's purpose, we shall consider deduction now, not in terms of its form, but in relation to the matter used in the deductive process. Therefore, we shall be concerned, not with the structural formation sought in the deductive process, but with the kind of matter obtained by the teacher's deductive method.

a. Science

In his definition of the teacher, Aristotle clarifies the kind of matter that the instructor should seek to give his students. In stating that "the people who instruct us are those who tell the causes of each thing,"[15] the Philosopher points out that the teacher should aim to give his pupils material which contains a knowledge of the causes of the things being taught. Thus the instructor giving his students a knowledge of the principle *every triangle has its exterior angles equal to the opposite interior angles* must explain the cause of this truth. This means that the teacher must show by a geometrical construction that the three-sided nature of the triangle is the cause of the truth of the given theorem. When the teacher gives his pupils material containing the cause of the thing being taught, he is achieving, according to Aristotle, the purpose of the deductive procedure from a material standpoint.

To give the student a knowledge of the thing's causes, however, is to give him scientific material, for scientific knowing is defined as that kind of knowledge in which one knows "the cause on which the fact depends, as the cause of that fact and of no other, and, further, that the fact could not be other than it is."[16] Thus one knowing scientifically that the moon is eclipsed must understand the following: (1) He must have a knowledge of the fact that the earth can interpose itself between the moon and the sun. (2) He must know that this interposition is the actual cause of the eclipse of the moon. (3) He must know that, if this cause is present, the eclipse of the moon will occur. He must understand that, given the cause, the eclipse of the moon cannot be otherwise.[17]

Since (according to Aristotle) "we think we have scientific knowledge when we know the cause,"[18] the teacher giving his students a knowledge of the thing's causes, will be giving them scientific material. Therefore we can say that the teacher's ultimate purpose in the deductive method is to give his pupils scientific knowledge.

Scientific knowledge, whether it concerns natural things, mathematical objects, or being in general, is by definition a mode of knowing which is certain. Thus Aristotle says that "scientific knowledge and its object differ from opinion and the object of opinion in that scientific knowledge is commensurately universal and proceeds by necessary connexions, and that which is necessary cannot be otherwise."[19] Since science, by its very nature, is knowledge of a necessary cause-effect relationship, it is a modality of knowing which is certain, which cannot be otherwise. Thus, if one knows the conclusion *all material things are corruptible* by means of the cause of its truth, namely, that all material things have parts, then one has certain knowledge. Such a conclusion is certain, for corruptibility necessarily inheres in material things because the premises from which it is concluded are necessarily connected. Scientific conclusions are by nature in a necessary mode, for they proceed from necessary premises.[20]

b. Opinion

Although the teacher's ultimate purpose in the deductive method is to give his students such scientific conclusions, he is often unable to achieve this goal. The reason is that many times one is able to have only an opinion about things, rather than scientific or certain knowledge. Thus one can hold as probable that dark clouds are a sign of rain, but he cannot be certain of this fact. One's knowledge includes opinion, as well as scientific knowledge, for

> the acts of reason resemble, in a certain respect, the acts of nature. Whence art imitates nature to the extent to which it is able. In the acts of nature there is found a threefold diversity. For in certain of them, nature acts with necessity, in such a way that it cannot fail [such as the eclipse of the moon caused by the interposition of the earth between it and the sun]. In certain other acts nature operates for the most part, although it can at times fail in its proper act. Whence, in such circumstances there must be a twofold act: one which is for the most part, as when from seed there is generated a perfect animal; the other when nature fails in that which is according to it, as when from seed there is generated something monstrous because of the corruption of some principle.[21]

Just as nature has that which is with necessity, that which is for the most part, and that which is deficient, so one's knowing includes these same three possibilities in relation to necessity. In human knowledge there is truth which is certain, that degree of knowing which is probable, and finally that deviation from truth called falsehood. This condition exists in human knowing, for one's thinking reflects the things that he knows, which are produced necessarily, for the most part, or in a defective way.

When one has only probable knowledge about a thing, it is called opinion, which is defined as that type of knowledge in which "the reason inclines wholly to one side of a contradiction, with fear of the other."[22] Thus one with an opinion that rain is threatening is inclined toward the affirmative side of this proposition, but he still fears the negative position, namely, that it may not rain.

Opinion is that kind of knowledge which is concerned with contingent reality, rather than with necessary things. The object of this mode of knowing is anything which may change, and therefore the knowledge about such a thing is of the same stability, i.e., it is a form of knowing which is only probable or can be otherwise. As an indication that such a definition of opinion is sound, Aristotle refers both to the common viewpoint about opinion and to each individual's experience in the matter. He says that

> this view [of opinion] also fits the observed facts, for opinion is unstable, and so is the kind of being we have described as its object. Besides, when a man thinks a truth incapable of being otherwise he always thinks that he knows it, never that he opines it. He thinks that he opines when he thinks that a connexion, though actually so, may quite easily be otherwise; for he believes that such is the proper object of opinion, while the necessary is the object of knowledge.[23]

Although the object of opinion is that which can be otherwise, it is possible for one to have only an opinion about something in reality which is actually necessary. A person might only believe, for example, the proposition *the human being has the power to laugh*, although this property necessarily inheres in human beings. Such a person possesses only probable knowledge about an actually necessary proposition either because he does not know the proper reason for the fact or, if he does, he does not realize that the given reason is the proper one. One has only opinion about the actually necessary if he "should proceed to the immediate through middles which are true, but which nevertheless are not in the things essentially of which they are said, as definitions which are predicated substantially and signify the species of the thing, or...[if he] should not take them as being thus inherent."[24] Therefore we can see that often, although opinion is a kind of knowledge of the contingent, it is also the mode of knowing that one can have about the actually necessary.

One frequently has only opinion about the actually necessary, for the movement of one's mind in knowing is from potency to act, which is a gradual movement toward perfect knowledge. Since anything gradually acquiring perfection moves from the imperfect to the perfect, and one of the imperfect stages in human knowing is a probable understanding or opinion, one naturally tends to have first an opinion about the necessary things of reality, rather than a scientific knowledge of them.

Only later does he reach a scientific mode of knowing, which is "commensurately universal and proceeds by necessary connexions."[25] In the knowledge of the revolution of the earth around the sun, for example, the scientists held this position (the Copernican theory) first as something probable and only later as a scientific fact. Therefore, since the human mind moves from potency to act, it is normal for one to know the actually necessary first as something probable.

Aristotle holds that the probable stage in human knowing falls under the province of the teacher's deductive procedure, for this tentative mode of knowing is ordered to a later scientific understanding. Hoping for a certain understanding of the necessary things of reality, one formulates opinions about what he sees in order that he may gradually arrive at the real truth about these things. Thus, in attempting to understand the relationship existing between the earth and the sun, the scientists formulated working hypotheses for the purpose of gradually arriving at a better understanding.

Therefore, since that which is ordered to an end falls under its domain, one's first tentative understanding of things, as ordered to a more certain knowledge, falls under the province of the teacher assisting the student to arrive at a knowledge of the causes of things. The following quotation reveals that Aristotle orders one's first probable understanding of reality to a later scientific understanding and thus would place such a mode of knowing as a provisional goal of the teacher:

> We must say for how many and for what purposes the treatise [on dialectical or probable reasoning] is useful. They are three—intellectual training, casual encounters, and the philosophical sciences.... For the study of the philosophical sciences it is useful, because the ability to raise searching difficulties on both sides of a subject will make us detect more easily the truth and error about the several points that arise.[26]

At this point we shall summarize what we have treated in this section concerning the purpose of the teacher who is proceeding deductively. In general, the instructor's aim in this procedure is to lead the student from potential to actual knowledge. Expressed from a formal viewpoint, his purpose is to help the pupil make an application of his general knowledge to particular cases contained therein.

If we examine deduction from a material standpoint, Aristotle holds that the teacher should strive to give his students a knowledge of causes, or scientific knowledge. Under such a purpose, however, the Philosopher would also include opinion or dialectical knowledge, insofar as it is ordered to a later scientific understanding, an understanding which would culminate in the highest reasoned science, metaphysics.

B. Deduction's Materials

With an understanding of the teacher's purpose in deduction, we are prepared to discuss the materials needed to accomplish such a purpose. According to Aristotle, the materials needed for the syllogistic procedure are the definition of the subject, a nominal notion of the property in relation to this subject, and the knowledge of the universal principle. In the words of Aquinas: "It is necessary that, before the knowledge of the conclusion is had, in some way the subject and the passion should be known. And likewise it is necessary that the principle be foreknown, since from the knowledge of the principle, the conclusion is made known."[27] Since the nominal definition of the property (as related to the subject) has been treated in chapter 4,[28] we shall discuss in this section only the definition of the subject and the knowledge of the principle.

1. The Universal Principle

If the teacher wishes to proceed deductively, part of the needed background for the student is the knowledge of the universal principle pertinent to the topic being treated. Thus the student learning deductively the conclusion *all human beings have the power to laugh* must rely on his knowledge of the universal principle *whatever is rational has the power to laugh*, as well as his definition of the human being as rational. The universal principles needed for the process of deduction will have different characteristics according to the purpose of the teacher.

If the instructor is leading the student to scientific knowledge, he must rely on universal principles capable of generating scientific conclusions in the minds of his pupils. If the teacher's purpose is to reach at best a dialectical understanding, however, his class will need to know only dialectical principles. Since the teacher's purpose in deduction, according to Aristotle, is to generate science ideally and to instill dialectical knowledge as leading to science, let us examine the characteristics of the principles needed for such a purpose.

a. For Science

Since scientific knowledge is the ideal toward which the teacher should aim, we shall treat first the requirements for the universal principles capable of generating science in those being taught. As we do so, we must remember that scientific knowledge is the ideal, and that very frequently the human being, whose intellectual power can be likened to the eyes of bats peering into the sun, is unable to attain such a goal. Nevertheless, since the ideal is that toward which each person should strive, we shall examine first the characteristics of universal principles needed for science.

According to Aristotle, universal principles leading to scientific conclusions must be true, primary, and immediate. As he expresses it, "the premises of demonstrated knowledge must be true, primary, immediate, better known than and prior to the conclusion, which is further related to them as effect to cause."[29] First of all, the universal principle known by the student must be true, for that which is false has no real existence. Thus one can affirm mentally that material things are not corruptible, but such a falsehood has no correspondence to anything in reality. Obviously, however, what does not exist cannot be known in a scientific way. Therefore false principles will never lead to scientific knowledge; or, expressed in a positive mode, a basic condition of the universal principles leading to science is that they must be true.

Secondly, the universal principles leading to science must be first or primary, i.e., they must not be dependent upon any other principles. These principles must not be dependent on any others or proved by means of other principles, for scientific knowledge, as that which is certain, must resolve or prove whatever part of its chain of reasoning is yet open to proof. Since "a person does not have science unless he has a demonstration of those things which can be demonstrated,"[30] the very principles from which such knowledge proceeds cannot be those which are yet open to further proof. If they are, they must be resolved or proved, until one finally rests in principles not requiring further proof.

Such principles would be those which are not dependent on any others, and, as such, are first or primary in the order of demonstration. Ultimately only first or primary principles can lead to scientific conclusions, although it is true that a particular conclusion can rest on a nonprimary principle which, however, must be capable of being resolved to a first principle. Therefore we can see that the principles leading to science must not only be true but also first in the order of demonstration.

Since the principles leading to science must be first in the order of demonstration, it follows that such principles must be immediate or self-evident. This characteristic of immediacy is a consequence of the prior nature of the principles, for only indemonstrable, immediate, or self-evident principles (as incapable of demonstration) are prior in the order of demonstration. These immediate or self-evident principles are those in which one term is in the definition of the other, or in which the predicate is identical with the subject.[31] Thus the proposition *the human being is an animal* is self-evident, for the predicate is part of the definition of the subject *human being*. Such propositions can be described as self-evident or immediate, for they are clear as soon as their terms are understandable, and they do not require any mediating or middle link to make them evident.

Thus far we have seen that the universal principles leading to science must be true, first, and therefore immediate or self-evident. From our discussion, we know that such principles must fulfill at least one of the following conditions proper to self-evident propositions: (1) The predicate is identical with the subject, as in the statement *the human being is a rational animal.* (2) The predicate is in the definition of the subject, as in the statement *the human being is an animal.* (3) The subject is in the definition of the predicate, as in the statement *every number is either odd or even.* Only insofar as principles fulfill one of these conditions and are thereby described as self-evident, can they be the type leading to scientific conclusions.

Since universal principles leading to science must be self-evident, they are therefore also necessary principles. This characteristic is proper to self-evident or immediate principles, for these principles, such as those in which one term is in the definition of the other, are by this fact necessarily connected. These principles are such that, if the subject exists, the predicate cannot not exist in it. Thus, granted the existence of the subject *human being*, the predicate *animal* must belong to such a subject, for it is part of the essence and definition of human being. This means, of course, that the subject *human being* has a necessary connection with the predicate *animal*. Therefore we can see that self-evident principles, by their very nature, are thereby necessary principles. In the words of Aristotle: "Attributes attaching essentially to their subjects attach necessarily to them: for essential attributes are either elements in the essential nature of their subjects, or contain their subjects as elements in their own essential nature."[32]

Self-evident or immediate principles, as we noted in chapter 4, admit of a twofold division: they can be self-evident to all or just to the wise. Thus the proposition *the whole is greater than the part* is self-evident to all, while the proposition *two right angles equal one straight angle* is self-evident just to those understanding such terminology. As these examples indicate, this division is based on the kinds of terms found in the propositions.

If the terms are part of the common vocabulary of all people, then the propositions composed of such terms are self-evident to all; while, if the terms are more specialized in nature, the propositions resulting from them are immediately clear only to those understanding such vocabulary. Naturally, however, the latter propositions, although not self-evident at first to those with no experience in such vocabulary, will be clear to these individuals as soon as the terms are defined.[33]

If a particular person is to have an immediate knowledge of a self-evident principle, he must be able to grasp the definition of the terms of the given universal principle. If there is something, however, of which the human being is incapable of knowing the essential definition, then it is not possible for him to possess any self-evident principles about such a thing. The human being, for example, cannot know any self-evident principles about God, for the object of the human intellect is the essence of material things, and God is not part of the material order. Since the human person properly knows the essence of only material things, he does not possess any self-evident principles about the immaterial order as such.

Because of this limitation, we must specify that the self-evident principles leading to science must be those self-evident to the human intellect. This limits such principles to those whose immediacy is derived from the essence of material things. Thus, in natural science, the principle *every material thing is composed of parts* can be immediately known to human beings, for the definition of material things makes it evident that composition inheres in such beings. Again, in mathematics, the proposition *two right angles equal one straight angle* can be self-evident to the human intellect, for the definition of the subject (derived by an abstraction from matter) reveals that the predicate is immediately true of it.

Finally, in metaphysics (known again by an abstraction from matter) the principle *the whole is greater than its parts* is one of the common principles self-evident to all people, for the definition of whole immediately shows that it is greater than any of its parts. Aristotle points out that the principles leading to science must be those self-evident to the human being, when he says that they must be "better known than and prior to the conclusion."[34]

Thus far we have seen that the universal principles leading to science must be those self-evident to the human intellect. Since these principles are immediate and therefore are concerned with definition, they will be statements of the causes of things. Thus, in the statement *the human being is an animal*, the predicate denotes that which is derived from the material cause of the subject. These principles are concerned with the causes of things, for definition, ideally speaking, gives the causes of that defined.

Thus the following definition of a house explains it in terms of its material and final causes: a house is a covering made from some sturdy material for the purpose of protecting human beings from the elements. Since self-evident principles have one term in the definition of the other, these principles will give the causes of the thing treated. For this reason Aristotle says that scientific conclusions deriving from true, first, and immediate principles are "related to them [the principles] as effect to cause."[35]

Although it is true that principles leading to science must be propositions about the causes of things, often one does not know a given thing's cause, but rather only the effect of such a cause. Thus one can easily see the effect of an eclipse of the sun, namely, less sunlight in a particular area, but he may be completely ignorant of the cause of such a phenomenon. When one knows the effect of a cause better than the cause itself, he must demonstrate by means of this effect (rather than the cause), for he must always advance in knowledge by that which is known to him.

When a person demonstrates in this fashion, he does not know the cause of his conclusion; rather, by means of the cause's effect, he knows that a cause of this effect exists. Such a demonstration is called quia (that), while a demonstration through the cause is denominated propter quid (because of which).[36]

As an example of the quia demonstration, Aristotle cites the proof in which it is concluded that the moon is spherical because of the phases through which it passes in the course of its revolution around the earth. He says that "another example [of quia demonstration] is the inference that the moon is spherical from its manner of waxing. Thus: since that which so waxes is spherical, and since the moon so waxes, clearly the moon is spherical."[37] This is a quia demonstration, for the moon is shown to be spherical by its manner of waxing and waning, which is an effect of such sphericity, rather than the cause of such a shape.

Quia demonstrations are very frequent in natural science, where one, first knowing the outer effects of natural things, proceeds from these to a knowledge of their inner natures. These demonstrations must also be used in metaphysics, whenever the cause in a given proof is the Universal Cause of all being, which is a cause above the material order. In order to demonstrate, one must use principles about the effects of things, if these effects are better known to him. Although this kind of demonstration is not ideal, it is most useful, for, by means of it, one knows that a cause must exist. Since it is ordered to a later strictly scientific understanding, this quia demonstration, with its principles about effects rather than causes, must be understood by the teacher.

At this point we have seen that the principles leading to science must give the causes of things. Since such principles are definitions, we can immediately see the vital role that definition plays in acquiring scientific knowledge. When one possesses a principle giving the definition, he thereby has a true, first, immediate, and necessary principle. Since such characteristics are needed for principles leading to science, the principle giving the definition is required for scientific knowledge.

If the person wishing to arrive at scientific knowledge has a true, first, immediate, and necessary principle, he will possess a proposition that is true at all times, places, and instances of the principle. The person thus possesses the principle which is universally true, taking here the strictest meaning of universality. This meaning is expressed by Aristotle as follows:

> I call 'true in every instance' what is truly predicable of all instances—not of one to the exclusion of others—and at all times, not at this or that time only; e.g. if animal is truly predicable of every instance of man, then if it be true to say 'this is a man', 'this is an animal' is also true, and if the one be true now the other is true now.[38]

The person possessing a necessary principle has one which is universally true, for necessary principles, being those in which one term is in the definition of the other, are such that, given the existence of one term, the other term cannot not exist. Because of this necessary connection between the subject and the predicate, such principles are universally true at all times, places, and instances. Thus, in the proposition *the human being is an animal*, the predicate *animal* will always inhere in the subject *human being*, for the predicate is part of the definition of the subject.

Not only must the principles leading to science be necessarily connected and therefore always true, but also they must be commensurately universal or prime. Such propositions are those in which the predicate inheres in its proper or primary subject. Thus the universal principle *the human being is sentient* fails to be prime, because being sentient inheres in the human being, not because he is a human being, but because he is an animal. On the other hand, the proposition *every animal is sentient* is a prime or commensurately universal principle, for the predicate inheres in the first thing to which it properly belongs.

Universal principles, then, are prime if the predicate belongs to its primary subject. In the words of Aristotle: "An attribute belongs commensurately and universally to a subject when it can be shown to belong to any random instance of that subject and when the subject is the first to which it can be shown to belong."[39] As an example of such a proposition, Aristotle gives the principle *every triangle has its angles equal to two right angles.*. This is a commensurately universal proposition, for *triangle*, rather than *figure* or even *isosceles triangle*, is the primary subject to which this predicate belongs.

Aristotle maintains that principles leading to science must be commensurately universal or proper principles, for the person seeking science desires to know the proper reason for his conclusion. Because of this, he must utilize principles which have a commensurately universal or proper relationship. In this way the one who is demonstrating will obtain the proper cause for the problem at hand.

Since scientific reasoning proceeds from proper principles, it does not utilize any principles more common than the problem to be proved. This means, for example, that the first common principles of all knowledge are not the specific premises used in any given demonstration. Nevertheless, the chief of all these first principles, the principle of contradiction, is presupposed in every proper principle used in a scientific demonstration. Thus the proper principle *the human being is an animal* implicitly maintains the contradictory proposition *the human being is not a nonanimal.* If such an implication were not understood, the proposition *the human being is an animal* would have no validity. Thus one could simultaneously hold that the human being is both an animal and a nonanimal. As this example illustrates, the principle of contradiction stands behind the validity of every proper principle. As the first of all immediate principles, it is most obvious to all people and is the source from which all proof ultimately proceeds.[40]

At this point we have completed our discussion of the nature of the principles leading to scientific knowledge. Let us now summarize the characteristics proper to such principles, characteristics which must be known by the teacher assisting his students in the acquisition of science. These principles can be described as true, first, immediate to the human intellect, causal, necessary, commensurately universal, and proper. Since all these characteristics belong to those principles in which one term is in the definition of the other or in which the predicate is identical with the subject, it is evident that principles of this nature have a key role to play in the material needed for the acquisition of science.

b. For Opinion

In addition to knowing the characteristics of the principles leading to scientific knowledge, the teacher must understand the nature of those principles which will produce only opinion. The instructor must be aware of the kind of principles producing dialectical knowledge, for his purpose in deductive reasoning includes not only scientific knowledge for his students but also probable knowledge as leading to science. In fact, much of the teacher's work lies in the realm of assisting his students to reach a sound opinion about the matter under discussion, for "since the human soul occupies the lowest place in the order of intellective substances, it has the least intellective power."[41] Since often the student is able to obtain only an opinion on a given topic, we must treat the nature of the principles leading to dialectical or probable conclusions.

Aristotle defines dialectical knowledge or opinion as knowledge "concerned with that which may be true or false, and can be otherwise."[42] One possesses only an opinion if he thinks that his knowledge, although actually true or false at a given moment, may not continue to be such. Thus a person has no more than belief or opinion if he holds that a certain remedy is good for colds but he also sees that it may not be effective in all cases of such a disease. As the kind of knowledge which may be otherwise, opinion differs from scientific knowledge which is concerned with necessary things.

Since opinion is not the necessary mode of knowledge that science is, the premises from which it proceeds do not require the rigid characteristics proper to the principles leading to science. Rather Aristotle holds that the principles producing dialectical knowledge need be only those which are generally accepted. To be given general acceptance, a principle must be "accepted by every one or by the majority or by the philosophers—i.e. by all, or by the majority, or by the most notable and illustrious of them."[43] As an illustration of the principles accepted by all or by most people, we could cite the proverb *a stitch in time saves nine*, while the theories of Einstein on relativity would be examples of propositions held by a notable scientist.

Aristotle holds that generally accepted propositions are not only those held by all or most people but also those proposed by the most illustrious of a given society, for the reputation of this latter group commands the respect of the multitude. Therefore a generally accepted proposition can be that proposed by a single person, if he holds a position meriting such acceptance. For this reason also, Aristotle says that

> all opinions that are in accordance with the arts are dialectical propositions; for people are likely to assent to the views held by those who have made a study of these things, e.g. on a question of medicine they will agree with the doctor, and on a question of geometry with the geometrician; and likewise also in other cases.[44]

Thus we see that the propositions will be probable if they are accepted by all or most people or by those few whose reputation commands acceptance from the many.

Since propositions leading to dialectical conclusions are those given general acceptance, it is necessary to point out that one of the most powerful means of gaining the acceptance of the group is precisely the personal character of the one presenting the proposition. Thus a student body in a given college is inclined to accept the doctrines proposed by the faculty member who has an unquestioned moral and intellectual reputation among those students. In the following quotation Aristotle points out the importance of one's personal character if one hopes to gain general acceptance of a given proposition:

> We believe good men more fully and more readily than others: this is true generally whatever the question is, and absolutely true where exact certainty is impossible and opinions are divided.... It is not true, as some writers assume in their

treatises on rhetoric, that the personal goodness revealed by the speaker contributes nothing to his power of persuasion; on the contrary, his character may almost be called the most effective means of persuasion he possesses.[45]

Just exactly what this personal character should include, Aristotle reveals in the following quotation:

> There are three things which inspire confidence in the orator's own character—the three, namely, that induce us to believe a thing apart from any proof of it: good sense, good moral character, and goodwill.... Men either form a false opinion through want of good sense; or they form a true opinion, but because of their moral badness do not say what they really think; or finally, they are both sensible and upright, but not well disposed to their hearers, and may fail in consequence to recommend what they know to be the best course. These are the only possible cases.[46]

Having seen that principles leading to dialectical conclusions need to be only those generally accepted, we shall now point out the particular kinds of generally accepted propositions which Aristotle says are most helpful in argumentation. These propositions can be found in three general fields of knowledge,

> for some are ethical propositions, some are on natural philosophy [as including metaphysics], while some are logical. Propositions such as the following are ethical, e.g. 'Ought one rather to obey one's parents or the laws, if they disagree?'; such as this are logical, e.g. 'Is the knowledge of opposites the same or not?'; while such as this are on natural philosophy, e.g. 'Is the universe eternal or not?'[47]

Dialectical propositions abound in the fields of moral science, natural science, and logic, for many parts of these subject matters are concerned with either contingent things or such obscure matters that the mind often reaches no more than an opinion about them. An illustration of matters of a contingent nature would be whether or not federal welfare programs hamper private initiative, while the problems of evolution and of the nature of the atom are examples of questions which are difficult to solve.

In the subject matters just mentioned, the teacher leading his students to dialectical conclusions should help them to acquire a fund of generally accepted propositions. According to Aristotle, one part of this dialectical knowledge should include propositions about the principles of a given science, for their wide applicability makes them useful for many problems. He says that

> in arguments it is a great advantage to be well up in regard to first principles, and to have a thorough knowledge of premises at the tip of one's tongue. For just as in a person with a trained memory, a memory of things themselves is immediately caused by the mere mention of their *loci*, so these habits too will make a man readier in reasoning, because he has his premises classified before his mind's eye, each under its number. It is better to commit to memory a premise of general

application than an argument: for it is difficult to be even moderately ready with a first principle, or hypothesis.[48]

In the foregoing quotation Aristotle notes that, although one should have a fund of the first principles of the different sciences, it is difficult to have even an opinion about them. The reason is that these principles are had by defining the terms, an operation which requires both intuitive ability and experience with the things to be defined.[49] Although it is not easy to know the basic principles of the different sciences, one must strive to have at least an opinion about them because of their universal application in argumentation. Thus the student attempting to proceed dialectically in the different sciences will be helped by some dialectical positions on the principles of natural things, on the meaning of motion, on the nature of the soul, on the essence of goodness, and on the nature of happiness.

Not only should the student hoping to argue dialectically have some probable propositions on the first principles of the sciences about the different kinds of being, but also he should have some notions about the attributes common to all being. Thus the student should have some dialectical propositions on those characteristics proper to being as being, such as sameness and difference, likeness and unlikeness, contrariety, and priority and posteriority.[50] By means of such principles, the pupil can arrive at a dialectical understanding of many problems in the various sciences. Thus, in order to know more about the passion of hatred, the student might argue "that hatred is in the concupiscible appetite, in which love is, from the fact that contraries are concerned with the same thing."[51]

In order to proceed dialectically in all the different sciences, therefore, the student should have a fund of generally accepted propositions about the first principles of these sciences. Thus he might hold the following concerning the nature of human happiness: "Chiefest of blessings is health for a man,...this being the general opinion."[52] If it is possible, he should also acquire some probable positions about those problems which are most frequent in a given science, and particularly about those which are ultimate. This means that the student should have the spirit of inquiry about such problems as the temporal beginning of the universe, the existence of a First Cause of all things, and the immortality of the human soul.

By means of some dialectical positions on the perennial problems of the different subject matters, the student can gradually become more experienced about these problems and more capable of judging them. Aristotle emphasizes the importance of dialectical principles about the constant questions of the sciences in his statement that "it is best to know by heart arguments upon those questions which are of most frequent occurrence, and particularly in regard to those propositions which are ultimate: for in discussing these answerers frequently give up in despair."[53]

Let us now summarize what we have discussed about the dialectical knowledge which the teacher will employ to help his students arrive at probable conclusions in the different subject matters. We have seen that dialectical propositions are those which are generally accepted, an acceptance which can be engendered because it is the thinking of one prominent individual. We have also pointed out that the teacher should help the student to acquire such generally accepted propositions about both the opening topics of a science and its most frequent problems, particularly those which are ultimate. Utilizing this fund of dialectical propositions, the instructor can help his students deduce conclusions of a comparable mode of certainty. In this deductive procedure leading only to opinion, the teacher's hope is that his class may later advance from these dialectical beginnings to a scientific understanding of the problem at hand.

2. Definition of Subject

In addition to knowing some universal principles, the student who is proceeding deductively must be able to define his subject as falling under such universal principles. Since the definition of the subject is part of the needed material for the deductive procedure, we shall now treat this part of the knowledge necessary for the deductive method. In our treatment we shall speak first of the type of definition of the subject needed for scientific knowledge and then of the kind of definition leading to only opinion.

a. For Science

If the teacher is helping his students to arrive at a scientific conclusion, he must employ a definition of the subject which gives at least one of the thing's causes. Thus, if the instructor is helping his pupils to conclude that thunder is a rumbling sound in the heavens, he can accomplish his purpose through a definition giving the efficient cause, i.e., through the fact that thunder is something produced by a discharge of lightning from the clouds.[54] The teacher cannot make use of a definition through accidents or effects because he is leading the students to science, which is knowledge about the proper causes of things. In the words of Aquinas: "Since we think ourselves to know scientifically when we know the cause, as was stated in the First Book, and a demonstration is a syllogism causing scientific knowledge, consequently the middle of demonstration is a cause."[55]

To assist his students to know scientifically, the teacher may employ any one of the four causes in his deductive procedure. To illustrate that all of the four causes may be used as the definition of the subject (and also of the passion), Aquinas, in his commentary on Aristotle's doctrine, gives the following demonstrations:

Material cause
Whatever is composed of contraries is corruptible.
A stone is composed of contraries.
∴ A stone is corruptible.

Formal cause
The sum of two angles drawn in a semicircle equals a right angle.
The angle inscribed in the semicircle equals such angles.
∴ The angle inscribed in the semicircle equals a right angle.
Efficient cause
Whoever attacks first will himself be attacked.
The Athenians attacked the Sardians first.
∴ The Athenians were themselves attacked.
Final cause
Whoever permits digestion will be healthy.
One walking after dinner permits digestion.
∴ One walking after dinner will be healthy.[56]

In each of the above demonstrations there is a definition of the subject by means of one of the four causes. Only if the student has such a causal definition will he be able to arrive at scientific knowledge.

It is possible for the student, if he has a definition of the subject by means of a certain one of its causes, to obtain in his conclusion a definition of this subject in terms of another one of its causes. Thus the pupil is able to conclude to the fact that a house must be made of sturdy material (material cause) from the fact that it is a structure protecting human beings from the elements (final cause).[57] The pupil can arrive at one cause of the subject by means of a definition containing another one of its causes, for a definite causal relationship exists among the four causes.

To explain this relationship we must first note that matter and form are intrinsic to the thing, while the efficient and final causes have an extrinsic relationship to the given object. These extrinsic causes are in a way the causes of the form and matter, for the agent, acting because of a given purpose, educes the form from the matter. In relation to the production of a chair, for example, the carpenter, desiring to create an artistic product for a certain customer, educes a certain style of chair from a particular kind of lumber. As this illustration points out, a definite order of causality exists among the four causes: acting because of a given purpose, the agent educes the form from matter, a matter which exists for the sake of the given form.[58]

Since there is a definite order among the four causes, it is possible to conclude from one of the causes to another one following from it. Thus, from the efficient cause acting with necessity, the student can conclude to the formal cause. The following demonstration illustrates this type of reasoning:

Whatever follows a lightning discharge is an aerial rumbling sound.
Thunder follows a lightning discharge.
∴ Thunder is an aerial rumbling sound.[59]

In the foregoing demonstration the student is able to conclude, from his knowledge of the efficient cause of thunder (a discharge of lightning from clouds), that thunder is an aerial rumbling sound (its formal cause). It is also possible for the pupil to arrive at the knowledge of a thing's efficient and material causes by definitions giving prior causes. Thus, if the student is concluding that a house must be built of sturdy material because it protects the human being from the elements, he is obtaining the material cause of the house through reasoning employing a definition from the final cause.

Although the student may conclude to the material, formal, and efficient causes from causes prior to these particular three, it is not possible to arrive at the final cause by the demonstrative process. The final cause precludes demonstration, for it is the first of the causes in the chain of causality. The student, therefore, may obtain a knowledge of this cause only by the inductive process. There is no other way to arrive at the understanding of the final cause, for "the definition of *immediate* things, i.e., of things not having causes, is as a certain indemonstrable laying down of the *quod quid est* [whatness of the thing]."[60] Although the student may obtain the other three causes in the conclusion of a demonstration, he can arrive at the final cause only by induction.

Thus far we have seen that the teacher assisting the student to arrive at scientific knowledge needs a causal definition of the subject. To obtain such a definition the student may employ both the inductive and deductive procedures for the material, formal, and efficient causes of a given thing, but the final cause may be known only by the process of induction.

Quite frequently, however, the pupil may be unable to discover the proper causes of a thing; instead he may know only some of the outer characteristics of the thing's inner nature. Thus he may be able to define an elephant only as an animal with large flappy ears and a long trunk. Often the student is forced to define a thing by the outer effects of its inner nature, for it is difficult for the human intellect, which moves from potency to act, to understand the thing's essence immediately. Therefore, "sometimes necessity compels us to use accidental differences in place of essential differences inasmuch as accidental differences are the signs of certain essential differences unknown to us."[61]

b. For Opinion

In his attempts to describe or define a given thing, the student may use accidents peculiar or proper to the object, or he may employ accidents which are not peculiar to the thing. An example of the former type could be the definition of yellow jaundice as a disease turning the skin yellow, while a case of the latter might be the description of a balloon as something which is colored blue. If the pupil in his reasoning process uses a definition through a nonproper accident, his conclusion can be only an opinion about a given thing. Thus the student, defining education as that which leads to unpopularity, may reason as follows:

Unpopularity is undesirable.
Education leads to unpopularity.
∴ Education is undesirable.[62]

The above syllogism can lead to only an opinion about education, for the definition employed is one giving a characteristic which is not peculiar to the educational process. Since the pupil is proceeding from knowledge which is only accidentally connected with the thing, he cannot arrive at scientific knowledge in his conclusion. In the words of Aristotle: "As often as we have accidental knowledge that the thing exists, we must be in a wholly negative state as regards awareness of its essential nature; for we have not got genuine knowledge even of its existence, and to search for a thing's essential nature when we are unaware that it exists is to search for nothing."[63] The student cannot know the essential nature (have scientific knowledge) of a rabbit, for example, from the fact that he sees a fast motion in the bushes; for this knowledge, being purely accidental to rabbits, will not even reveal the existence of such an animal.[64]

c. For Quia Demonstration

Although a definition through a nonproper accident cannot give even a definite knowledge of a thing's existence, a definition through an accident peculiar to the thing or through some part of the thing's essence will enable the student to demonstrate that the thing truly exists. This type of demonstration called quia will not reveal the essential nature of the thing under discussion, but it will establish with certitude the existence of this thing. Thus the pupil can truly demonstrate that an eclipse of the moon exists, if he knows an accident peculiar to the eclipse, such as that the full moon in eclipse casts no shadow. The reasoning of this particular quia demonstration is as follows:

Whenever the full moon casts no shadow, it is eclipsed.
Now the full moon casts no shadow.
∴ Now the full moon is being eclipsed.

In reasoning such as the above example, the student can really demonstrate that a given thing exists, although he cannot know its essential nature, i.e., what it is or why it is such. In order to answer the questions what and why and thus arrive at scientific knowledge, the student must know the proper causes of the thing, such as the fact that the cause of an eclipse is the interposition of the earth between the moon and the sun.

If the pupil knows only some part of the thing's essence or a property peculiar to it, however, he can conclude from such knowledge only to the existence of the thing. As Aristotle expresses it: "We are aware whether a thing exists or not sometimes through apprehending an element in its character,...as, for example, when we are aware of thunder as a noise in the clouds, of eclipse as a privation of light, or of man as some species of animal, or of the soul as a self-moving thing."[65] In order to know not only the existence but also the essence of the thing (which is scientific knowledge), the student must possess a definition through the proper causes of the thing.

We have now completed our discussion of the definition of the subject, which is part of the material needed for the deductive process. In our treatment of this section we pointed out that the student can reach a scientific conclusion about a thing only if he has a causal definition. If he has a description of the thing which is only accidentally related to it, he can arrive at no more than an opinion about the given object. By means of a definition giving part of the thing's essence or some accident proper to it, however, the student can have a true demonstration concerning the existence of the given thing. Ideally, of course, he should try to obtain the proper causes of the thing, for only by such a definition can he reach scientific knowledge.

C. Deduction's Procedure

Having discussed both the purpose and the materials of the teacher in the deductive process, let us now treat the instructor's procedure as he works to achieve his purpose through these materials. Ideally, the purpose of the teacher is to help his students arrive at scientific conclusions through the use of commensurately universal principles and of causal definitions. Although scientific knowledge for the student is the primary goal of the teacher, he does not neglect probable conclusions obtained from generally accepted premises, for dialectical knowledge is usually the first stage in the human effort to arrive at science. Therefore the purpose of the teacher includes both dialectical and scientific knowledge for the student.

In order to achieve these two purposes, the teacher must employ different kinds of premises, but his general manner of procedure is the same in both cases. Since the teacher's general method is similar for both probable and scientific knowledge, we will not discuss a separate procedure for these two kinds of knowledge. Rather we will speak of the teacher's general procedure in deductive reasoning, a procedure applicable to both science and opinion.

1. Statement of Problem

If the teacher wishes to proceed carefully in assisting the student to secure a scientific or probable conclusion, he must first state the problem to be solved or to be brought to a satisfactory conclusion. Just as he does in the inductive method, the teacher must place the unknown before the minds of the students first. It is imperative that the class have a statement of the problem at the very beginning of the deductive process, for all those

> who inquire without first stating the difficulties are like those who do not know where they have to go; besides, a man does not otherwise know even whether he has at any given time found what he is looking for or not; for the end is not clear to such a man, while to him who has first discussed the difficulties it is clear.[66]

Therefore, since the teacher does have a definite goal which he hopes that the students will achieve, he must first tell them the problem of the particular lesson.

To illustrate this first step of the teacher's deductive method, let us take the following problem: Why does the preservation of animals require that they possess the sense of touch? In the beginning of the class, the instructor must place this problem before his students and stimulate their curiosity about it. To do this, he may simply state the problem and then cite cases indicating that animal preservation demands the sense of touch, such as the short life span of babies born without any tactile nerves and the difficulties in survival experienced by idiots, whose sense of touch is very poor.

Through questions about these cases, such as why babies without any tactile sense seldom survive, the teacher can deepen his students' awareness of the problem. As the students see the problem, the teacher can ask them to wonder about its solution. He might stimulate their thinking by questions such as the following: Does animal preservation require the sense of touch because of some characteristic found in all animals? If so, what is this particular quality? Would this quality necessarily be one that has a definite connection with the sense of touch?

2. Definition of Subject

In the foregoing questions the teacher is helping the students to seek some characteristic or definition of all animals which will solve the problem about animals' reliance upon a sense of touch. Having given the initial statement of the problem, the teacher's procedure now is to help the students find a definition of the subject (animal), so that they will see the subject as falling under a general principle about the sense of touch. Appropriately, after stating the problem, the teacher helps the students define the subject, for the deductive process is simply the application of a general principle to a particular case falling under such a principle. In the words of Aristotle: "Every demonstration proves a predicate of a subject as attaching or as not attaching to it."[67]

In order for the general principle to be applied to the particular subject, it is necessary to see the subject as a particular case of this principle, i.e., to define the subject as falling under this principle. Thus, if one will know why material things are corruptible, one must define them as things composed of parts. Immediately, then, one can place material things under the general principle *whatever has parts is corruptible* and see the conclusion *material things are corruptible*. Therefore, since deduction consists in an application such as this example illustrates, the teacher, having stated the problem, must help the students to define the subject.

To help the students seek some characteristic or definition of all animals making them reliant upon touch, the teacher must observe the following: (1) He must possess the correct answer himself. (2) He should first ask for suggestions from the students, thus obtaining a clear idea of their experiential background.

(3) If he receives the correct answer or an answer containing some of the correct elements, he should continue the clarification for those who could not have given such an answer. (4) If the teacher does not receive any suitable response, he must suggest possible solutions, one of which is the correct one.

In the circumstance that a given class is unaware of the characteristic of animals which makes them rely for their preservation upon the sense of touch, the teacher can suggest the following solutions: In order to live, do animals need touch because their bodies come in actual contact with many objects which are hot or cold, wet or dry, hard or soft? Or perhaps do animals need touch for survival because their bodies move from place to place? Again, do animals require touch because their bodies have weight? Finally, do animals, in order to preserve themselves, need touch because their bodies require some sense to permeate the whole body?

As the students are faced with various characteristics about animal bodies, such as contact with other bodies, weight, local movement, and overall sensitivity, they must choose the correct factor for solving the problem. Since their response must be the connecting link or middle term between animal preservation and the sense of touch, the pupils must survey the given characteristics, guided by the knowledge that their choice must be precisely such a connecting link. Therefore, by testing each suggestion for its worth as a middle term, the students should be able to see that animal preservation requires touch because the animal has constant contact with other bodies.

Contact with other bodies (together with a subsequent reaction) is the middle term of the problem, for, in order to survive, animals contacting other objects must be able to react to these objects and thus avoid those which are dangerous (such as fire) and accept those which are beneficial (such as water). If these animals could not react in such a way, they would not be able to preserve their existence. Since this reaction occurs through the sense of touch, all animals must have the tactile sense in order to survive. The syllogistic form of this particular problem is as follows:

> Whatever contacts other bodies needs a survival reaction.
> Animal bodies contact other bodies.
> ∴ Animal bodies need a survival reaction.
> Such survival reaction occurs from the sense of touch.
> ∴ Animal bodies need the sense of touch.[68]

To solve the foregoing problem by finding the correct middle term, the students made use of the following steps: (1) They first wondered about the problem. (2) They then sought to define the subject as falling under a general principle. To do this, they considered the teacher's suggested characteristics in the light of their own experience and of the fact that they were seeking a link between animal preservation and the sense of touch.

In addition to experience and the knowledge that they were seeking a middle term, however, the students required intuitive ability or native intelligence. In fact, Aristotle holds that this insight is a crucial factor in the process of defining the subject as falling under a general principle. He says that

> quick wit is a faculty of hitting upon the middle term instantaneously. It would be exemplified by a man who saw that the moon has her bright side always turned towards the sun, and quickly grasped the cause of this, namely that she borrows her light from him; or observed somebody in conversation with a man of wealth and divined that he was borrowing money, or that the friendship of these people sprang from a common enmity. In all these instances he has seen the major and minor terms and then grasped the causes, the middle terms.[69]

Aided by the suggestions of the teacher, their own experience, and most of all by their own intuitive ability, the students are able to find the middle term, i.e., to define the subject as falling under the general principle. At this moment the problem is solved, for, since the subject is so defined, the student can instantly see that the general principle is applicable to it. The fact that this particular definition of the subject solves the problem is pointed out in the following quotation:

> If, however, a term [a middle] is assumed in the *minor* proposition, concerning which it is manifest that it is contained under the universal in the major proposition, the truth of the *minor* proposition is evident, because that which is taken under the universal is under the knowledge of the universal, and thus the knowledge of the conclusion is had immediately.[70]

In our discussion of the deductive method of the teacher, which entails first a statement of the problem and then a definition of the subject as falling under a general principle, we have presumed that the general principle is known by the student. In the event that such is not the case, the teacher will be unable to proceed deductively in a given problem. First it will be necessary to establish the needed general principle, either by induction or deduction. Only after the students possess the needed foreknowledge of the general principle can the teacher proceed with the deductive method just outlined.

3. Needed Syllogistic Rules

In order to proceed accurately with the foregoing deductive method, the teacher must remember the various rules leading to correct form in the reasoning process. These rules include those which underlie the entire syllogistic process and those which pertain specifically to the three figures of the syllogism. Especially important for the teacher, however, are the general rules of the syllogism, for these basic principles contain potentially the specific rules of the three figures. By reason of the power of these basic principles, it is possible for the teacher to move correctly in various specific cases, although he would not find the converse to be true. Therefore, because of the essential character of these basic principles and because of the limitations imposed by the scope of this book, we shall discuss only the general rules that the teacher must know to have a correct syllogistic form for his deductive method of teaching.

Aristotle defines the syllogism as "discourse in which, certain things being stated, something other than what is stated follows of necessity from their being so."[71] The syllogistic procedure is one in which an individual moves from known premises to a hitherto unknown conclusion following from such premises. Expressed in relation to the material treated in this chapter, the syllogism is a mental formation which proceeds from a universal principle and a definition of a particular subject to a conclusion applying the predicate of the general principle to the particular subject. This application of the predicate to the subject is made possible by the definition of the subject, which forms a connecting link or middle term between them. An illustration of this syllogistic formation is as follows:

Whatever has parts	(M)	is corruptible.	(P)
Material things	(S)	have parts.	(M)
∴ Material things	(S)	are corruptible.	(P)

Since the syllogistic procedure is one which applies a predicate to a subject by means of a connecting middle term, the first and most basic rule of the syllogism is that it may have only three terms.[72] In the words of Aristotle: "Every demonstration and every syllogism will proceed through three terms only."[73] The very nature of the syllogism demands that it have only three terms, for its purpose is to attribute one thing to another by means of a common middle term. If the subject and the predicate were related to two different terms, it would be impossible to attribute the predicate to the subject, there being no common link between them. Consequently, from the very nature of the syllogistic procedure, we have the first rule that the teacher must observe in his deductive method: There may be only three terms in the syllogism.

Although on the surface this first rule may not seem difficult to observe, it can be easily violated because of the use of equivocation in language. Since a person often uses one word to mean two things, such as *pen* meaning a pig's shelter or a writing instrument, the one syllogizing may mean two different things as he repeats the same word for his middle term. As a result, although he has three words, he actually has four meanings or terms. Thus one might syllogize:

'Evils are good: for what needs to be is good, and evils must needs be.' For 'what needs to be' has a double meaning: it means what is inevitable, as often is the case with evils, too (for evil of some kind is inevitable), while on the other hand we say of good things as well that they 'need to be'.[74]

As this example illustrates, one's tendency to use words equivocally makes it a simple matter for him to violate the rule about only three terms in the syllogism.

In order to avoid the danger of equivocation and thus observe the need for only three terms in the deductive method of teaching, the instructor must make sure that the meaning or definition of the middle term is the same in both premises. If the teacher does not clarify the meaning of both usages of the middle term, he can easily violate the most basic rule of the syllogism. Thus, if he does not explain both usages of this term, he might syllogize as follows:

> The educational process is for moral and intellectual virtue.
> The teacher is the agent of the educational process.
> ∴ The teacher is the agent for moral and intellectual virtue.

Since education refers to the entire human development in the major premise, but only to the process of schooling in the minor premise, this particular term is used at best in only an analogous sense. As a result, this syllogism has more than three terms, and the conclusion is not valid. In order to avoid this danger of more than three terms, the teacher must always be careful about the meaning of the middle term in his deductive method of teaching. The instructor must not neglect to ask himself "the question whether in using the ambiguous term he has a simple meaning in view."[75]

The second syllogistic rule to be observed by the teacher is that the middle term must be taken universally at least once.[76] This means that either the subject or predicate must be connected with the middle term taken in a universal sense. This rule can be exemplified as follows:

> Everything with parts (*universal meaning*) is corruptible.
> All material things have parts.
> ∴ All material things are corruptible.

If neither the subject nor the predicate is related to the middle term taken universally, they would both be related to this term taken in a particular sense, and thus these two could be connected to two different parts of the middle term. To illustrate this:

> All petunias are plants.   (*one kind*)
> All maple trees are plants.   (*another kind*)
> ∴ Maple trees are not petunias, for they are different plants.

From the foregoing example we can see that, unless the middle term is taken universally at least once, the subject and predicate can be related to different parts of this middle. As a result there would be no real connecting link or middle term between them, and it would be impossible to have a conclusion attributing the predicate to the subject. Therefore it is absolutely necessary that the teacher proceeding deductively observe the following rule: The middle term must be taken universally at least once.

Failure to observe this second syllogistic rule results in a very common error in the reasoning process called the fallacy of consequence.[77] In this particular fallacy the individual, neglecting to observe this second rule, reaches his conclusion from the presumption that the predicate (consequent) has the same extension as the middle term (antecedent). Thus a person might syllogize as follows:

All rain makes the ground wet.
The streets of this city are wet.
∴ The streets of this city have had rain.

The conclusion of this particular syllogism is invalid, for the person does not have any case of the middle term taken universally, and he has concluded from the presumption that the middle term (*wet*) and the predicate (*rain*) have the same extension. Obviously, however, these two terms do not have equal extension, for the ground may become wet from other causes than rain, such as the overflowing of a river. Since it is not possible to hold automatically that the predicate and middle term have equal extension or are convertible, one must carefully observe the rule about the universality of the middle term in order to have a valid conclusion.

Is it ever possible for an individual to presume that his predicate and middle term are convertible and therefore to syllogize without apparently observing the rule about the universality of the middle term? This possibility can occur only if the predicate is peculiar to the middle term, i.e., if the predicate is a definition or a property of the given middle term.[78] Since the predicate is proper only to this middle term, one can proceed without any apparent universality taken in the middle term. To exemplify this:

Whatever can laugh is rational.
The human being is rational.
∴ The human being can laugh.

In the above syllogism the lack of universality in the middle term is only apparent, however, for the major premise can be converted as follows:

Whatever is rational can laugh.
The human being is rational.
∴ The human being can laugh.

As the present form of the above syllogism reveals, this syllogism does not violate the rule about the universality of the middle term. Since the predicate is convertible with the middle term, the need for universality of the middle term is observed and the conclusion is valid.

In his deductive method of teaching, the instructor must carefully observe the rule that the middle term must be taken universally at least once. Especially in reasoning from the outer effects or signs of things to their proper causes, the teacher must be vigilant concerning this rule.[79] Since the presence of a certain sign in a thing does not automatically mean that it is present only in this thing and therefore convertible with it, the teacher, in utilizing effects as middle terms, must see that this middle term has the proper universality. Otherwise the conclusions to which he leads his students will have no value. An example of a failure to observe this rule about the middle would be the following syllogism:

> A Communist sympathizer attends Communist-front organizations.
> The Jones family attend such organizations.
> ∴ The Jones family are Communist sympathizers.

Although the conclusion of the foregoing syllogism is often accepted, it is invalid because of a failure to observe the rule about the universality of the middle term. If the teacher wishes to avoid this common type of fallacy, he must check the way that he uses the middle term in his deductive method of teaching.

A third rule that the teacher must observe in his deductive procedure is the principle that two negative premises will yield no conclusion. The instructor cannot lead his students to any conclusion from two negative premises, for in such premises both the subject and the predicate are separated from the middle term. Since these two have no connecting link, there can be no conclusion applying the predicate to the subject. The following syllogism illustrates this:

> No human being is irrational.
> No cow is a human being.
> (These premises prove nothing about the cow.)

In the preceding syllogism no conclusion can be drawn, for there is no link established between the subject and the predicate. In order to proceed deductively, the teacher cannot utilize two negative premises; rather, "in every syllogism one of the premises must be affirmative."[80]

With this discussion of the third general rule of the syllogistic process, we have completed this section concerning the teacher's procedure in the deductive method. We have seen that this procedure is twofold: (1) a presentation of the problem; (2) a definition of the subject as falling under the general principle.

In order to insure that this procedure will not lead to invalid conclusions, the teacher must know at least the general rules for the formation of syllogisms. The most basic of these are as follows: (1) The syllogism may have only three terms. (2) The middle term of the syllogism must be taken universally at least once. (3) No conclusion can be drawn from two negative premises. Although the teacher should know many more specific rules in order to polish his deductive method, the foregoing twofold procedure, as well as the three basic rules of the syllogism, will give him the foundation for a real artistry in the deductive process of teaching.

Chapter 7

Conclusion

The purpose of this book has been to understand the activity of teaching by means of the doctrine of Aristotle. To accomplish this purpose we have examined teaching in general, treated the natural acquisition of knowledge, and finally considered the twofold procedure of teaching. In each of these three sections, we have emphasized the following order: (1) a statement of purpose, (2) a consideration of the needed materials, (3) an explanation of the procedure required to accomplish the purpose with the given materials.

We have used this order because Aristotle maintains that both nature and art work by starting with a given purpose, then collecting the needed materials, and finally moving into the proper procedure. Thus a building company first secures a blueprint, then buys the materials, and finally begins actual operations. Therefore, having completed the above mentioned three parts of the book in the order recommended by Aristotle, let us now summarize what we have been able to learn about teaching.

In our summarization we shall speak briefly about the most important points of the three sections of the book. Then we shall give a final statement about teaching taken from the material of the three sections. Since this statement will be drawn from the three parts of the summary, it will represent the principal thought about teaching as understood through Aristotle's doctrine.

As the principal point of the book, this final statement will be the theme which has permeated the whole work and will show its unity. Seen in the light of this statement, the separate parts of the book will be more understandable. Having served to provide the material for this principal point, these parts can now be understood as important sections of the pervading theme about teaching.

The first section of this book was a general examination of the definition, purpose, materials, and procedure of teaching. According to Aristotle, the teacher is one who gives his students a knowledge of the causes of things. The primary reason for the instructor's activity is to help his pupils know the proper causes of a thing and ultimately to lead his class to an understanding of the First Cause of all reality. This purpose of the teacher is a very lofty goal, for the primary reason for the human being's entire existence is the knowledge of the First Cause. All people naturally desire to know, for

> each thing naturally desires its own perfection. Hence matter is also said to desire form as any imperfect thing desires its perfection. Therefore, since the intellect, by which man is what he is, considered in itself is all things potentially, and becomes them actually only through knowledge, because the intellect is none of the things that exist before it understands them, as is stated in Book III of *The Soul*; so each man naturally desires knowledge just as matter desires form.[1]

To know is the very reason for human existence. Therefore, since the teacher's purpose for his students is the same as that of the whole of life, his work is one of real importance.

To accomplish his purpose, the teacher relies on two kinds of material: the native potential of his students and his own knowledge of the subject matter. Within each of the pupils being instructed is an active force called the agent intellect, through which each one is able to abstract the natures of sensible things from their individuating principles. This power in each student "actualises the intelligible notions themselves, abstracting them from matter, i.e., bringing them from potential to actual intelligibility."[2] Through this abstractive force, the pupils naturally understand the first concepts and principles of all knowledge, the chief of which are the concept of being and the principle of contradiction. These seeds of knowledge, grasped immediately when the reason begins to function, stand as the foundation upon which all later knowledge is built.

In addition to the potential of the student, the teacher's second material for his activity of teaching is his own knowledge of the subject matter. The instructor cannot give his students the proper causes of things unless he possesses this knowledge himself, "for what exists potentially must always be brought to actuality by an agent, which is an actual being. Hence what is potentially a man becomes actually a man as a result of the man who generates him, who is an actual being."[3]

Therefore the teacher must actually understand that which he is teaching. If possible, he must know his subject matter scientifically, i.e., he must know the proper causes, method, and chief conclusions of the subject matter. At this point he knows theoretically the method for explaining this subject, but he also needs experience in teaching it. This practice is needed, "for men of experience act more effectively than those who have the universal knowledge of an art but lack experience."[4]

Neither the potential of the student nor the knowledge and experience of the teacher can be omitted from the teaching process. Each has its own importance. Because of the abstractive power of his agent intellect, the student is able to listen to the spoken words of the teacher, abstract the essential meaning from these sensible signs, and thus advance in knowledge. Without this power, the student would be forced to remain in the sense order of sounds and motions through which his teacher is communicating to him. Thanks to the student's agent intellect, however, the teacher is able to set "before the pupil signs of intelligible things, and from these the agent intellect [of the pupil] derives the intelligible likenesses and causes them to exist in the possible intellect."[5]

Although the student is gifted with native abstractive ability, he still relies heavily on the knowledge of the teacher. The reason is that at first the pupil only potentially possesses the knowledge of the given lesson. Therefore he can easily fall into error about a given problem. To avoid this danger, the pupil needs the help of one who actually knows. Therefore, since the student only potentially understands the problem which is already clear to the teacher, the knowledge of the instructor is absolutely necessary for the teaching process. With his clear grasp of the subject matter, the teacher can "help him [the student] towards knowledge, leading him step by step from principles he already knows to conclusions hitherto unknown to him. Nor would this external aid be necessary if the human mind were always strong enough to deduce conclusions from the [first] principles it possesses by nature."[6]

To lead the student to the proper causes of things by relying on the student's native potential and his own knowledge of the subject, the teacher must operate in accordance with the correct procedure or method. According to Aristotle, the basic methodological principle to be used by the teacher and every other artist is that all art must imitate nature. In order to be successful the instructor must "look at the things which are of nature, and use them to bring about...[his] own work."[7]

Insofar as the teacher examines the student's natural procedure for acquiring knowledge, employs the sense objects of the natural world surrounding the student, and proceeds in accordance with the knowledge he has gleaned about the workings of the student's mind, he is using the basic methodological principle of teaching and can hope to accomplish his purpose.

In the second section of this text, we examined the student's natural procedure for acquiring knowledge. In this examination we treated first the objects of knowledge and then the procedure by which the student obtains an understanding of things. This order from object to procedure was deliberately chosen, for "the *type* of every act or operation is determined by an object."[8] Thus the process of building is determined by the object in which it terminates, namely, the finished dwelling. Since every procedure is determined by an object, we considered first the objects of knowledge and then the natural procedure for acquiring it.

Aristotle has two major principles concerning the objects of the human being's natural activity of knowing. The first is that human knowledge begins with the sense objects, "since all of the objects of our understanding are included within the range of sensible things existing in space, that is to say, that none seems to have that sort of distinct existence apart from things of sense which particular things of sense have apart from one another."[9]

The Philosopher's second principle about the objects of knowledge is that, although human knowing begins with the sense order, the proper object of his intellectual power is the essence of the material thing. Since the thing's essence

is precisely its proper causes, it is clear that the person's intellectual power seeks
to know the causes of things. This desire will never be satisfied until it rests in
the knowledge of the First Cause of all things.

To reach the object desired by his intellectual power, one follows a definite
natural procedure. In general, this procedure is a movement from potency to act,
for the human mind at first is "like a sheet of paper on which no word is yet
written, but many can be written."[10] Gifted with the abstractive power of his
agent intellect, however, the human being is able to actualize this potential state,
an actualization which is a reception of form without matter. Because one is
able to receive the forms of things without matter, he is able to actually know or
to be assimilated with the object of his knowledge.

Because of the assimilation proper to knowing Aristotle says that "the soul is
in a way all existing things."[11] By this he does not mean that the soul is

> simply identical with the things it knows; for not stone itself, but its formal like-
> ness exists in the soul. And this enables us to see how intellect in act *is* what it
> understands; the form of the object is the form of the mind in act.
> Thus the soul resembles the hand. The hand is the most perfect of organs, for it
> takes the place in man of all the organs given to other animals for purposes of de-
> fence or attack or covering. Man can provide all these needs for himself with his
> hands. And in the same way the soul in man takes the place of all the forms of
> being, so that through his soul a man is, in a way, all being or everything; his soul
> being able to assimilate all the forms of being—the intellect intelligible forms and
> the sense sensible forms.[12]

To assimilate the forms of things to itself, the human intellect follows the
twofold procedure of induction and deduction. Relying on both his sense and
intellectual powers, one obtains his first intellectual knowledge by an inductive
procedure. This process is one in which a person first senses and remembers a
given sense object. Following this, his cogitative power coalesces similar succeeding memories into experience by organizing them around the initial, stable
memory. As one's experience grows, his agent intellect is able to abstract from
such experience a universal concept or principle. This inductive procedure is
one which begins in sense knowledge and ends, because of the power of the
agent intellect, in a knowledge of the essence of the material thing.

By means of this inductive method, one is able to move from sense knowledge to the universal level. On this level the human being advances from the
known to the unknown by means of the reasoning or deductive process. This
reasoning procedure "is an argument in which, certain things being laid down,
something other than these necessarily comes about through them."[13] Having
reached the universal level, one reasons to the unknown by means of certain
things which he lays down or knows. Through knowledge of a general principle
and of a particular case defined as falling under this principle, one is able to apply the principle to the given case.

Since the definition of the subject constitutes a middle term between the universal principle and the given subject, one is able to connect these two, i.e., to apply the predicate of the principle to the subject. By this reasoning process the human being advances from the known to the unknown, seeking always the causes of things, and above all, the knowledge of the First Cause.

This deductive method, anchored to a firm sense foundation by means of the inductive method, constitutes the natural procedure that the human being follows when he acquires intellectual knowledge. According to Aristotle, these two methods are the human being's way of never neglecting sense knowledge and of arriving ultimately at the causes of things. The Philosopher shows that these two procedures are the human way of acquiring knowledge when he says that "every belief comes either through syllogism or from induction."[14]

In the third section of the book we examined the instructor's twofold method of teaching, which must imitate the student's natural manner of acquiring knowledge. Because of the teacher's reliance on the pupil's natural way of knowing, his procedure for explaining a subject matter will utilize the inductive and deductive techniques. By the inductive method the instructor can help the student obtain either definitions or universal propositions. To do this, the teacher must proceed in the following manner: (1) He must first give the class a statement of the problem, i.e., of the definition or proposition to be secured. (2) He must provide a sufficient number of singular cases of the given problem so that the students can abstract the needed universal.

In choosing his examples, the teacher should select those which are clear and striking so that these illustrations will make an impression upon the student's memory. As he presents these examples, the instructor should first utilize similar cases so that the students can intuit the desired universal; then he should present contrasting examples so that the class will see the point more clearly. As the students are first aware of the particular problem and then study the examples given to them, they will be able to arrive at the definition or universal proposition according to their degree of intuitive ability. Thus the teacher's purpose as he proceeds inductively is accomplished.

By the deductive method of teaching, the teacher is able to lead his students to scientific conclusions or at least to dialectical inferences preparatory to a later scientific understanding. Such conclusions can be obtained in all the arts and sciences, which are the various kinds of universal knowledge as contrasted with the singular knowledge of experience. Since the deductive method is one in which a universal principle is applied to a particular case falling under that principle, the teacher's materials for this method include both universal principles and the definition of the particular case.

In order to lead his students to scientific or dialectical conclusions by means of the above materials, the instructor's procedure must be as follows: (1) As in the inductive method, the teacher must give his class a statement of the problem. (2) Following this, he must help them to define the particular subject as falling under the universal principle. To assist the pupils in this process, the teacher may suggest possible definitions and then ask the students to consider these suggestions for their value as connecting links or middle terms between the subject and the principle. As the students consider the given problem and survey the possible middle terms before them, they will be able to select the correct definition according to their power of intuition. Having defined the subject as falling under the principle, the students can instantly see that the principle is applicable to the subject, and thus the problem is solved.

In helping the students to define the subject as falling under the universal principle, the teacher must carefully observe the various rules for the formation of the syllogism. Otherwise, no real link will be established between the principle and the subject, and the conclusion will be invalid. The most basic of the rules needed by the teacher (and also by the students) are as follows: (1) There may be only three terms in the syllogism. (2) The middle term must be taken universally at least once. (3) No conclusion follows from two negative premises. If the teacher wishes to lead his students to valid conclusions in his deductive method, he must be aware of at least these general rules.

With this explanation of the deductive method, we have completed our summary of the three sections of the book. We must now state the chief thought underlying all of these parts. As we consider the nature of the material that we have treated, we can formulate the principal point of the book as follows: According to Aristotle's doctrine, the teacher is one who leads his students to knowledge of the proper causes of things by means of both the students' potential and his own knowledge. To help his pupils learn about the causes of things and, above all, about the First Cause, the teacher will work in harmony with the students' natural way of knowing and thus will employ both the inductive and deductive methods. All the essential parts of this principal point are contained in the following quotations found at the beginning of the book:

1. All instruction given or received by way of argument proceeds from pre-existent knowledge.[15]
2. All teaching starts from what is already known, as we maintain in the *Analytics* also; for it proceeds sometimes through induction and sometimes by syllogism.[16]
3. The people who instruct us are those who tell the causes of each thing.[17]

More briefly stated, the principal point of this analysis of teaching by means of the doctrine of Aristotle is that the teacher is one who leads his students to a knowledge of causes and, to the degree that this is possible, to an understanding of the First Cause.

Appendix

Sample Lesson Plans

Outlines for Detailed Lesson Plan

Inductive	Deductive
A. Purpose	A. Purpose
B. Type (presentation/activity/review)	B. Type (presentation/activity/review)
C. Matter 　1. Lesson topic 　2. Teaching aids	C. Matter 　1. Lesson topic 　2. Teaching aids
D. Procedure 　1. Review 　　a. General 　　b. Specific 　2. Presentation 　　(Activity/Review) 　　a. State purpose 　　b. Fulfill purpose 　　　1) Singular cases 　　　　a) Initial case 　　　　b) Additional cases 　　　2) Abstraction 　3. Oral recall 　4. Assignment 　　(classwork/homework)	D. Procedure 　1. Review 　　a. General 　　b. Specific 　2. Presentation 　　(Activity/Review) 　　a. State purpose 　　b. Fulfill purpose 　　　1) Define subject under principle 　　　2) Refer to principle 　　　3) Grasp conclusion 　3. Oral recall 　4. Assignment 　　(classwork/homework)

This appendix was written and applied by Marie Granger, OP.

Inductive Lesson: Biological Science

A. Purpose: to observe that animals called mammals have hair or fur.

B. Type: presentation.

C. Matter
    1. **Lesson topic**: mammals, pp. 38-39.
    2. **Teaching aids**: live mouse in cage, pictures.

D. Procedure
    1. **Review**
        a. **General**: Recall animals as living things.
        b. **Specific**: Recall differences in shape and size of animals.
    2. **Presentation**
        a. **State purpose**: Tell students that today they will see that animals called mammals have fur or hair on their bodies.
        b. **Fulfill purpose**
            1) **Singular cases**
                a) **Initial case**: Observe the live mouse in the cage. Note that it has fur.
                b) **Additional cases**: Using textbook pictures of various mammals, observe that
                    (1) The bear, rabbit, and beaver have fur.
                    (2) The horse, elephant, and pig have hair.
            2) **Abstraction**: Tell students that all animals called mammals have hair or fur on their bodies.
    3. **Oral recall**: Give the names of various animals and ask the students to select the ones which have hair or fur.
    4. **Activity/Assignment**: Ask the students to find or draw two or more pictures of animals which have hair or fur. Mount pictures on colored construction paper. Place on bulletin board with caption: Animals called mammals have hair or fur.

(Each sample of a detailed lesson plan may be easily condensed to fit into the teacher's plan book.)

Inductive Lesson: Grammar

A. Purpose: to explain the definition of a descriptive adjective.

B. Type: presentation/activity.

C. Matter
   1. **Lesson topic**: descriptive adjective, pp. 138-39.
   2. **Teaching aids**: text, chalkboard, activity sheets, grammar review sheet.

D. Procedure
   1. **Review**: Recall the definition of noun and verb. Elicit examples of each from students.
   2. **Presentation**
      a. **State purpose**: Tell students that they are going to learn the definition of a descriptive adjective. Tell them that a descriptive adjective is a word that describes a noun.
      b. **Fulfill purpose**
         1) **Singular cases**
            a) **Initial case**: Place the phrase *sour lemon* on chalkboard. Point out that *sour* is a word that describes lemon. (It describes the taste of the lemon; it tells what kind of lemon it is.) Tell them that *sour* is a descriptive adjective because it describes *lemon* which is a noun.
            b) **Additional cases**
               (1) In chalkboard columns, separate adjectives from the noun:
               --ripe, sweet, red, chocolate, large (cherry),
               --tall, strong, feeble, smiling, old (man).
               Point out that each of the words in the first column describes the noun *cherry*; that each of the words in the second column describes the noun *man*.
               (2) Place the nouns *mother* and *tree* on the chalkboard. Elicit several descriptive adjectives for each noun from the students.
         2) **Abstraction**: Tell students that a descriptive adjective is a word that describes a noun.
   3. **Activity**: Complete the following: a textbook exercise orally; an adjective grammar review sheet.
   4. **Oral recall**: Ask several students to define and exemplify a descriptive adjective.
   5. **Assignment**: Ask students to complete each of the adjective activities which was begun in class.

Deductive Lesson: Physical Science

A. Purpose: to prove that the wind has force.

B. Type: presentation/activity.

C. Matter
   1. **Lesson topic**: wind, pp. 2-5.
   2. **Teaching aids**: text, chalkboard, fan, leaves, scraps of paper, boat, pan of water, pinwheel.

D. Procedure
   1. **Review**
      a. **General**: Recall the seasons of the year.
      b. **Specific**: Recall the definitions of wind and force.
   2. **Presentation**
      a. **State purpose**: Tell students that they will learn why the wind has force.
      b. **Fulfill purpose**
         1) **Define subject under principle**: Wind has the power to move things. The wind (a fan) moves leaves, scraps of paper, and boats.
         2) **Refer to principle**: Whatever has power to move things has force.
         3) **Grasp conclusion**: Therefore the wind has force.
   3. **Oral recall**: Ask a student to recall why the wind has force.
   4. **Activity**: Make a pinwheel. Show that the wind (a fan) can make it move.
   5. **Assignment**: Perform an experiment at home to show that the wind has force. Illustrate the experiment.

Deductive Lesson: Biological Science

A. Purpose: to prove that the grasshopper is an insect.

B. Type: presentation.

C. Matter
   1. Lesson topic: insects, pp. 217-22.
   2. Teaching aids: text, chalkboard, diagram or picture of grasshopper, over-
      head projector.

D. Procedure
   1. Review
      a. General: Recall the major divisions of living things studied thus far in
        chapter 8.
      b. Specific: Recall the class of crayfish. List several.
   2. Presentation
      a. State purpose: Tell students that they will learn why the grasshopper is
        an insect.
      b. Fulfill purpose
        1) Define subject under principle: Use overhead projector to view
          enlargement of a grasshopper. Pointing to the illustration, ask the
          students to observe that the grasshopper has:
          a) a hard outer skeleton (no back bone),
          b) a body with three parts: head, thorax, abdomen,
          c) three pairs of legs,
          d) two pairs of wings,
          e) two antennae,
          f) a number of spiracles on the abdomen,
          g) two compound eyes.
        2) Refer to principle: Any arthropod which has three distinct body
          parts, three pairs of jointed legs, wings (with few exceptions), one
          pair of antennae, spiracles and tracheal tubes (with some excep-
          tions), and eyes (usually both compound and simple) is an insect.
          (Clarify, if necessary.)
        3) Grasp conclusion: Tell students that the grasshopper is an insect
          because it has the above characteristics.
   3. Oral recall: Ask two or three students to recall the characteristics of in-
      sects.
   4. Assignment: For homework, ask the students to memorize the character-
      istics of insects.

Notes

Preface

1. Aristotle *Metaphysica* 1.2.982a29-30. This and all subsequent texts of Aristotle have been taken from the W. D. Ross translation, first edition (1910-31).
2. Aristotle *Ethica Nicomachea* 6.3.1139b26-28.
3. Aristotle *Physica* 2.2.194a22.
4. Aristotle *Analytica Posteriora* 2.19; *Metaphysica* 1.1.

Chapter 1: Teaching in General

1. Aristotle *Physica* 1.1.184a22-25.
2. Aristotle *De Partibus Animalium* 1.1.639b13-20.
3. Aristotle *Analytica Posteriora* 1.1.71a1-2.
4. Aristotle *Ethica Nicomachea* 6.3.1139b26-28.
5. Aristotle *Metaphysica* 1.2.982a29-30.
6. Aquinas *Summa Theologica* 1.117.1.c. This and all subsequent texts from the *Summa Theologica* have been taken from the English Dominican translation (1947-48).
7. Aquinas *Metaphysics* 9.7.1848; cf. Aristotle *Metaphysica* 9.8.1049b24-26.
8. Aquinas *De Anima* 2.11.372.
9. Aristotle *Rhetorica* 2.23.1398b9-16.
10. Aristotle *Topica* 1.12.105a13-16.
11. Aristotle *De Caelo* 2.14.297b31-298a5.
12. Usually the movement from the known to the unknown refers to the deductive process. The following quotation illustrates this particular usage of the phrase: "Now when anyone applies these universal principles to certain particular things, the memory or experience of which he acquires through the senses; then by his own research advancing from the known to the unknown, he obtains knowledge of what he knew not before" (Aquinas *Summa Theologica* 1.117.1.c.).
   In this book, however, we shall use the phrase *known to the unknown* as including both induction and deduction, unless the context indicates otherwise.
13. Aristotle *Topica* 1.1.100a25-26.
14. Aristotle *Analytica Priora* 2.23.68b10-14.
15. Aristotle *Ethica Nicomachea* 6.3.1339b27-30; cf. Aristotle *Analytica Posteriora* 1.18.81b6-9.
16. Aristotle *Metaphysica* 1.2.982a29-30.
17. Aquinas *Posterior Analytics* 1.4.5; cf. Aristotle *Metaphysica* 2.1.993b19-30.
18. Aristotle *Metaphysica* 1.1.981a25-29.

19. Aquinas *Metaphysics* 1.1.29. (The word *only* was in brackets in the original quotation.) Cf. Aristotle *Metaphysica* 1.1.981b7-9.

20. Aristotle *Analytica Posteriora* 1.2.71b8-12.

21. Aquinas *Posterior Analytics* 2.7.8; cf. Aristotle *Analytica Posteriora* 2.8.93a28-93b8.

22. Aristotle *Metaphysica* 1.2.982a29-30.

23. Aristotle *De Partibus Animalium* 1.1.639a2-13.

24. Aquinas *Metaphysics* 1.2.36; cf. Aristotle *Metaphysica* 1.2.982a8-10.

25. Aquinas *Metaphysics* 1.1.35.; cf. Aristotle *Metaphysica* 1.1.981b27-982a2.

26. Aquinas *Metaphysics* 11.1.2146.

27. Aquinas *De Anima* 3.8.701; cf. Aristotle *De Anima* 3.4.429b5-9.

28. Aristotle *Ethica Nichomachea* 2.6.1106a15-19; cf. Aquinas *Summa Theologica* 1-2.55.2.c.

29. Aristotle *Metaphysica* 1.2.982a29-30.

30. Aristotle *Ethica Nicomachea* 2.1.1103a14-15.

31. Aristotle *De Partibus Animalium* 1.5.644b32-645a1; cf. Aquinas *Truth* 3.27.2.c.

32. Aristotle *Ethica Nicomachea* 1.1.1094a21-22.

33. Ibid. 13.1102a5-1103a10.

34. Aristotle *Politica* 7.13.1332b9-10.

35. Aristotle *Ethica Nicomachea* 1.7.1098a8-17.

36. Ibid. 2.6.1106a16-17.

37. Aristotle *Politica* 7.15.1334b14-28.

38. Ibid.

39. Aristotle *Ethica Nicomachea* 10.7.1178a1-3.

40. Aquinas *Politics* 1.1.33 (quoted in Conway, *Principles*, 11).

41. Aquinas *Posterior Analytics* 1.1.1; cf. Aristotle *Metaphysica* 1.1.980b25-27.

42. Aristotle *Ethica Nicomachea* 1.7.1097b26-29.

43. Ibid. 1098a16-17.

44. Aristotle *Ethica Nicomachea* 10.7.1177a20-1177b4.

45. Ibid. 1.1.1094a21-22.

46. Aristotle *De Partibus Animalium* 1.1.639b27-31.

47. Aquinas *Truth* 2.11.4.c.

48. Aristotle *Analytica Posteriora* 2.19.100a13-14.

49. Aristotle *Metaphysica* 9.8.1050a1.

50. Ibid. 5.12.1019a15-18.

51. Ibid. 20-22.

52. Ibid. 15-22.

53. Aquinas *Metaphysics* 5.14.955.

54. Aristotle *Physica* 8.4.254b25-27; cf. Aquinas *Physics* 8.7.1024-28.

55. The potential of the student can be defined as the source of the movement toward knowledge only if we use movement in the broad sense of the term. In fact, "least strictly of all, and indeed only by a metaphor, is movement to be ascribed to the act of the intellect, in which there is no movement of the material substance, as in the case of vegetative activities, nor even any alteration of the subject of 'spiritual' operations, as in the case of sense-awareness. There is only an activity which is *called* movement simply because the mind goes from potency into act. This differs from movement proper; for whereas the latter connotes an imperfection in the moving subject, this activity proceeds from the subject as already perfect and complete." (Aquinas *De Anima* 1.10.160).

56. Aristotle *Analytica Posteriora* 2.19.100a13-14.

57. Aquinas *De Anima* 3.10.728; cf. Aristotle *De Anima* 2.5.430a10-13.

58. Aquinas *De Anima* 3.7.681; cf. Aristotle *De Anima* 3.4.429a22-24.

59. Aquinas *De Anima* 3.7.680.

60. Ibid. 3.10.730; cf. Aristotle *De Anima* 3.5.430a14-17.

61. Aquinas *De Anima* 3.10.739.

62. For a more complete treatment of first concepts and principles, see pp. 106-12.

63. Aquinas *Truth* 2.11.1.c.; cf. Aristotle *Analytica Posteriora* 2.19.

64. Aristotle *De Sensu et Sensibili* 1.437a12; cf. Aquinas *Metaphysics* 1.1.12.

65. Aquinas *Truth* 2.11.1.ad11; cf. Aristotle *De Anima* 3.4.429b5-24.

66. Aquinas *De Unitate Intellectus* 5.51 (quoted in Conway, *Principles*, 149).

67. Aristotle *Metaphysica* 1.1.981a16-20; cf. Aquinas *Metaphysics* 1.1.20.

68. Aristotle *Physica* 8.5.257a13.

69. Aristotle *De Anima* 2.5.417b12-14.

70. Aristotle *Metaphysica* 1.1.981b7-8; 2.982a29-30.

71. Aquinas *Metaphysics* 9.7.1848; cf. Aristotle *Metaphysica* 9.8.1049b24-26.

72. Aquinas *Metaphysics* 1.1.29; cf. Aristotle *Metaphysica* 1.1.981b7-8.

73. Aquinas *Physics* 8.9.1047; cf. Aristotle *Physica* 8.5.257a13-14.

74. Aristotle *De Partibus Animalium* 1.1.639a6-7.

75. Aquinas *Metaphysics* 1.1.35; cf. Aristotle *Metaphysica* 1.1.981b27-28.

76. Aristotle *Analytica Posteriora* 1.2.71b10-12.

77. Aristotle *Ethica Nicomachea* 6.3.1139b33-34.

78. Ibid. 1.3.1094b15-28; cf. Aquinas *De Trinitate* 6.1.c.

79. Aristotle *De Anima* 2.5.417b13-14.

80. Aquinas *Metaphysics* 2.5.335; cf. Aristotle *Metaphysica* 2.3.995a12-14.

81. Aristotle *De Anima* 1.1.403a29-403b4; cf. Aquinas *De Anima* 1.2.24-30.

82. Aquinas *Metaphysics* 2.5.335; cf. Aristotle *Metaphysica* 2.3.995a12-14.

83. Aristotle *Analytica Priora* 2.23.68b10-14; cf. Aristotle *Analytica Posteriora* 1.1.71a1-10.

84. Aristotle *De Anima* 3.8.432a3-7.

85. Aquinas *De Anima* 3.4.631.

86. Aristotle *Ethica Nicomachea* 6.3.1139b26-28.

87. Aquinas *Summa Theologica* 1.117.1.c.; cf. Aristotle *Ethica Nicomachea* 6.3.1139b26-28.

88. Aristotle *Metaphysica* 1.1.981b7-8.

89. Ibid. 981a13-15. When Aristotle says that men of experience have more success than those with only theory, he is speaking solely about the practical order, concerned with theory and application. He is not referring to the speculative order, in which there is only theory, only the consideration of the truth. For this reason, this quotation does not apply to the contemplative part of teaching, to the part concerned with the teacher's study of the speculative sciences in order to understand them, but only to the active part of this activity, namely, the giving of such truth to the student.

90. Aquinas *Metaphysics* 1.1.19; cf. Aristotle *Metaphysica* 1.1.981a7-12.

91. Aquinas *Metaphysics* 1.1.20; cf. Aristotle *Metaphysica* 1.1.981b13-15.

92. Aquinas *De Anima* 3.9.722; cf. Aristotle *De Anima* 3.4.429b33-430a2.

93. Aquinas *De Anima* 3.4.624; cf. Aristotle *De Anima* 3.3.427b1-3.

94. Aquinas *De Anima* 2.11.372; cf. Aristotle *Ethica Nicomachea* 6.3.1139b26-30.

95. Aristotle *Ethica Nicomachea* 2.1.1103a14-15.

96. Ibid. 1.7.1098b6-7.

97. Aristotle *De Sophisticis Elenchis* 2.165b3.

98. Aquinas *Posterior Analytics* 1.1.6; cf. Aristotle *De Anima* 3.3.428a20-428b8.

99. Aquinas *Posterior Analytics* 1.3.6.
100. Aquinas *Truth* 2.14.10.c.; cf. Aristotle *Metaphysica* 9.8.1049b18-28.
101. Aristotle *Ethica Nicomachea* 1.3.1094b29-30.
102. Ibid. 6.1.1139a7-9.
103. Aquinas *Metaphysics* 2.2.290; cf. Aristotle *Metaphysica* 2.1.993b19-23.
104. Aquinas *Ethics* 10.14.2138; cf. Aristotle *Ethica Nicomachea* 10.9.1179a35-1179b3.
105. When we cite this possibility, we are referring to the teacher who is studying a speculative science, such as mathematics or natural science. The teacher, both in his study and in his teaching of a practical subject (such as engineering), is ordained to the practical order.
106. Aristotle *Metaphysica* 9.8.1050a18-19.
107. Ibid. 5.2.1013b26-27.
108. Ibid. 9.8.1050a18-19; cf. Aquinas *Truth* 2.11.4.c.
109. Aquinas *Ethics* 10.14.2138.
110. Aquinas *Metaphysics* 7.6.1381-82; cf. Aristotle *Metaphysica* 7.7.1032a11-12.
111. Aristotle *Metaphysica* 1.1.981b7-9.
112. Aristotle *Ethica Nicomachea* 6.4.1140a9-11.
113. Ibid. 11-14.
114. Ibid. 14-15.
115. Aquinas *Summa Theologica* 1-2.57.3.c.
116. Aquinas *Metaphysics* 9.8.1862; cf. Aristotle *Metaphysica* 9.8.1050a23-29.
117. Aquinas *Metaphysics* 6.1.1152.
118. Aristotle *Ethica Nicomachea* 6.4.1140a20-23.
119. Aquinas *Summa Theologica* 1-2.49.4.c.
120. Aristotle *De Anima* 2.5.417b12-14; cf. Aquinas *Truth* 2.11.2.c.
121. Aristotle *Metaphysica* 1.2.982a30.
122. Aquinas *Truth* 2.11.1.c.
123. Aquinas *Posterior Analytics* 1.1.1.
124. Aristotle *Metaphysica* 1.1.981a5-12.
125. Aristotle *Physica* 2.2.194a22.
126. Aquinas *Politics* Prooem.2 (quoted in Conway, *Principles*, 36).
127. Aristotle *Meteorologica* 4.3.381b3-8.
128. Aquinas *Physics* 2.4.171.
129. Ibid. 2.14.268; cf. Aristotle *Physica* 2.8.199b28-31.
130. Aquinas *Summa Contra Gentiles* 2.75.

Chapter 2: Natural Objects in Knowing

1. Aristotle *De Anima* 2.4.415a15-23; cf. Aquinas *De Anima* 2.6.304-5.
2. Aquinas *De Anima* 3.7.676; cf. Aristotle *De Anima* 3.4.429a12-17.
3. Aristotle *De Anima* 2.4.416a15-18; cf. Aquinas *De Anima* 2.8.332.
4. Aquinas *De Anima* 2.6.305; cf. Aristotle *De Anima* 2.4.415a15-23.
5. Aristotle *De Anima* 2.4.415a15-23; cf. Aquinas *De Anima* 1.8.111.
6. Aquinas *De Anima* 2.3.259; cf. Aristotle *De Anima* 2.2.413b1-5.
7. De Koninck, "Abstraction," 187.
8. Aristotle *De Anima* 2.6.418a7-25.
9. Aquinas *De Anima* 2.13.384; cf. Aristotle *De Anima* 2.6.418a10-18.
10. Aquinas *De Anima* 2.13.386; cf. Aristotle *De Anima* 2.6.418a18-20.
11. Aquinas *De Anima* 3.1.577; cf. Aristotle *De Anima* 3.1.425a15-30.

12. Aquinas *De Anima* 2.13.393; cf. Aristotle *De Anima* 2.6.418a20-25.
13. Aquinas *De Anima* 3.1.577; cf. Aristotle *De Anima* 3.1.425a15-30.
14. De Koninck, "Abstraction," 170.
15. The following quotation clarifies the fact that quantity is the immediate subject of quality: "Since all accidents are related to substance as form to matter, and since the nature of every accident is to depend on substance, any accidental form cannot possibly be separated from substance. Accidents, however, befall substance in a definite order. Quantity comes first, then quality, then passions and motion. So quantity can be considered in substance before the sensible qualities, in virtue of which matter is called sensible, are understood in it." (Aquinas *De Trinitate* 5.3.c.).
16. Aquinas *De Anima* 2.13.395; cf. Aristotle *De Anima* 2.6.418a20-25.
17. Aquinas *De Anima* 2.13.396.
18. Ibid. 398.
19. Ibid. 384; cf. Aristotle *De Anima* 2.6.418a11-13.
20. Aristotle *De Anima* 2.6.418a15-17.
21. Aquinas *De Anima* 3.6.661; cf. Aristotle *De Anima* 3.3.428b18-30.
22. Aquinas *Truth* 1.1.11.c.
23. Aristotle *De Anima* 3.6.429b26-430a5; cf. Aquinas *Truth* 1.1.3.c.
24. Aristotle *De Anima* 2.6.418a15-17; cf. Aquinas *Metaphysics* 4.12.672-73.
25. Aquinas *De Anima* 2.1.215; cf. Aristotle *De Anima* 2.1.412a6-12.
26. Aquinas *Metaphysics* 7.2.1277; cf. Aristotle *Metaphysica* 7.3.1029a3-5.
27. Aquinas *Posterior Analytics* 1.2.5; cf. Aristotle *Analytica Posteriora* 1.1.71a10-15.
28. Aquinas *Metaphysics* 7.2.1302,1304.
29. Aristotle *Metaphysica* 9.9.1051a22-30.
30. Aquinas *De Anima* 2.1.215.
31. Aquinas *Metaphysics* 5.2.775; cf. Aristotle *Metaphysica* 5.2.
32. Aquinas *Metaphysics* 3.8.435.
33. Aristotle *De Anima* 3.4.429b10-23; cf. Aquinas *Summa Theologica* 1.84.1.c.
34. Aquinas *Summa Theologica* 1.7.1.c.; cf. Aristotle *Metaphysica* 10.9.
35. Aquinas *De Anima* 2.5.283.
36. Ibid. 3.8.706.
37. Aquinas *Metaphysics* 5.8.876.
38. Ibid. 7.15.1626; cf. Aristotle *Metaphysica* 7.15.1040a23-28.
39. Aquinas *Summa Theologica* 1.7.1.c.; cf. Aquinas *Metaphysics* 7.15.1618.
40. Aquinas *De Anima* 3.8.706; cf. Aristotle *Metaphysica* 7.10.1035a1-35.
41. Aristotle *De Anima* 2.5.417b22-23.
42. Aquinas *De Anima* 2.12.377.
43. Aquinas *Summa Theologica* 1.84.2.c.; cf. Aristotle *De Anima* 2.12.424a17-23.
44. Aquinas *Summa Theologica* 1.84.2.c.
45. Aquinas *Truth*.1.1.1.c.; cf. Aristotle *De Anima* 3.2.425b26-426a26.
46. De Koninck, "Abstraction," 167.
47. Aquinas *Summa Theologica* 1.84.7.c.
48. Aquinas *De Anima* 3.13.791; cf. Aristotle *De Anima* 3.8.432a2-8.
49. De Koninck, "Abstraction," 169.
50. Aristotle *De Caelo* 3.7.306a16-18.
51. Aquinas *Truth* 2.12.3.ad2.
52. De Koninck, "Abstraction," 186.
53. Aristotle *Metaphysica* 1.1.980a27-28.
54. Aristotle *De Sensu et Sensibili* 1.437a11-12.

55. Aristotle *De Anima* 3.13.435a16.
56. Aristotle *De Sensu et Sensibili* 1.437a5-10; cf. Aquinas *Metaphysics* 1.1.8.
57. Aquinas *Metaphysics* 1.1.8. (The section in brackets is part of the quotation.)
58. Aristotle *De Anima* 2.7.418b5-13; cf. Aquinas *De Anima* 2.14.
59. Aristotle *De Sensu et Sensibili* 1.437a7-11.
60. Ibid. 11-12.
61. Aristotle *De Interpretatione* 1.16a3-4; cf. Aquinas *Truth* 2.11.1.ad11.
62. Aristotle *De Sensu et Sensibili* 1.437a11-12.
63. Ibid. 1. 437a3-16.
64. Aquinas *De Anima* 3.18.865; cf. Aristotle *De Anima* 3.13.435a12-19.
65. Aristotle *De Anima* 3.12.434b18-22.
66. Aquinas *De Anima* 3.17.861.
67. De Koninck, "Abstraction," 187.
68. Aquinas *De Anima* 3.13.791; cf. Aristotle *De Anima* 3.8.432a2-8.
69. Aristotle *De Generatione and Corruptione* 1.2.316a10.
70. Aristotle *De Caelo* 3.7.306a9.
71. Aristotle *De Anima* 4.2.426b8-17; cf. Aquinas *De Anima* 3.3.603.
72. Aquinas *De Anima* 3.3.609.
73. Ibid; cf. Aristotle *De Anima* 3.2.426b10-14.
74. Aquinas *De Anima* 3.3.601; cf. Aristotle *De Anima* 3.2.426b8-17.
75. Aquinas *Summa Theologica* 1.78.4.ad2.
76. Ibid.; cf. Aristotle *De Anima* 3.2.426b16-28.
77. Aquinas *De Anima* 3.12.773; cf. Aristotle *De Anima* 3.7.431a20-30.
78. Aquinas *De Anima* 3.3.612.
79. Reith, *Psychology*, 102; cf. Aquinas *Summa Theologica* 1.14.2.ad1.
80. Aquinas *Summa Theologica* 1.78.4.ad2.
81. Aristotle *De Anima* 2.6.418a20-25; cf. Aquinas *De Anima* 2.13.390.
82. Aquinas *De Anima* 3.6.659; cf. Aristotle *De Anima* 3.3.428b10-18.
83. Aquinas *De Anima* 3.6.658.
84. Ibid. 659.
85. Lennon, "Nature of Experience," 73.
86. Aquinas *Summa Theologica* 2-2.173.2.c.; cf. Aristotle *De Anima* 3.3.427b18-20.
87. Aquinas *De Anima* 3.6.664; cf. Aristotle *De Anima* 3.3.428b18-30.
88. Aquinas *Summa Theologica* 1.78.4.c.
89. Aquinas *De Anima* 2.13.393; cf. Aristotle *De Anima* 2.6.418a20-25.
90. Aquinas *Summa Theologica* 1.78.4.c.
91. Ibid.
92. Aquinas *Metaphysics* 1.1.15. (The section in brackets is part of the quotation.) Cf. Aristotle *Metaphysica* 1.1.980b25-30.
93. Aquinas *Posterior Analytics* 2.20.11; cf. Aristotle *Analytica Posteriora* 2.19.100a1-6.
94. Aquinas *Truth* 2.14.1.ad9.
95. Aquinas *Metaphysics* 1.1.15; cf. Aristotle *Metaphysica* 1.1.980b25-27.
96. Aquinas *Posterior Analytics* 2.20.14; cf. Aristotle *Analytica Posteriora* 2.19.100a14-100b3.
97. Aquinas *De Anima* 2.13.398.
98. Ibid.
99. Aquinas *Summa Theologica* 1-2.3.8.c.; cf. Aristotle *Metaphysica* 1.2.982b11-983a23.
100. Aristotle *Metaphysica* 5.2.1013b25-28; cf. Aquinas *Metaphysics* 5.3.782.

101. Aquinas *Summa Theologica* 1.84.6.c.
102. Aquinas *Metaphysics* 1.1.14; cf. Aristotle *Metaphysica* 1.1.980b25-27.
103. Aquinas *Posterior Analytics* 2.20.14; cf. Aristotle *Analytica Posteriora* 2.19.100a14-100b4.
104. Aristotle *De Memoria et Reminiscentia* 1.449b26-28.
105. Aquinas *Summa Theologica* 1.79.6.c.; cf. Aristotle *Physica* 4.11.
106. If, however, we consider memory only as the ability to retain the forms of things, not as individuated by a time element, then it is found in the intellect. "For what is received into something is received according to the conditions of the recipient. But the intellect is of a more stable nature, and is more immovable than corporeal matter. If, therefore, corporeal matter holds the forms which it receives, not only while it actually does something through them but also after ceasing to act through them, much more cogent reason is there for the intellect to receive the species unchangeably and lastingly, whether it receive them from things sensible, or derive them from some superior intellect. Thus, therefore, if we take memory only for the power of retaining species, we must say that it is in the intellectual part" (Aquinas *Summa Theologica* 1.79.6.c.).
107. Ibid. 2-2.49.1.ad2; cf. Aristotle *De Memoria et Reminiscentia* 2.451b13-16.
108. Aquinas *Summa Theologica* 1.78.4.c.
109. Aquinas *De Anima* 2.18.397.
110. Aquinas *Summa Theologica* 1.78.4.c.
111. Aristotle *De Memoria et Reminiscentia* 2.453a10-13. (The section in brackets is part of the quotation.)
112. Aquinas *Metaphysics* 5.10.902; cf. Aristotle *Metaphysica* 5.8.1017b22-23.
113. Aquinas *On Being and Essence* chap.1.
114. Aristotle *De Anima* 2.5.417b22-23.
115. It must be emphasized here that we do not know ideas or images, but that we know by means of them. See Aristotle *Metaphysica* 7.6.1031b12-22; cf. Aquinas *De Anima* 3.8.718.
116. Guralnik, *Webster's Dictionary*, 864.
117. Aquinas *De Anima* 3.8.706; cf. Aristotle *Metaphysica* 7.10.1035a1-35.
118. Aquinas *Summa Theologica* 1.84.1.c; cf. Aristotle *Metaphysica* 1.6.
119. Aristotle *Physica* 5.3; cf. Aquinas *Physics* 2.5.
120. Aristotle *Metaphysica* 1.7.988a34-35.
121. Aquinas *De Anima* 3.8.705. See Aristotle *Metaphysica* 7.6; Aquinas *Metaphysics* 7.5.
122. Aquinas *De Anima* 3.8.717.
123. Aquinas *Summa Theologica* 1.84.1.c.
124. Aquinas *De Anima* 3.8.717; cf. Aristotle *Metaphysica* 1.6.
125. Aristotle *De Anima* 3.3.427b7-15.
126. Aquinas *Metaphysics* 1.1.15; cf. Aristotle *Metaphysica* 1.1.980b25-26.

Chapter 3: Natural Way Knowing Occurs

1. Reith, *Psychology*, 78.
2. Aquinas *Truth* 1.2.2.c.
3. Ibid. 1.1.1.c.; cf. Aristotle *De Anima* 3.2.425b18-426a26.
4. Aquinas *De Anima* 3.2.590; cf. Aristotle *De Anima* 3.2.425b26-426a26.
5. Aquinas *De Anima* 3.9.723; cf. Aristotle *De Anima* 1.2.404b8-29.
6. Plato *Meno* 81a-81e.

7. Aquinas *Posterior Analytics* 1.3.2; cf. Aristotle *Analytica Posteriora* 1.1.71a28-30; Aquinas *Truth* 2.11.1.c.

8. Aristotle *Analytica Posteriora* 1.1.71b6-7; see Aristotle *Metaphysica* 9.9.1051a22-30.

9. Aristotle *Analytica Posteriora* 1.1.71a26-71b8; cf. Aquinas *Posterior Analytics* 1.3.1.

10. Aquinas *De Anima* 1.4.43; cf. Aristotle *De Anima* 3.2.425b18-426a26.

11. Aquinas *De Anima* 2.10.351; cf. Aristotle *De Anima* 1.1.404b7-15.

12. Aristotle *De Anima* 3.3.427a21-27.

13. Aquinas *De Anima* 3.7.675. (Italics mine.) Cf. Aristotle *De Anima* 3.4.429a13-18.

14. Aquinas *De Anima* 3.10.728. (Italics mine.) Cf. Aristotle *De Anima* 3.5.430a10-14.

15. Aristotle *De Anima* 2.5.417a3-6.

16. Ibid. 3-9; cf. Aquinas *Summa Theologica* 1.84.3.c.

17. Aristotle *De Generatione et Corruptione* 1.7.323b3-324a25; cf. Aquinas *De Anima* 2.10.351,357.

18. Aquinas *De Anima* 2.10.351; cf. Aristotle *De Anima* 2.5.417a17-21.

19. Aristotle *De Anima* 2.5.416b33-417a3; cf. Aquinas *De Anima* 2.10.350,354.

20. Aristotle *Physica* 1.1.184a22-25.

21. Aristotle *De Anima* 1.2.403b20-23.

22. Ibid. 2.12.424a17-18.

23. Aquinas *De Anima* 3.7.676; cf. Aristotle *De Anima* 3.4.429a13-19.

24. Aquinas *De Anima* 2.11.359; cf. Aristotle *De Anima* 2.5.417a23-25.

25. Aquinas *De Anima* 2.11.361; cf. Aristotle *De Anima* 2.5.417a26-31.

26. Aquinas *De Anima* 2.12.373-74; cf. Aristotle *De Anima* 2.5.417b17-19.

27. Aquinas *De Anima* 2.12.373.

28. Ibid. 1.12.183; cf. Aristotle *De Anima* 2.5.416b33-35.

29. Aquinas *De Anima* 2.14.418; cf. Aristotle *De Anima* 2.12.424b12-13.

30. Aquinas *De Anima* 2.12.375; cf. Aristotle *De Anima* 2.5.417b24-25.

31. Aristotle *Metaphysica* 5.12.1019a20-24; cf. Aquinas *Metaphysics* 5.14.956-58.

32. Aquinas *Metaphysics* 5.14.958; cf. Aristotle *De Anima* 2.5.417b2-8.

33. Ibid.

34. Ibid.; see Aquinas *De Anima* 2.11.365-66.

35. Aquinas *Metaphysics* 5.14.963; cf. Aristotle *Metaphysica* 5.12.1019b1-6.

36. Aristotle *Analytica Posteriora* 2.19; cf. Aquinas *Posterior Analytics* 2.20.

37. Aquinas *De Anima* 2.11.372; cf. Aristotle *Analytica Posteriora* 1.1.71a11-28.

38. Aquinas *De Anima* 2.11.366; cf. Aristotle *De Anima* 2.5.417b6-8.

39. Aristotle *De Anima* 2.5.417b7.

40. Ibid. 3.7.431a4-6.

41. Ibid. 1.4.408b8-17; cf. Aquinas *De Anima* 1.10.157-60.

42. Aquinas *De Anima* 2.24.553; cf. Aristotle *De Anima* 2.12. 424a17-23.

43. Aristotle *De Anima* 2.12.424a17-23.

44. Ibid. 17-18.

45. Aquinas *Truth* 1.1.1.c.; cf. Aristotle *De Anima* 3.2.425b26-426a26.

46. Aristotle *De Anima* 2.5.417b7.

47. Aquinas *De Anima* 2.5.283; cf. Aristotle *Metaphysica* 10.9.1058b1-20.

48. Aquinas *Metaphysics* 7.15.1626; cf. Aristotle *Metaphysica* 7.15.1040a23-28.

49. Aristotle *De Anima* 2.12.424a17-18.

50. Aquinas *Truth* 1.2.2.c.; cf. Aristotle *De Anima* 2.12.424a17-424b2.

51. This in no way indicates that the sense is an incorporeal faculty like the intellect. Rather it is the form of a bodily organ, causing it to receive species without matter, but under the individuating conditions of matter. "For a sense-organ, e.g. the eye, shares the same being with the faculty or power itself, though it differs in essence or definition, the faculty being as it were the form of the organ.... So he [Aristotle] goes on to say 'an extended magnitude', i.e. a bodily organ is 'what receives sensation', i.e. is the *subject* of the sense-faculty, as matter is subject of form; and yet the magnitude and the sensitivity or sense differ by definition, the sense being a certain ratio, i.e., proportion and form and capacity, of the magnitude." (Aquinas *De Anima* 2.24.555). See Aristotle *De Anima* 2.12.424a24-28.

52. Aquinas *Summa Theologica* 1.78.3.c.; cf. Aristotle *De Anima* 2.12.424a17-23.

53. Aquinas *De Anima* 3.2.591; cf. Aristotle *De Anima* 3.2.425b26-27.

54. Aristotle *De Anima* 3.8.431b22-23.

55. Ibid. 2.425b26-426a2.

56. Ibid. 8.431b21.

57. Aquinas *De Anima* 3.13.789-90; cf. Aristotle *De Anima* 3.8.431b20-432a3.

58. Aquinas *De Anima* 3.12.766; cf. Aristotle *De Anima* 3.7.431a1-8.

59. Aquinas *De Anima* 3.2.592; cf. Aristotle *De Anima* 3.2.425b26-426a15.

60. Aristotle *De Anima* 3.8.431b21.

61. Aquinas *Truth* 1.2.2.c.

62. Aquinas *De Anima* 3.7.675; cf. Aristotle *De Anima* 3.4.429a13-17.

63. Aquinas *De Anima* 3.7.680; cf. Aristotle *De Anima* 3.4.429a18-24.

64. Aquinas *De Anima* 2.11.366; cf. Aristotle *De Anima* 2.5.417b2-8.

65. Aquinas *De Anima* 3.9.722; cf. Aristotle *De Anima* 3.4.429b29-430a2.

66. Aquinas *De Anima* 3.7.684.

67. Ibid.; cf. Aristotle *De Anima* 3.4.429a24-28.

68. Aristotle *De Anima* 3.5.430a20-25; cf. Aquinas *De Anima* 3.10.743.

69. Aquinas *De Anima* 1.2.21; cf. Aristotle *De Anima* 1.1.403a10-16.

70. Ibid.

71. Aquinas *De Anima* 3.10.728; cf. Aristotle *De Anima* 3.5.430a10-14.

72. Aquinas *De Anima* 3.10.729; cf. Aristotle *De Anima* 3.5.430a14-17.

73. Aquinas *Truth* 2.11.1.c.

74. Aristotle *Physica* 1.1.184a22-26, 184b9-14; cf. Aquinas *De Anima* 3.10.729.

75. Aquinas *De Anima* 3.10.731; cf. Aristotle *Metaphysica* 1.6.

76. Aquinas *De Anima* 3.10.733; cf. Aristotle *De Anima* 3.5.430a17-19.

77. Aquinas *De Anima* 3.10.732; cf. Aristotle *De Anima* 3.5.430a17-19.

78. Aquinas *De Anima* 2.1.228.

79. Aquinas *Metaphysics* 9.7.1848; cf. Aristotle *Metaphysica* 9.8.1049b18-27.

80. Aquinas *De Anima* 3.10.739.

81. Ibid. 13.791; cf. Aristotle *De Anima* 3.8.432a3-8.

82. Aquinas *De Anima* 3.10.739.

83. Aristotle *De Anima* 3.5.430a15-16.

84. Aquinas *Truth* 2.11.1.c.

85. Ibid.

86. Aquinas *Summa Theologica* 1.84.7.c.; cf. Aristotle *De Anima* 3.4.429b10-23.

87. Aristotle *Metaphysica* 7.6; cf. Aquinas *Metaphysics* 7.5.

88. Aristotle *Metaphysica* 7.11.1037a22-1037b7; cf. Aquinas *Metaphysics* 7.11.1535-36.

89. Aquinas *Summa Theologica* 1.78.4.c.; cf. Aristotle *De Anima* 3.2.425b24-25.

90. Aristotle *De Anima* 3.3.428b10-17.

91. Ibid. 8.432a2-8; cf. Aquinas *De Anima* 3.13.791.

92. Aristotle *De Anima* 3.4.429a18-28; cf. Aquinas *De Anima* 3.7.

93. For the fact that accidents have an essence in a qualified sense, see Aristotle *Metaphysica* 7.4.1030a18-27; cf. Aquinas *Metaphysics* 7.4.1332.

94. Aquinas *De Anima* 2.12.379.

95. Aquinas *Metaphysics* 7.13.1572; cf. Aristotle *Metaphysica* 7.13.1038b10-11.

96. Aquinas *De Anima* 2.12.380; cf. Aristotle *Metaphysica* 7.13.1038a8-15.

97. Aristotle *De Anima* 3.5.430a14-17; cf. Aquinas *De Anima* 3.10.733,831.

98. Conway, *Principles*, 144.

99. Aquinas *Summa Theologica* 1.85.2.ad3; cf. Aristotle *Metaphysica* 7.5.1031a12-13.

100. Aquinas *Summa Contra Gentiles* 1.53.

101. Aquinas *De Anima* 3.8.718; cf. Aristotle *De Anima* 3.4.429b10-23.

102. For the proof of this position, see Aquinas *Summa Theologica* 1.85.2.c.

103. Aquinas *De Anima* 3.13.791; cf. Aristotle *De Anima* 3.8.432a3-8.

104. Aquinas *Summa Theologica* 1.85.5.c.; cf. Aristotle *De Anima* 3.4.429b29-430a2.

105. Aristotle *De Anima* 3.6; cf. Aquinas *Summa Theologica* 1.79.8.c

106. Conway, *Principles*, 36-37.

Chapter 4: Natural Order in Knowing

1. Aquinas *De Anima* 2.7.675; cf. Aristotle *De Anima* 3.4.429a12-18.

2. Aristotle *De Anima* 3.4.429b30-430a2.

3. Aquinas *Physics* 1.1.11; cf. Aristotle *Physica* 1.1.184a22-26.

4. Aquinas *Summa Theologica* 1.85.5.c.; cf. Aristotle *De Anima* 3.6.430a26-32.

5. Aquinas *Summa Theologica* 1.85.5.c.; cf. Aristotle *Metaphysica* 9.10.1051a34-1052a11.

6. Aquinas *Truth* 2.15.1.c.; cf. Aristotle *Topica* 1.1.100a25-26.

7. Aquinas *Metaphysics* 12.11.2621-22; cf. Aristotle *Metaphysica* 12.9.1075a5-11.

8. Aristotle *De Anima* 3.6; cf. Aristotle *Analytica Posteriora* 1.1.71a1-10.

9. Aquinas *Truth* 2.15.1.c.; cf. Aristotle *Analytica Posteriora* 1.2.71b19-33; 2.19.100b5-17.

10. Aristotle *De Caelo* 3.7.306a18.

11. Aquinas *Posterior Analytics* 1.1.8-9.

12. Aristotle *Analytica Posteriora* 2.19.99b24-26.

13. Aquinas *Truth* 2.11.1.c.; cf. Aristotle *Analytica Posteriora* 2.19.100a13.

14. Aristotle *Analytica Posteriora* 2.19.99b26-27.

15. Aquinas *Posterior Analytics* 2.20.4.

16. Ibid. 6.

17. Aristotle *Analytica Posteriora* 1.1.71a1-2.

18. Aquinas *Posterior Analytics* 2.20.5.

19. Aristotle *Metaphysica* 2.1.993b9-11.

20. Ibid. 1.1.980a22.

21. Aquinas *Metaphysics* 1.1.2.

22. Aristotle *De Partibus Animalium* 1.5.644b32-645a1; cf. Aquinas *Truth* 3.27.2.c.

23. Aquinas *De Anima* 3.10.729; cf. Aristotle *De Anima* 3.5.430a14-17.

24. Aquinas *De Anima* 3.10.739.

25. Aristotle *De Anima* 3.5.430a16-17.

26. Aquinas *De Anima* 3.10.730.

27. Aquinas *Truth* 2.11.1.c.; cf. Aristotle *Ethica Nicomachea* 10.7.1177b26-31.

28. Aquinas *De Anima* 3.10.739.

29. Aristotle *Metaphysica* 1.1.980b25-26.

30. Aquinas *Truth* 2.11.1.c.

31. Aquinas *De Anima* 3.10.729; cf. Aristotle *De Anima* 3.5.430a14-17.

32. Aristotle *De Partibus Animalium* 1.1.639b13-20.

33. Aristotle *Analytica Posteriora* 1.1.71a1-2.

34. Aquinas *De Anima* 3.10.740; cf. Aristotle *Metaphysica* 9.8.1049b4-1050b6.

35. Aquinas *Metaphysics* 9.7.1848.

36. Aristotle *Ethica Nicomachea* 1.4.1095b3.

37. Aquinas *Metaphysics* 7.2.1301.

38. Aquinas *Physics* 1.1.7; cf. Aristotle *Metaphysica* 7.3.1029b1-12.

39. Aquinas *Metaphysics* 7.2.1304.

40. Ibid. 1305; cf. Aquinas *Posterior Analytics* 1.4.16.

41. Aquinas *Metaphysics* 7.2.1305; cf. Aristotle *Physica* 1.1.184a16-22.

42. Aquinas *Physics* 1.1.7; cf. Aristotle *Physica* 1.1.184a22-23.

43. Ibid.

44. Aquinas *Metaphysics* 1.2.46; cf. Aristotle *Metaphysica* 10.2.1053b21; 11.3.1061a15-18. When we say that the intellect's first concept is being, we must point out that this is a knowledge of being as something that is said about things, as something that can be predicated of things. This is not a knowledge of being as the universal cause of all things. In other words, the human being knows the most universal in predication first, but not the most universal in causation.

45. Aquinas *Metaphysics* 4.6.605; cf. Aristotle *Metaphysica* 4.3.1005b8-34.

46. Aquinas *Metaphysics* 4.6.597.

47. Ibid. 599.

48. Aristotle *Metaphysica* 4.3.1005b31.

49. Aquinas *Metaphysics* 4.6.602.

50. Ibid. 604.

51. Aquinas *Truth* 2.11.1.c.; cf. Aristotle *Analytica Posteriora* 2.19.

52. Aquinas *Metaphysics* 4.5.595; cf. Aristotle *Analytica Posteriora* 1.2.72a7-14; 1.4.73a34-73b2.

53. Aristotle *Analytica Posteriora* 1.2.72a15-19.

54. Aquinas *Metaphysics* 4.5.595.

55. Aquinas *Posterior Analytics* 1.5.7.

56. Aquinas *Metaphysics* 4.5.591; cf. Aristotle *Metaphysica* 4.3.1005a25-27.

57. Aristotle *Ethica Nicomachea* 1.7.1098b6-8.

58. Aristotle *Analytica Posteriora* 2.19.99b35-36.

59. Aquinas *Metaphysics* 1.1.10; cf. Aristotle *Metaphysica* 1.1.980a28-29.

60. Aquinas *Posterior Analytics* 2.20.10; cf. Aristotle *Analytica Posteriora* 2.19.100a1-4.

61. Aristotle *Analytica Posteriora* 2.19.99b34-36.

62. The process being described applies to the acquisition of not only the first concepts and principles but also later ones. The following distinction, however, can be admitted. If the principle is not a definition (which is a principle in an extended sense) nor a first principle, then it may be also acquired by the syllogistic process. Since the process under discussion applies to both primary and posterior principles, we shall illustrate it from the latter type because of their more particular nature.

63. Aquinas *Summa Theologica* 1.78.4.c.

64. Aquinas *Posterior Analytics* 2.20.11.

65. Ibid.

66. Ibid.; cf. Aristotle *Analytica Posteriora* 2.19.100a11-13.

67. Aquinas *Posterior Analytics* 2.20.11; cf. Aristotle *Analytica Posteriora* 2.19.100a1-8.

68. Aquinas *Posterior Analytics* 2.20.11.

69. Aristotle *Physica* 3.6; cf. Aquinas *Summa Theologica* 1.7.2.c.; 86.2.c.

70. Aristotle *Analytica Posteriora* 1.1.71b3-5; cf. Aquinas *Posterior Analytics* 1.3.5.

71. Aquinas *Summa Theologica* 1-2.51.3.c.

72. Aquinas *Posterior Analytics* 2.4.4; cf. Aristotle *Analytica Posteriora* 2.5.91b12-25.

73. Aristotle *Metaphysica* 4.4.1006a6-10.

74. Aquinas *De Anima* 3.9.722; cf. Aristotle *De Anima* 3.4.429b30-430a1.

75. Aquinas *Posterior Analytics* 1.3.6; cf. Aristotle *Analytica Posteriora* 1.1.71b5-8.

76. Aquinas *De Anima* 3.4.631; cf. Aristotle *De Anima* 3.3.427b14.

77. Aquinas *De Anima* 3.14.812; cf. Aristotle *Metaphysica* 1.2.982a18.

78. Aristotle *Analytica Posteriora* 1.1.71a18-19.

79. Ibid. 1-2.

80. Aquinas *Posterior Analytics* 1.25.6; cf. Aristotle *Analytica Posteriora* 1.13.79a14-15.

81. Aristotle *Topica* 1.1.100a25-27.

82. Aristotle *Ethica Nicomachea* 6.3.1139b27-30.

83. Aristotle *Analytica Priora* 1.4.25b35-37.

84. Strictly speaking, the definition of the property (which, in our example, is the same phrase *all things having parts*) is considered to be the middle term. "The *per se* middle of demonstrations is *the reason of the ultimate*, i.e., the definition of the major extreme" (Aquinas *Posterior Analytics* 2.19.2; cf. Aristotle *Analytica Posteriora* 2.17.99a2-3). For the explanation of the middle term considered as the definition of the property, see Aquinas *Posterior Analytics* 2.1; Aristotle *Analytica Posteriora* 2.2.

85. Here we are considering the reasoning process as including both the material of argumentation and the form that such a reasoning process takes.

86. Aristotle *Metaphysica* 12.10.1075a16-19; cf. Aquinas *Metaphysics* 12.12.2629-37.

87. Conway, *Logic*, S-106.

88. Aristotle *Metaphysica* 1.2.983a14-17; cf. Aquinas *Metaphysics* 1.3.54-55.

89. Aquinas *Metaphysics* 3.1.340; cf. Aristotle *Metaphysica* 3.1.995a23-995b3.

90. Aristotle *Metaphysica* 3.1.995a35.

91. Ibid. 995a36-995b1.

92. Aristotle *Analytica Posteriora* 2.7.92b11-16; cf. Aquinas *Posterior Analytics* 2.6.

93. Aristotle *Politica* 2.1.1260b28-29.

94. Aquinas *Posterior Analytics* 1.2.2; cf. Aristotle *Analytica Posteriora* 1.1.71a11-16.

95. Aquinas *Posterior Analytics* 1.2.7.

96. Ibid. 2.6.3; cf. Aristotle *Metaphysica* 12.8.1074a32-39.

97. Aquinas *Metaphysics* 7.4.1341; cf. Aristotle *Metaphysica* 7.4.1030b3-13.

98. Aquinas *Posterior Analytics* 1.2.3; cf. Aristotle *Analytica Posteriora* 1.1.71a11-16.

99. Strictly speaking, the definition of the property (which, in our illustration, is the same phrase *all things having parts*) is considered to be the middle term. See note 84.

100. Aquinas *Posterior Analytics* 1.2.3.

101. Here we are discussing the kind of knowledge that one has of the property as it is related to the subject. Because one must prove that it exists in the subject, his knowledge of the property as related to the subject is only a nominal definition of such a property. Thus, in such a respect, he will have only a nominal description of corruptibility.

In respect to the general principle, however, one has more than a nominal definition of the property. Rather, one knows that the principle is true and that the property exists in the given subject. Thus he knows that corruptibility actually exists in all things having parts.

102. Aquinas *Posterior Analytics* 1.2.5.
103. Aristotle *Analytica Posteriora* 2.7.92b4-7.
104. Aquinas *Posterior Analytics* 1.2.5; cf. Aristotle *Metaphysica* 4.4.
105. Aristotle *Analytica Posteriora* 1.1.71a11-16; cf. Aquinas *Posterior Analytics* 1.2.
106. Aristotle *Metaphysica* 6.1.1025b14; cf. Aquinas *Metaphysics* 6.1.1149.
107. Aristotle *De Partibus Animalium* 1.1.639b27-31.
108. Aquinas *Metaphysics* 6.1.1149; cf. Aristotle *Metaphysica* 6.1.1025b1-18.
109. Aquinas *Metaphysics* 1.1.4; cf. Aristotle *Metaphysica* 1.1.980a22.

Chapter 5: Inductive Process of Teaching

1. Aquinas *Ethics* 10.14.2138; cf. Aristotle *Ethica Nicomachea* 10.9.1179a35-1179b1.
2. Aquinas *Politics* Prooem.2 (quoted in Conway, *Principles*, 36).
3. Aristotle *De Partibus Animalium* 1.1.639b17-20.
4. Aquinas *De Anima* 2.6.305; cf. Aristotle *De Anima* 2.4.415a14-23.
5. Aquinas *De Anima* 3.13.791; cf. Aristotle *De Anima* 3.8.432a2-8.
6. Aristotle *De Anima* 2.6.418a15-17.
7. Aquinas *Truth* 1.1.11.c.
8. Aristotle *Metaphysica* 4.5.1009b1-1010a14; cf. Aquinas *Metaphysics* 4.11,12.
9. Aquinas *Summa Theologica* 1-2.3.8.c.; cf. Aristotle *De Anima* 3.4.429b18-22.
10. Aquinas *Physics* 1.1.5.
11. Aquinas *Metaphysics* 1.3.54; cf. Aristotle *Metaphysica* 1.2.982b11-17.
12. Aquinas *Metaphysics* 1.1.2.
13. Aristotle *Topica* 8.1.156a6-7.
14. Aristotle *De Anima* 2.5.417a6-7.
15. Ibid. 2 12.424a17-18.
16. Ibid. 3.5.430a14-16.
17. Aristotle *Analytica Posteriora* 2.19.100a4-9.
18. Aristotle *Topica* 1.1.100a25-27.
19. Aristotle *Analytica Priora* 2.23.68b13-14.
20. Aristotle *Metaphysica* 1.1.980b25-27.
21. Aquinas *Summa Theologica* 1.85.5.c.; cf. Aristotle *De Anima* 3.6.430a26-28.
22. In order to know, one relies also on the syllogism, the outlining of the process of reasoning. This formation of the mind is not mentioned at this point, however, for it is the result of the deductive process.
23. Aquinas *Metaphysics* 7.5.1378; cf. Aristotle *Metaphysica* 7.5.1031a12-14.
24. Aquinas *Summa Theologica* 1.84.7.c.; cf. Aristotle *De Anima* 3.4.429a10-17.
25. Aristotle *Physica* 1.1.184a22-25.
26. Aquinas *Physics* 1.1.11; cf. Aristotle *Physica* 1.1.184a25-184b14.
27. Aristotle *Metaphysica* 7.12.1037b28-1038a8; cf. Aquinas *Metaphysica* 7.12.1542-43.
28. Aquinas *Metaphysics* 7.12.1552; cf. Aristotle *Metaphysica* 7.12.1038a13.
29. Aristotle *Historia Animalium* 9.45.630a18-32.
30. Aquinas *Physics* 1.1.5.
31. Aquinas *Posterior Analytics* 1.16.5.

32. For Aristotle's treatment of the fact that there are only four causes, see *Physica* 2.7.198a13-23; Aquinas *Physics* 2.10.14-15.

33. Aristotle *Metaphysica* 5.2.1013a27-28; cf. Aquinas *Metaphysics* 5.2.764.

34. Conway, *Logic*, S-41; cf. Aquinas *Metaphysics* 7.17.1658.

35. Aristotle *Metaphysica* 9.9.1051a22-30; cf. Aquinas *Metaphysics* 7.2.1302, 1304.

36. Aristotle *Analytica Posteriora* 1.2.72a8-9.

37. The enunciation denotes either part of a contradiction indifferently, for it is simply the juxtaposition of the subject and predicate abstracting from whether one is affirming or denying. When the actual affirmation or negation is made, one has the proposition. Therefore the proposition is an enunciation that has been determined into either an affirmation or negation. If this determination has not been made, one has the enunciation. Thus Aquinas says that "enunciation embraces both parts of a contradiction" (*Posterior Analytics* 1.5.5.).

38. Ibid. 3.

39. Aristotle *Analytica Posteriora* 1.2.72a7-8.

40. Aquinas *Posterior Analytics* 1.5.4.

41. Aristotle *Analytica Posteriora* 1.4.73a34-73b2; cf. Aquinas *Posterior Analytics* 1.10.3-4.

42. Aquinas *Posterior Analytics* 1.5.7.

43. Aristotle *Analytica Posteriora* 2.3.90b23-27; cf. Aquinas *Posterior Analytics* 2.2.9; 2.8.10-11.

44. Aquinas *Metaphysics* 4.5.595.

45. Aquinas *Posterior Analytics* 1.5.2.

46. Aristotle *Topica* 1.12.105a13-16.

47. Aristotle *Analytica Posteriora* 2.19.100b3-5.

48. Aristotle *Topica* 1.12.105a13.

49. Aristotle *Analytica Posteriora* 2.19.100a4-6.

50. Aquinas *Physics* 1.1.11; cf. Aristotle *Physica* 1.1.184a22-184b14.

51. Aristotle *Physica* 1.1.184a25.

52. Aquinas *Posterior Analytics* 1.42.5; cf. Aristotle *Analytica Posteriora* 1.31.87b28-30.

53. Aquinas *Posterior Analytics* 1.23.6; cf. Aristotle *Analytica Posteriora* 1.13.78a22-78b2. In Aristotle's doctrine, this particular demonstration is used only as an example of the distinction between quia and propter quid demonstrations. It is important to realize Aristotle's purpose, for, in actual fact, one would first have to know that the planets were near before one could take their associated nontwinkling as a sign of each nearness.

54. Aquinas *Posterior Analytics* 1.23.6.

55. Ibid. 4.

56. Aristotle *Analytica Priora* 2.27.70a7-9.

57. Conway, *Logic*, S-131.

58. Aristotle *Rhetorica* 1.2.1357b14-19.

59. Aristotle *De Anima* 2.4.415a16-23.

60. Aquinas *De Anima* 3.13.791; cf. Aristotle *De Anima* 3.8.432a3-8.

61. Aquinas *Summa Theologica* 1.78.4.c.

62. Aquinas *Posterior Analytics* 2.20.11; cf. Aristotle *Analytica Posteriora* 2.19.100a9-13.

63. Aristotle *De Poetica* 4.1448b13-15.

64. Aquinas *Metaphysics* 1.1.3.

65. Aristotle *Ethica Nicomachea* 1.8.1099a1-6; cf. Aquinas *Metaphysics* 12.8.

66. Aristotle *Metaphysica* 1.1.980a27-28.

67. Aquinas *Summa Theologica* 1-2.32.8.c.; cf. Aristotle *Metaphysica* 1.2.982b11-23.
68. Aristotle *Ethica Nicomachea* 1.3.1094b15-17.
69. Aristotle *Metaphysica* 2.1.993b9-10.
70. Aristotle *Politica* 8.5.1339a29.
71. Aristotle *Ethica Nicomachea* 1.7.1098b6-7.
72. Aquinas *Summa Theologica* 1-2.9.2.ad2.
73. Aristotle *De Anima* 3.10.433a26-30; cf. Aquinas *De Anima* 3.15.827.
74. Aquinas *Summa Theologica* 1-2.34.1.c.
75. Ibid. 40.5.c.; cf. Aristotle *Ethica Nicomachea* 3.8.1117a10-11.
76. Aquinas *Summa Theologica* 1-2.40.2.c
77. Aristotle *Rhetorica* 3.14.1415b1-3.
78. Aristotle *Ethica Nicomachea* 10.4.1175a6-9.
79. Aristotle *Rhetorica* 3.2.1404b2-4; 3.10.1410b20-26.
80. Aristotle *Physica* 2.8.199a20-30.
81. Aristotle *Analytica Posteriora* 2.19.100a5-8.
82. Aquinas *Summa Theologica* 2-2.49.1.ad2.
83. Aristotle *Analytica Posteriora* 2.19.100a4-6.
84. Aquinas *Metaphysics* 3.1.339; cf. Aristotle *Metaphysica* 3.1.995a26-995b3.
85. Aristotle *Topica* 1.18.108b1-23.
86. It is natural for the student to abstract the universal from the sufficient number of cases presented to him. He does not have to make an effort to universalize, for he does so naturally. In connection with this, Aristotle says that "what knowledge apprehends is universals" (*De Anima* 2.5.417b23.).
87. Aristotle *Analytica Posteriora* 2.19.99b36-100b3.
88. Ibid. 2.19.100a7-8.
89. Aquinas *Posterior Analytics* 2.4.4; cf. Aristotle *Analytica Posteriora* 2.5.91b15.
90. Aristotle *Metaphysica* 1.1.981a5-7.
91. Aquinas *Posterior Analytics* 2.14.3; cf. Aristotle *Analytica Posteriora* 2.13.96b15-24. By these common things Aristotle means accidents which are "always in addition, but not outside the genus, up to the point that first each which is taken be by addition, but all be not by addition but convertible with the thing of which the *quod quid est* [definition] is sought" (Aquinas *Posterior Analytics* 2.13.4.).
92. Aristotle *Physica* 1.1.184b11-13.
93. Aquinas *Posterior Analytics* 2.16.3; cf. Aristotle *Analytica Posteriora* 2.13.97b17-21.
94. Aristotle *Analytica Posteriora* 2.13.97b23-25.
95. Aquinas *Posterior Analytics* 2.16.3.

Chapter 6: Deductive Process of Teaching

1. Aristotle *Topica* 1.12.105a13.
2. Ibid. 1.1.100a25-27.
3. Aquinas *De Anima* 2.11.372.
4. Aristotle *De Anima* 3.4.430a1-2.
5. Aquinas *Summa Theologica* 1.85.5.c.
6. Aristotle *Analytica Posteriora* 1.1.71a24-26.
7. Aquinas *Posterior Analytics* 1.38.7.
8. Aristotle *Analytica Posteriora* 1.24.86a24-27; cf. Aquinas *Posterior Analytics* 1.38.7.

9. Aquinas *Posterior Analytics* 1.3.6.
10. Aquinas *Metaphysics* 1.3.66; cf. Aristotle *Metaphysica* 1.2.98a13-21.
11. Aristotle *Ethica Nicomachea* 10.8.1178b31-32.
12. Aristotle *Analytica Posteriora* 2.3.90b34-35.
13. Aristotle *Analytica Priora* 1.1.24b18-20.
14. Aristotle *Metaphysica* 12.7.1072b25-29.
15. Ibid. 1.2.982a29-30.
16. Aristotle *Analytica Posteriora* 1.2.71b10-12.
17. Ibid. 2.8; cf. Aquinas *Posterior Analytics* 2.7.8.
18. Aristotle *Analytica Posteriora* 2.11.94a20-21.
19. Ibid. 1.33.88b30-33.
20. Ibid. 1.6; Aquinas *Posterior Analytics* 1.13.
21. Aquinas *Posterior Analytics* 1.1.5.
22. Ibid. 6; cf. Aristotle *Analytica Posteriora* 1.33.89a3-4.
23. Aristotle *Analytica Posteriora* 1.33.89a5-10.
24. Aquinas *Posterior Analytics* 1.44.9; cf. Aristotle *Analytica Posteriora* 1.33.89a18-21.
25. Aristotle *Analytica Posteriora* 1.33.88b31-32.
26. Aristotle *Topica* 1.2.101a25-37.
27. Aquinas *Posterior Analytics* 1.2.2.; cf. Aristotle *Analytica Posteriora* 1.1.71a11-16.
28. See foreknowledge of property, pp. 125-26.
29. Aristotle *Analytica Posteriora* 1.2.71b20-22.
30. Aquinas *Posterior Analytics* 1.4.14.
31. Ibid. 1.5.7.
32. Aristotle *Analytica Posteriora* 1.6.74b7-9.
33. Aquinas *Metaphysics* 4.5.595.
34. Aristotle *Analytica Posteriora* 1.2.71b21-22.
35. Ibid. 1.2.71b22.
36. Ibid. 1.13.78a22-79a15.
37. Ibid. 1.13.78b3-6.
38. Ibid. 1.4.73a27-32.
39. Ibid. 1.4.73b31-33.
40. Ibid. 1.11.77a10-35. Since the principle of contradiction is the first of all immediate principles, it is clearly incapable of being proved. It is possible, however, to show the validity of this principle by demonstration leading to the impossible. See Aristotle *Metaphysica* 4.4.1006a12-28; Aquinas *Metaphysics* 4.6.608-10.
41. Aquinas *Metaphysics* 2.1.285; cf. Aristotle *Metaphysica* 2.1.993a30-993b18.
42. Aristotle *Analytica Posteriora* 1.33.89a3.
43. Aristotle *Topica* 1.1.100b22-24.
44. Ibid. 1.10.104a33-38.
45. Aristotle *Rhetorica* 1.2.1356a5-13.
46. Ibid. 2.1.1378a7-14.
47. Aristotle *Topica* 1.14.105b20-25.
48. Ibid. 8.14.163b27-33.
49. Ibid. 8.3; Aristotle *Analytica Posteriora* 1.33.89b10-20.
50. Aquinas *Metaphysics* 5.11,12,13; cf. Aristotle *Metaphysica* 5.9,10,11.
51. Aquinas *Posterior Analytics* 1.20.5.
52. Aristotle *Rhetorica* 2.21.1394b13-14.
53. Aristotle *Topica* 8.14.163b17-19.
54. Aristotle *Analytica Posteriora* 2.8.93b9-14; cf. Aquinas *Posterior Analytics* 2.7.8.

55. Aquinas *Posterior Analytics* 2.9.2; cf. Aristotle *Analytica Posteriora* 2.11.94b20-24.
56. Aquinas *Posterior Analytics* 2.9; cf. Aristotle *Analytica Posteriora* 2.11.94a20-94b37.
57. Aquinas *Posterior Analytics* 1.16.5.
58. Ibid. 2.8.3.
59. Ibid. 2.8.9-10; cf. Aristotle *Analytica Posteriora* 2.10.93b38-94a13.
60. Aquinas *Posterior Analytics* 2.8.10; cf. Aristotle *Analytica Posteriora* 2.10.94a9-10.
61. Aquinas *Metaphysics* 7.12.1552; cf. Aristotle *Metaphysica* 7.12.1038a8-24.
62. Aristotle *Rhetorica* 2.23.1399a13-17.
63. Aristotle *Analytica Posteriora* 2.8.93a24-28.
64. Aquinas *Posterior Analytics* 2.7.6-7.
65. Aristotle *Analytica Posteriora* 2.8.93a21-24.
66. Aristotle *Metaphysica* 3.1.995a35-995b2.
67. Aristotle *Analytica Posteriora* 2.3.90b34-35.
68. Aristotle *De Anima* 3.12.434b9-18.
69. Aristotle *Analytica Posteriora* 1.34.89b10-16.
70. Aquinas *Posterior Analytics* 1.2.9; cf. Aristotle *Analytica Posteriora* 1.1.71a16-26.
71. Aristotle *Analytica Priora* 1.1.24b18-20.
72. Aristotle defines *term* as follows: "I call that a term into which the premiss is resolved, i.e., both the predicate and that of which it is predicated, 'being' being added and 'not being' removed, or vice versa" (*Analytica Priora* 1.1.24b17-19).
73. Ibid. 1.25.42a31-32.
74. Aristotle *De Sophisticis Elenchis* 4.165b34-39.
75. Ibid. 22. 178a27-28.
76. Aristotle *Analytica Priora* 1.24.41b6-35. Aristotle defines *universal* as follows: "By universal I mean the statement that something belongs to all or none of something else" (Ibid.1.1.24a17-18).
77. Aristotle *De Sophisticis Elenchis* 5.167b1-20.
78. Strictly speaking, the predicate will be a definition or property of the subject. See Aquinas *Posterior Analytics* 2.1.9.
79. Aristotle *De Sophisticis Elenchis* 5.167b4-13.
80. Aristotle *Analytica Priora* 1.24.41b6-7. Two additional rules may be deduced from the three treated in this book. They are as follows: (1) Two particular premises yield no conclusion. (2) The conclusion always follows the weaker part and may not have wider extension than the premises (Ibid. 1.24.41b6-35).

Chapter 7: Conclusion

1. Aquinas *Metaphysics* 1.1.2.
2. Aquinas *De Anima* 3.10.730; cf. Aristotle *De Anima* 3.5.430a14-17.
3. Aquinas *Metaphysics* 9.7.1848; cf. Aristotle *Metaphysica* 9.8.1049b24-26.
4. Aquinas *Metaphysics* 1.1.20; cf. Aristotle *Metaphysica* 1.1.981b13-15.
5. Aquinas *Truth* 2.11.1.ad11; cf. Aristotle *De Anima* 3.4.429b5-24.
6. Aquinas *De Anima* 2.11.372; cf. Aristotle *Ethica Nicomachea* 6.3.1139b26-30.
7. Aquinas *Politics* Prooem.2 (quoted in Conway, *Principles*, 36).
8. Aquinas *De Anima* 2.6.305; cf. Aristotle *De Anima* 2.4.415a14-23.
9. Aquinas *De Anima* 3.13.791; cf. Aristotle *De Anima* 3.8.432a2-8.
10. Aquinas *De Anima* 3.9.722; cf. Aristotle *De Anima* 3.4.429b33-430a2.
11. Aristotle *De Anima* 3.8.431b21.

12. Aquinas *De Anima* 3.13.789-90; cf. Aristotle *De Anima* 3.8.431b20-432a3.
13. Aristotle *Topica* 1.1.100a25-27.
14. Aristotle *Analytica Priora* 2.23.68b13-14.
15. Aristotle *Analytica Posteriora* 1.1.71a1-2.
16. Aristotle *Ethica Nicomachea* 6.3.1139b26-28.
17. Aristotle *Metaphysica* 1.2.982a29-30.

Bibliography

Aquinas, Thomas. *On Being and Essence.* Translated by Armand Maurer. Toronto, Canada: The Pontifical Institute of Medieval Studies, 1949.

_____. *Commentary on Aristotle's De Anima.* Translated by Kenelm Foster and Silvester Humphries. New Haven: Yale University Press, 1951.

_____. *Commentary on Aristotle's Physics.* Translated by Richard J. Blackwell, Richard J. Spath, and W. Edmund Thirlkel. New Haven: Yale University Press, 1963.

_____. *Commentary on the De Trinitate of Boethius (V-VI).* Translated by Armand Maurer as *The Division and Methods of the Sciences.* Toronto, Canada: The Pontifical Institute of Medieval Studies, 1953.

_____. *Commentary on the Metaphysics of Aristotle.* Translated by John P. Rowan. 2 vols. Chicago: Henry Regnery Company, 1961.

_____. *Commentary on the Nicomachean Ethics.* Translated by C. I. Litzinger. 2 vols. Chicago: Henry Regnery Company, 1964.

_____. *De Unitate Intellectus contra Averroistas Parisienses* in *Opuscula Omnia.* Edited by J. Perrier. Paris: Lethielleux, 1949.

_____. *Exposition of the Posterior Analytics of Aristotle.* Translated by Pierre Conway. Quebec: La Librairie Philosophique M. Doyon, 1956.

_____. *In Libros Politicorum Aristotelis Expositio.* Edited by R. Spiazzi. Turin: Marietti, 1951.

_____. *Summa Contra Gentiles.* Translated by Anton C. Pegis et al as *On the Truth of the Catholic Faith.* Image Books ed. 4 vols. Garden City, NY: Doubleday and Company, Inc., 1955-57.

_____. *Summa Theologica.* Translated by Fathers of the English Dominican Province. 3 vols. New York: Benziger Brothers, Inc., 1947-48. (Reprinted by Christian Classics, 1981.)

_____. *Truth.* Translated by Robert W. Mulligan et al. 3 vols. Indianapolis, IN: Hackett Publishing, Inc., 1994.

Aquinas, Thomas, and Cajetan. *Aristotle: On Interpretation.* Translated by Jean T. Oesterle. Milwaukee, WI: Marquette University Press, 1962.

Aristotle. *The Basic Works of Aristotle.* Edited by Richard McKeon. New York: Random House, 1941.

_____. *The Works of Aristotle.* Edited by W. D. Ross. 1st ed. 11 vols. London: Oxford University Press, 1910-31.

Ashley, Benedict M. *The Arts of Learning and Communication.* Dubuque, IA: The Priory Press, 1958.

Barzun, Jacques. *Begin Here: The Forgotten Conditions of Teaching and Learning.* Edited by Philipson Morris. Chicago, IL: University of Chicago Press, 1991.

Bigge, Morris L. and Shermis. *Learning Theories for Teachers.* 5th ed. Reading, MA: Addison-Wesley Longman, Inc., 1992.

Bruner, Jerome S. *Toward a Theory of Instruction.* Cambridge, MA: Belknap Press, 1974.

Catania, A. Charles. *Learning.* 4th ed. Paramus, NJ: Prentice-Hall, 1997.

Conway, Pierre. *Aristotelian Formal and Material Logic.* Edited by Mary Michael Spangler. Lanham, MD: University Press of America, 1995.

_____. "Induction in Aristotle and St. Thomas." *The Thomist* 22 (1959): 336-65.

_____. *Metaphysics of Aquinas.* Edited by Mary Michael Spangler. Lanham, MD: University Press of America, 1996.

_____. *Principles of Education.* Washington, DC: The Thomist Press, 1960.

_____. *Thomistic English—Logic.* Columbus, OH: College of St. Mary of the Springs, 1958.

De Koninck, Charles. "Abstraction from Matter: Notes on St. Thomas's Prologue to the *Physics.*" *Laval Théologique et Philosophique* 13 (1957): 133-96.

Donaldson, Margaret. *Children's Minds.* New York: W. W. Norton & Co., Inc., 1979.

Gagne, Ellen D. *The Cognitive Psychology of School Learning.* Reading, MA: Addison-Wesley Longman, Inc., 1993.

Glutz, Melvin. *The Manner of Demonstrating in Natural Philosophy.* River Forest, IL: Dominican House of Studies, 1956.

Gredler, Margaret. *Learning and Instruction.* 3rd ed. Paramus, NJ: Prentice-Hall, 1996.

Guralnik, David B., ed. *Webster's New World Dictionary of the American Language.* 2nd college ed. New York: Simon & Schuster, 1985.

Guzie, Tad W. "St. Thomas and Learning Theory: A Bibliographical Survey," *The New Scholasticism,* 34 (1960): 275-95.

Harris and Leahey, Thomas H. *Learning and Cognition.* 4th ed. Paramus, NJ: Prentice-Hall, 1996.

Ingardia, Richard. *Thomas Aquinas: International Bibliography, 1977-1990.* Bowling Green, OH: The Philosophy Documentation Center, 1993.

Kane, William H. *Scholastic Methodology: The Art of Philosophic Reasoning.* River Forest, IL: Dominican House of Studies, 1961.

Kiernan, Thomas P., ed. *Aristotle Dictionary.* New York: Philosophical Library, 1962.

Lennon, Joseph L. *The Nature of Experience and Its Role in the Acquisition of Scientific Knowledge According to the Philosophy of St. Thomas Aquinas.* Notre Dame: University of Notre Dame Dissertation, 1954.

Miethe, Terry L. and Bourke, Vernon J., eds. *Thomistic Bibliography, 1940-1978.* Westport, CT: Greenwood Press, 1980.

Montessori, Maria. *The Montessori Method.* Reprint of 1912 ed. Herndon, VA: Books International, Inc., 1996.

Organ, Troy Wilson. *An Index to Aristotle.* Princeton, NJ: Princeton University Press, 1949.

Plato. *Meno.* Translated by Benjamin Jowett. New York: The Liberal Arts Press, 1949.

Reith, Herman. *An Introduction to Philosophical Psychology.* Englewood Cliffs, NJ: Prentice-Hall, Inc., 1956.

Scheffler, Israel. *Reason and Teaching.* Indianapolis, IN: Hackett Publishing, Inc., 1981.

Smith, Vincent E. *The Elements of Logic.* Milwaukee, WI: The Bruce Publishing Company, 1957.

_____. *The General Science of Nature.* Milwaukee, WI: The Bruce Publishing Company, 1958.

_____. *The School Examined: Its Aim and Content.* Milwaukee, WI: The Bruce Publishing Company, 1960.

Smith, Vincent E., ed. *The Logic of Science.* New York: St. John's University Press, 1964.

Spangler, Mary Michael. *Logic: An Aristotelian Approach.* Revised ed. Lanham, MD: University Press of America, Inc., 1993.

Weisheipl, J. Athanasius. *Aristotelian Methodology.* River Forest, IL: Dominican House of Studies, 1958.

Index